The Big Book of Traditional House Plans

500+ Homes in Full Color
From 1,300 to 11,000 Square Feet

The Big Book of Traditional House Plans

hanley▲wood

Published by Hanley Wood
One Thomas Circle, NW, Suite 600
Washington, DC 20005

Distribution Center
PBD
Hanley Wood Consumer Group
3280 Summit Ridge Parkway
Duluth, Georgia 30096

Vice President, Home Plans, Andrew Schultz
Director, Marketing, Mark Wilkin
Associate Publisher, Development, Jennifer Pearce
Editor, Simon Hyoun
Assistant Editor, Kimberly Johnson
Publications Manager, Brian Haefs
Production Manager, Theresa Emerson
Senior Plan Merchandiser, Nicole Phipps
Plan Merchandiser, Hillary Huff
Graphic Artist, Joong Min
Product Manager, Susan Jasmin
Marketing Manager, Brett Bryant

Most Hanley Wood titles are available at quantity discounts with bulk purchases for educational, business, or sales promotional use. For information, please contact Andrew Schultz at aschultz@hanleywood.com.

VC Graphics, Inc.
Creative Director, Veronica Vannoy
Graphic Designer, Jennifer Gerstein
Graphic Designer, Denise Reiffenstein
Graphic Designer, Jeanne-Erin Worster

Photo Credits
Front Cover: Top (left to right): Plan HWEPL11283, design and photo by Garrell Associates, Inc.; Plan HWEPL06804, design by Studer Residential Designs, photo by Ron and Donna Kolb; Plan HWEPL00800, design and photo by HomePlanners. LLC. Blueprints for these homes are available online at www.eplans.com. Main: Plan HPK3200255 on page 211, design and photo by Stephen Fuller, Inc.
Back Cover: Top: Plan HPK3200204 on page 159, design and photo by Donald A. Gardner Architects, Inc.
Bottom: Plan HPK3200416 on page 343, design by Stephen Fuller, Inc, photo by Scott Moore.
Pages 6-10, photos by Phil Bell. Pages 101-105, photos by Brian Willy Photography.
Pages 212-216, photos by Exposures Unlimited, Ron & Donna Kolb. Pages 343-347, photos by Scott Moore.

10 9 8 7 6 5 4 3 2 1

Printed in the United States of America

Library of Congress Control Number: 2006935046

ISBN-10: 1-931131-73-2
ISBN-13: 978-1-931131-73-5

The Big Book of Traditional House Plans

CONTENTS

ONLINE EXTRA!

PASSAGEWAY

For access to bonus home plans, articles, online ordering, and more go to: **www.hanley woodbooks.com/BigBookTraditional**

Features of this site include:

- A dynamic link that lets you search and view bonus home plans
- Online related feature articles
- Built-in tools to save and view your favorite home plans
- A dynamic web link that allows you to order your home plan online
- Contact details for the Hanley Wood Home Plan Hotline
- Free subscriptions to Hanley Wood Home Plan e-news

hanley▲wood

Introduction

Bay windows, gables, and columned entries are a few of the many characteristics that define a traditional home. See more of this home on page 357.

RIGHT: Decorative ceilings, columns, and other design elements define living areas while letting the home maintain easy relationships between rooms.

Traditional Values

Unlike other house plan collections—of Victorian homes, two-story designs, or affordable plans—you're likely to find on bookstore shelves, a volume of traditional homes requires some explanation of purpose: What is a traditional home? Who is it for? What does it look like? The uncertainty stems from both the term's popularity and novelty—from its widespread and imprecise usage. For instance, a traditional home to some is merely a home with a historical exterior, an umbrella term comprising Colonials, Romantics, Victorians, and their subtypes. For others, a traditional—Traditional—is itself a principal architectural style with characteristic forms and material composition. For others still, what makes a home traditional is less substantive and more ineffable: a personal space with a familiar feeling and sounds from their own histories.

Traditionals, Inside and Out

We believe that the homes in the *The Big Book of Traditional House Plans* will satisfy all the above definitions

and expectations of a traditional home. These 530 plans certainly offer historically informed exteriors and regional accents: gabled dormers, well-trimmed windows, porches, and distinguished entries. But up close, these traditionals unexpectedly display modernist qualities: experimentation with technology, love of efficiency, and disdain for fussy period conventions. Exteriors confidently combine richer organics with worry-free siding. Windows are plentiful and the fenestration smartly designed. Formal interior rooms for dining and entertaining open into casual, family spaces. Lastly, these homes are dedicated to the pleasure of their owners: civilized personal spaces and attending amenities seek to deliver the full comforts of home.

Traditional House Plans

As always, we also believe that building a new home from predrawn blueprints offers the best of many worlds. Because it is a custom-built home, owners can change and personalize the design to taste; but unlike a custom-designed home, owners do not have to pay for a full-time architect. Just as a traditional home represents easy compromises between period aesthetics and modern construction, building from a predrawn plan spares owners from having to choose between good design and smart spending.

Using This Book

The book has been divided into four sections of house plans, arranged by square footage, and one section of landscape plans. Each plan has been assigned a plan number (e.g., HPK3200001), listed on the plan page, and a price tier (e.g., L3) that's listed on the long table on page 460. Match the price tier for your plan in the blueprint price schedule at the top of page 460 to find your pricing options. The plan numbers can also be used on our Web site—eplans.com—to find out more details about the plan and to browse any photos of the finished home.

Made to Fit

A small home with a luxurious side
aims to please new families.

Full-height windows frame the bed in the master suite.

A prominent gabled entry and matching front-loading garage help balance the front elevation of this thoughtfully designed small home. Alternating brick and stucco emphasize the variety of exterior forms and large windows.

First impressions continue to make an impact inside the home. Beyond the elevated entryway, a two-story foyer—remarkably spacious for a home of this size—brightens the forward spaces and showcases the attractive stairway, as well as art niches and a plant shelf. A deep reach-in closet and powder room add utility to the space.

The great room features a robust fireplace and large windows at both ends. Use the space as a singular gathering room or designate a formal dining area. Casual meals occur in the breakfast nook, which opens directly to the rear property. The large island kitchen is made for serious cooks. The built-in pantry and above-sink window are must-haves.

The master suite is conveniently located on the first level and includes a luxury-minded bath. The oversized walk-in and nearby laundry room are just what modern homeowners desire. Upstairs bedrooms are just as comfortable, each with a reach-in and views of the backyard. The full-sized bath is designed for easy sharing.

Starter Homes

RIGHT: A gable-topped covered stoop emphasizes the front entry. The courtyard design makes way for landscape features.

BELOW: Arched windows at both ends illuminate the central fireplace, which is topped with an art niche. The flexible space can be shared between the dining and conversation areas.

Casual meals are everyday treats in the naturally bright breakfast nook.

The no-mess kitchen provides generous amounts of cabinet and counter space.

Plan: HPK3200001

First Floor: 1,314 sq. ft.
Second Floor: 458 sq. ft.
Total: 1,772 sq. ft.
Bedrooms: 3

Bathrooms: 2 ½
Width: 52' - 0"
Depth: 51' - 4"

First Floor

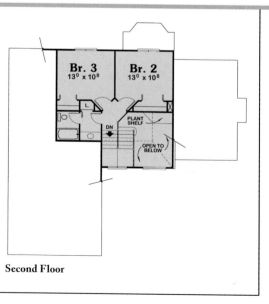

Second Floor

Plan: HPK3200002

Square Footage: 1,322
Bedrooms: 3
Bathrooms: 2
Width: 44' - 6"

Depth: 58' - 2"
Foundation: Crawlspace, Slab

A fine first impression is offered with the delightful chalet roofline on the entry of this efficient country design. A traditional foyer opens to the large living room. Accents include a sloped 10-foot ceiling, a snack bar from the kitchen and windows that frame the fireplace. The kitchen has a corner sink, island preparation area, and a dining nook. The front-facing master bedroom has a walk-in closet and a twin-sink vanity in the bath. Two family bedrooms share a hall bath. A hallway laundry center and a two-car garage discreetly sit at the rear of the house, completing the plan.

Starter Homes

Plan: HPK3200003

Square Footage: 1,360
Bedrooms: 3
Bathrooms: 2

Width: 40' - 0"
Depth: 49' - 10"
Foundation: Slab

Plan: HPK3200004

Square Footage: 1,373
Bedrooms: 3
Bathrooms: 2
Width: 50' - 4"

Depth: 45' - 0"
Foundation: Crawlspace,
Unfinished Walkout
Basement

Starter Homes

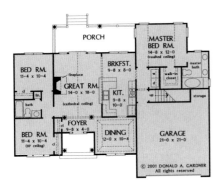

BONUS RM.
13-4 x 21-0

© 2001 Donald A. Gardner, Inc.

Plan: HPK3200005

Square Footage: 1,377	Bathrooms: 2
Bonus Space: 322 sq. ft.	Width: 57' - 8"
Bedrooms: 3	Depth: 44' - 0"

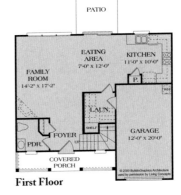

First Floor

Second Floor

Plan: HPK3200006

First Floor: 680 sq. ft.	Bathrooms: 2 ½
Second Floor: 714 sq. ft.	Width: 34' - 5"
Total: 1,394 sq. ft.	Depth: 31' - 3"
Bedrooms: 3	Foundation: Slab

Starter Homes

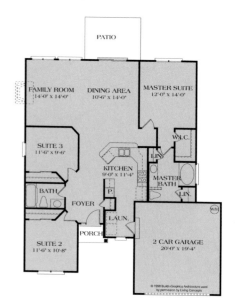

Plan: HPK3200007

Square Footage: 1,402
Bedrooms: 3
Bathrooms: 2

Width: 45' - 8"
Depth: 50' - 6"
Foundation: Slab

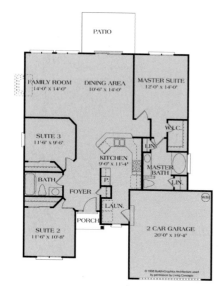

Plan: HPK3200008

Square Footage: 1,402
Bedrooms: 3
Bathrooms: 2

Width: 45' - 4"
Depth: 50' - 1"
Foundation: Slab

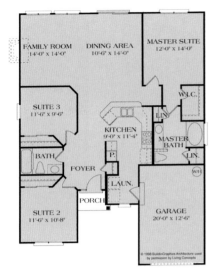

Plan: HPK3200009

Square Footage: 1,402
Bedrooms: 3
Bathrooms: 2

Width: 37' - 7"
Depth: 50' - 1"
Foundation: Slab

Plan: HPK3200010

Square Footage: 1,416
Bedrooms: 3
Bathrooms: 2

Width: 45' - 0"
Depth: 49' - 10"
Foundation: Slab

Starter Homes

First Floor

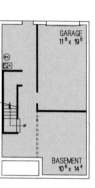

Second Floor

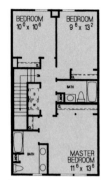

BASEMENT

Plan: HPK3200011

First Floor: 685 sq. ft.
Second Floor: 760 sq. ft.
Total: 1,445 sq. ft.
Bedrooms: 3
Bathrooms: 2 ½

Width: 21' - 0"
Depth: 36' - 0"
Foundation: Unfinished Basement

First Floor

Second Floor

Plan: HPK3200012

First Floor: 743 sq. ft.
Second Floor: 707 sq. ft.
Total: 1,450 sq. ft.
Bedrooms: 3
Bathrooms: 2 ½

Width: 49' - 4"
Depth: 34' - 0"
Foundation: Unfinished Basement

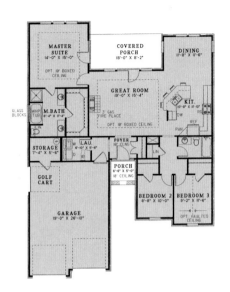

Plan: HPK3200013

Square Footage: 1,472
Bedrooms: 3
Bathrooms: 2
Width: 45' - 0"

Depth: 60' - 4"
Foundation: Crawlspace, Slab

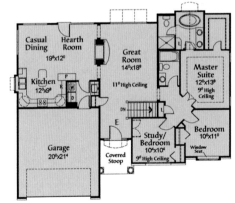

Plan: HPK3200014

Square Footage: 1,486
Bedrooms: 3
Bathrooms: 2
Width: 52' - 8"

Depth: 44' - 4"
Foundation: Unfinished Basement

Starter Homes

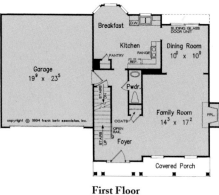

First Floor

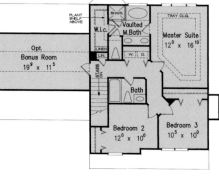

Second Floor

Plan: HPK3200015

First Floor: 767 sq. ft.
Second Floor: 738 sq. ft.
Total: 1,505 sq. ft.
Bedrooms: 3
Bathrooms: 2 ½

Width: 47' - 10"
Depth: 36' - 0"
Foundation: Crawlspace, Slab, Unfinished Walkout Basement

© 2005 Donald A. Gardner, Inc.

Plan: HPK3200016

Square Footage: 1,536
Bedrooms: 3
Bathrooms: 2

Width: 55' - 4"
Depth: 51' - 0"

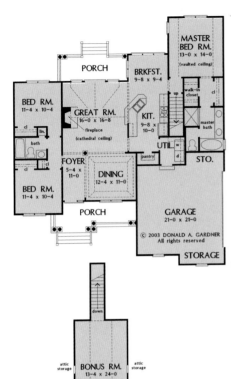

Plan: HPK3200017

Square Footage: 1,547
Bonus Space: 391 sq. ft.
Bedrooms: 3

Bathrooms: 2
Width: 51' - 8"
Depth: 59' - 0"

Plan: HPK3200018

Square Footage: 1,562
Bedrooms: 3
Bathrooms: 2 ½

Width: 85' - 4"
Depth: 27' - 4"
Foundation: Slab

Starter Homes

First Floor

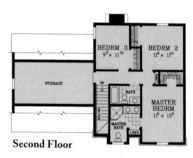

Second Floor

Plan: HPK3200019

First Floor: 798 sq. ft.
Second Floor: 765 sq. ft.
Total: 1,563 sq. ft.
Bedrooms: 3
Bathrooms: 2 ½

Width: 47' - 4"
Depth: 38' - 10"
Foundation: Unfinished Basement

Lower Level

Main Level

Plan: HPK3200020

Main Level: 1,504 sq. ft.
Lower Level: 68 sq. ft.
Total: 1,572 sq. ft.
Bedrooms: 3
Bathrooms: 2

Width: 51' - 2"
Depth: 32' - 4"
Foundation: Unfinished Walkout Basement

DECK

spa

MASTER BED RM.
13-4 x 13-8

master bath

skylights

BED RM.
11-4 x 11-0

GREAT RM.
15-4 x 16-10
(cathedral ceiling)

fireplace

BRKFST.
11-4 x 7-8

walk-in closet

storage

KITCHEN
11-4 x 10-0

FOYER
8-2 x 5-10

GARAGE
20-0 x 19-8

bath

DINING
11-4 x 11-4

PORCH

BED RM./
STUDY
11-4 x 10-4

B. NATHAN.

Plan: HPK3200021

Square Footage: 1,576
Bedrooms: 3
Bathrooms: 2

Width: 60' - 6"
Depth: 47' - 3"

Plan: HPK3200022

Main Level: 1,083 sq. ft.
Lower Level: 512 sq. ft.
Total: 1,595 sq. ft.
Bedrooms: 3
Bathrooms: 2

Width: 36' - 0"
Depth: 32' - 0"
Foundation: Unfinished Basement

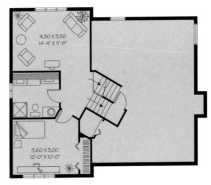

4.30 X 3.50
14'-4" X 11'-8"

3.60 X 3.00
12'-0" X 10'-0"

Lower Level

12'-4"x 12'-0"
3.70 x 3.60

9'-0"x 10'-0"
2.70 x 3.00

10'-4"x 12'-4"
3.10 x 3.70

17'-0"x 14'-4"
5.10 x 4.30

12'-4"x 10'-0"
3.70 x 3.00

Main Level

Starter Homes

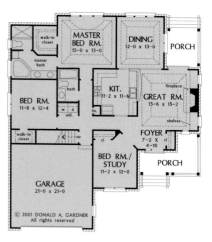

Plan: HPK3200023

Square Footage: 1,610   Bathrooms: 2
Bonus Space: 353 sq. ft.   Width: 49' - 11"
Bedrooms: 3   Depth: 55' - 1"

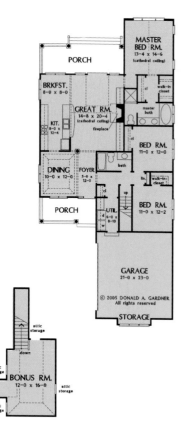

Plan: HPK3200024

Square Footage: 1,611   Bathrooms: 2
Bonus Space: 300 sq. ft.   Width: 37' - 4"
Bedrooms: 3   Depth: 82' - 6"

First Floor

Second Floor

Plan: HPK3200025

First Floor: 1,005 sq. ft.
Second Floor: 620 sq. ft.
Total: 1,625 sq. ft.
Bedrooms: 2
Bathrooms: 2 ½

Width: 30' - 0"
Depth: 44' - 6"
Foundation: Finished
Walkout Basement

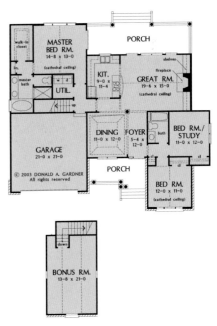

Plan: HPK3200026

Square Footage: 1,628
Bonus Space: 300 sq. ft.
Bedrooms: 3

Bathrooms: 2
Width: 56' - 0"
Depth: 50' - 4"

Starter Homes

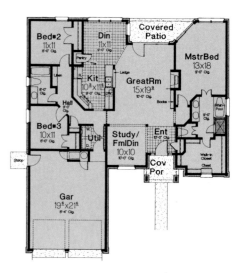

Plan: HPK3200027

Square Footage: 1,640
Bedrooms: 3
Bathrooms: 2

Width: 50' - 0"
Depth: 55' - 4"
Foundation: Slab

© 2004 Donald A. Gardner, Inc.

Plan: HPK3200028

Square Footage: 1,640
Bedrooms: 3
Bathrooms: 2

Width: 55' - 10"
Depth: 55' - 6"

Plan: HPK3200029

Square Footage: 1,644
Bedrooms: 3
Bathrooms: 2

Width: 55' - 0"
Depth: 41' - 10"
Foundation: Slab

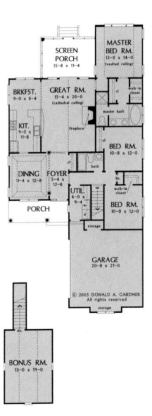

Plan: HPK3200030

Square Footage: 1,651
Bonus Space: 264 sq. ft.
Bedrooms: 3

Bathrooms: 2
Width: 38' - 8"
Depth: 79' - 2"

Starter Homes

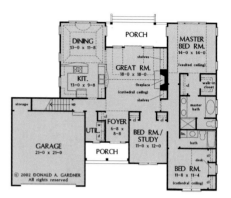

Plan: HPK3200031

Square Footage: 1,654
Bonus Space: 356 sq. ft.
Bedrooms: 3

Bathrooms: 2
Width: 60' - 4"
Depth: 47' - 10"

First Floor

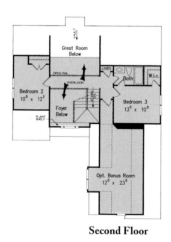

Second Floor

Plan: HPK3200032

First Floor: 1,179 sq. ft.
Second Floor: 479 sq. ft.
Total: 1,658 sq. ft.
Bonus Space: 338 sq. ft.
Bedrooms: 3
Bathrooms: 2 ½

Width: 41' - 6"
Depth: 54' - 4"
Foundation: Crawlspace,
Slab, Unfinished Walkout
Basement

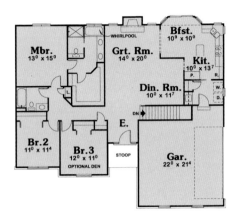

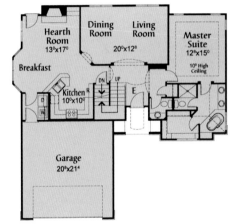

Whirlpool

Mbr.
13⁰ x 15⁰

Grt. Rm.
14⁰ x 20⁰

Bfst.
10⁹ x 10⁰

Kit.
10⁰ x 13⁷

Din. Rm.
10⁰ x 11⁷

E.

Br.2
11⁰ x 11⁴

Br.3
12⁰ x 11⁰
OPTIONAL DEN

STOOP

Gar.
22⁰ x 21⁴

Den
12⁰ x 11⁰

Optional Layout

Plan: HPK3200033

Square Footage: 1,660
Bedrooms: 3
Bathrooms: 2

Width: 54' - 4"
Depth: 48' - 4"

Hearth Room
13⁰x17⁰

Dining Room

Living Room
20⁰x12⁸

Master Suite
12⁸x15⁰

10⁰ High Ceiling

Breakfast

Kitchen
10⁰x10⁰

Garage
20⁰x21⁴

First Floor

Bedroom
11⁸x10⁴

Bedroom
10⁸x12⁸

Four Bedroom Option Available

Open to Below

Second Floor

Plan: HPK3200034

First Floor: 1,233 sq. ft.
Second Floor: 433 sq. ft.
Total: 1,666 sq. ft.
Bedrooms: 3
Bathrooms: 2 ½

Width: 49' - 0"
Depth: 47' - 4"
Foundation: Unfinished Basement

Starter Homes

First Floor

Second Floor

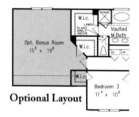

Optional Layout

Plan: HPK3200035

First Floor: 882 sq. ft.
Second Floor: 793 sq. ft.
Total: 1,675 sq. ft.
Bonus Space: 416 sq. ft.
Bedrooms: 3
Bathrooms: 2 ½

Width: 49' - 6"
Depth: 35' - 4"
Foundation: Crawlspace,
Slab, Unfinished Walkout
Basement

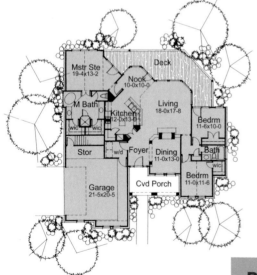

Plan: HPK3200036

Square Footage: 1,675
Bedrooms: 3
Bathrooms: 2
Width: 57' - 5"

Depth: 59' - 6"
Foundation: Crawlspace,
Slab, Unfinished
Basement

Starter Homes

Plan: HPK3200037

Square Footage: 1,684
Bedrooms: 3
Bathrooms: 2 ½
Width: 55' - 6"

Depth: 57' - 6"
Foundation: Unfinished
Walkout Basement

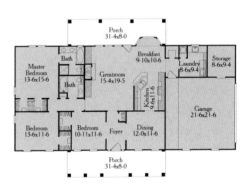

Plan: HPK3200038

Square Footage: 1,688
Bedrooms: 3
Bathrooms: 2
Width: 70' - 1"

Depth: 48' - 0"
Foundation: Crawlspace,
Slab, Unfinished
Basement

Starter Homes

First Floor

Plan: HPK3200039

First Floor: 1,235 sq. ft.
Second Floor: 459 sq. ft.
Total: 1,694 sq. ft.
Bonus Space: 236 sq. ft.
Bedrooms: 3

Bathrooms: 2 ½
Width: 48' - 6"
Depth: 42' - 4"
Foundation: Slab

Second Floor

First Floor

Plan: HPK3200040

First Floor: 780 sq. ft.
Second Floor: 915 sq. ft.
Total: 1,695 sq. ft.
Bedrooms: 3
Bathrooms: 2 ½

Width: 41' - 0"
Depth: 41' - 0"
Foundation: Unfinished
Walkout Basement

Second Floor

Plan: HPK3200041

Square Footage: 1,699   Width: 50' - 0"
Bedrooms: 3   Depth: 51' - 0"
Bathrooms: 2   Foundation: Crawlspace

Plan: HPK3200042

Square Footage: 1,701   Width: 45' - 0"
Bedrooms: 3   Depth: 68' - 2"
Bathrooms: 2   Foundation: Slab

Starter Homes

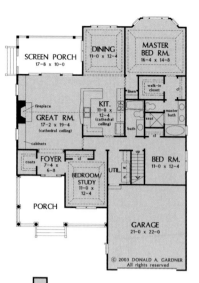

SCREEN PORCH 17-8 x 10-0

DINING 11-0 x 12-4

MASTER BED RM. 16-4 x 14-8

GREAT RM. 17-2 x 19-4 (cathedral ceiling)

KIT. 11-0 x 12-4 (cathedral ceiling)

FOYER 7-4 x 6-8

BEDROOM/ STUDY 11-0 x 12-4

PORCH

BED RM. 11-0 x 12-4

UTIL.

GARAGE 21-0 x 22-0

BONUS RM. 13-4 x 22-0

attic storage   attic storage

Plan: HPK3200043

Square Footage: 1,727
Bonus Space: 346 sq. ft.
Bedrooms: 3

Bathrooms: 2
Width: 46' - 0"
Depth: 66' - 4"

First Floor

Patio

Covered Porch

Breakfast 10'6" x 13'6"

Kitchen 8'7" x 11'6"

Great Room 12'9" x 17'10" 12' ceiling

Bath

Laun.

Foyer

Porch

Dining Room 11'6" x 12'

WALK-IN CLOSET

Two-Car Garage 21' x 25'

Second Floor

Bedroom 11'3" x 11'6"

Bath

Great Room Below

Foyer Below

Hall

Master Bedroom 12'2" x 16'

TRAY CEILING

Bedroom 11'6" x 9'7"

PLANT SHELF

SLOPE   SLOPE

Bath

WALK-IN CLOSET

ATTIC STORAGE

Plan: HPK3200044

First Floor: 941 sq. ft.
Second Floor: 786 sq. ft.
Total: 1,727 sq. ft.
Bedrooms: 3
Bathrooms: 2 ½

Width: 57' - 10"
Depth: 42' - 4"
Foundation: Unfinished Basement

Plan: HPK3200045

Square Footage: 1,732
Bonus Space: 243 sq. ft.
Bedrooms: 3
Bathrooms: 2

Width: 52' - 0"
Depth: 63' - 10"
Foundation: Crawlspace, Slab

© Stephen Fuller, Inc.

Plan: HPK3200046

Square Footage: 1,733
Bedrooms: 3
Bathrooms: 2 ½
Width: 55' - 6"

Depth: 57' - 6"
Foundation: Unfinished Walkout Basement

Starter Homes

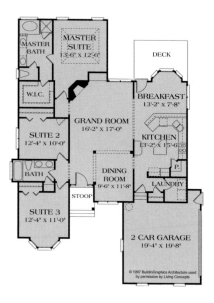

© 1997 BuildinGraphics Architecture used by permission by Living Concepts

Plan: HPK3200047

Square Footage: 1,734	Width: 48' - 0"
Bedrooms: 3	Depth: 65' - 3"
Bathrooms: 2	Foundation: Crawlspace

Plan: HPK3200048

Square Footage: 1,736	Width: 50' - 0"
Bedrooms: 3	Depth: 62' - 10"
Bathrooms: 2	Foundation: Slab

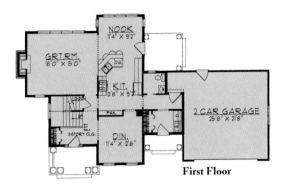

First Floor

Second Floor

Plan: HPK3200049

First Floor: 1,032 sq. ft.
Second Floor: 716 sq. ft.
Total: 1,748 sq. ft.
Bedrooms: 3
Bathrooms: 2 ½

Width: 64' - 8"
Depth: 37' - 0"
Foundation: Unfinished Basement

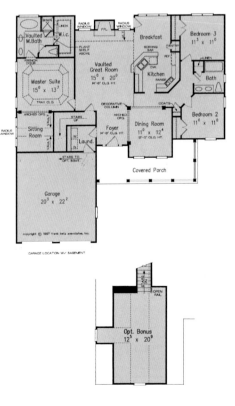

Plan: HPK3200050

Square Footage: 1,749
Bonus Space: 308 sq. ft.
Bedrooms: 3
Bathrooms: 2
Width: 54' - 0"

Depth: 56' - 6"
Foundation: Crawlspace, Slab, Unfinished Walkout Basement

Starter Homes

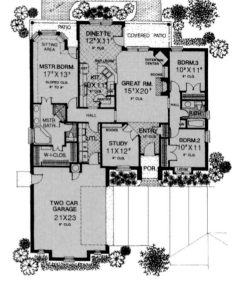

Plan: HPK3200051

Square Footage: 1,760
Bedrooms: 3
Bathrooms: 2

Width: 50' - 0"
Depth: 65' - 4"
Foundation: Slab

First Floor

Second Floor

Plan: HPK3200052

First Floor: 1,210 sq. ft.
Second Floor: 555 sq. ft.
Total: 1,765 sq. ft.
Bedrooms: 3
Bathrooms: 2 ½

Width: 43' - 4"
Depth: 37' - 0"
Foundation: Unfinished Basement

Gables and a multilevel roof create the soft charm of this design. The foyer provides views into both the great room with a warming hearth and the dining room with a vaulted ceiling. The great room features a fireplace and access to the rear deck. The kitchen offers a spacious work area and opens to the adjacent breakfast room. Enter the master suite through large double doors and behold a tray ceiling and French doors leading to a private deck. Bedrooms 2 and 3 share a full bath.

Plan: HPK3200053

Square Footage: 1,770
Bedrooms: 3
Bathrooms: 2 ½
Width: 48' - 0"

Depth: 47' - 0"
Foundation: Unfinished Walkout Basement

Starter Homes

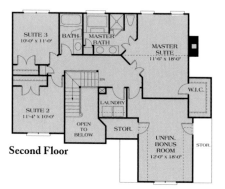

First Floor

© 1992 BuildinGraphics Architecture used by permission by Living Concepts

Second Floor

Plan: HPK3200054

First Floor: 854 sq. ft.
Second Floor: 919 sq. ft.
Total: 1,773 sq. ft.
Bonus Space: 278 sq. ft.
Bedrooms: 3

Bathrooms: 2 ½
Width: 45' - 10"
Depth: 37' - 5"
Foundation: Crawlspace, Slab

Plan: HPK3200055

Square Footage: 1,775
Bedrooms: 3
Bathrooms: 2
Width: 52' - 0"

Depth: 52' - 0"
Foundation: Crawlspace, Slab

Optional Layout

Plan: HPK3200056

Square Footage: 1,779
Bedrooms: 3
Bathrooms: 2
Width: 57' - 0"

Depth: 56' - 4"
Foundation: Crawlspace,
Unfinished Walkout
Basement

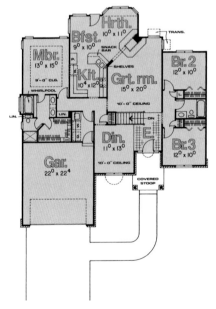

Plan: HPK3200057

Square Footage: 1,782
Bedrooms: 3
Bathrooms: 2

Width: 52' - 0"
Depth: 59' - 4"

Starter Homes

First Floor

Second Floor

Plan: HPK3200058

First Floor: 1,108 sq. ft.
Second Floor: 677 sq. ft.
Total: 1,785 sq. ft.
Bedrooms: 3

Bathrooms: 2 ½
Width: 26' - 1"
Depth: 80' - 2"
Foundation: Slab

Plan: HPK3200059

Square Footage: 1,792
Bedrooms: 3
Bathrooms: 2
Width: 68' - 0"

Depth: 62' - 0"
Foundation: Crawlspace,
Slab, Unfinished
Basement

Order blueprints anytime at
eplans.com or 1-800-521-6797

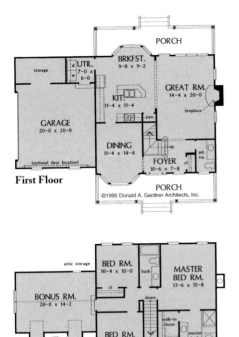

First Floor

©1995 Donald A. Gardner Architects, Inc.

Second Floor

© 1995 Donald A. Gardner Architects, Inc.

Plan: HPK3200060

First Floor: 959 sq. ft.	Bedrooms: 3
Second Floor: 833 sq. ft.	Bathrooms: 2 ½
Total: 1,792 sq. ft.	Width: 52' - 6"
Bonus Space: 344 sq. ft.	Depth: 42' - 8"

© 2002 Donald A. Gardner, Inc.

First Floor

© 2002 DONALD A. GARDNER All rights reserved

Second Floor

Plan: HPK3200061

First Floor: 1,345 sq. ft.	Bedrooms: 3
Second Floor: 452 sq. ft.	Bathrooms: 2 ½
Total: 1,797 sq. ft.	Width: 63' - 0"
Bonus Space: 349 sq. ft.	Depth: 40' - 0"

Starter Homes

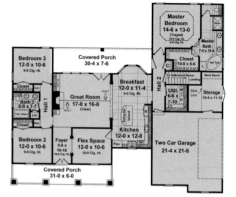

Plan: HPK3200062

Square Footage: 1,800
Bonus Space: 302 sq. ft.
Bedrooms: 3
Bathrooms: 2

Width: 65' - 0"
Depth: 56' - 8"
Foundation: Crawlspace, Slab

Plan: HPK3200063

Square Footage: 1,800
Bedrooms: 3
Bathrooms: 2

Width: 62' - 2"
Depth: 53' - 5"

Plan: HPK3200064

First Floor: 927 sq. ft.	Bedrooms: 3
Second Floor: 880 sq. ft.	Bathrooms: 2 ½
Total: 1,807 sq. ft.	Width: 58' - 4"
Bonus Space: 117 sq. ft.	Depth: 38' - 8"

A large covered porch at the back of this home will be a great place to grill out, entertain or enjoy a few moments of quiet solitude. The floor plan includes a flex room, allowing the formal dining room to easily convert to a den. With either arrangement, a lovely triple window brings in plenty of natural light and invites a peaceful state of mind. Just inside the entry, the breakfast area can function formally or informally and connects with a centrally positioned walk-through kitchen. Three family bedrooms—including a generous master suite—reside on the second floor.

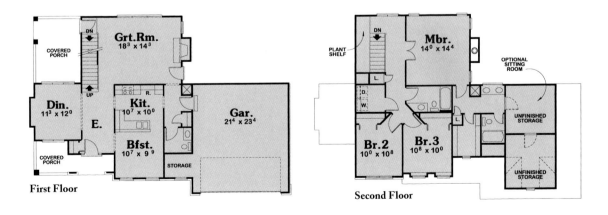

First Floor

Second Floor

Starter Homes

Plan: HPK3200065

Square Footage: 1,807	Width: 74' - 0"
Bedrooms: 3	Depth: 44' - 0"
Bathrooms: 2 ½	Foundation: Slab

The striking European facade of this home presents a beautiful stone exterior, complete with stone quoins, a shingled rooftop, and French-style shutters on the front windows. Step inside the great room where a 10-foot ceiling and fireplace will greet you. A large island in the kitchen provides plenty of much-needed counter space for the cook of the family. An element of privacy is observed with the master suite separated from the other two bedrooms, which share a full bath. An oversized two-car garage and a covered patio are just some of the added amenities.

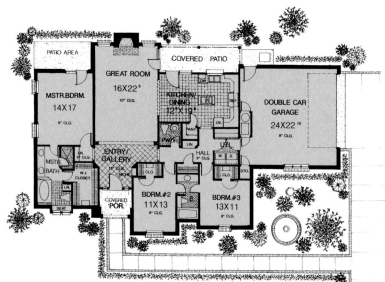

This modest three-bedroom home offers the charm of brick and siding and all the comforts of a true family home. Upon entry, the dining room is on the left, defined by columns and an arch. Continue to the island kitchen that offers a rounded eating bar for fun, casual meals. A vaulted nook is a great place to take in the morning sun. The hearth-warmed living room is inviting and open. The master suite grants homeowners a lavish spa bath and an 11-foot ceiling. Two family bedrooms share a full bath on the opposite side of the home.

Plan: HPK3200066

Square Footage: 1,810
Bedrooms: 3
Bathrooms: 2

Width: 55' - 0"
Depth: 48' - 0"

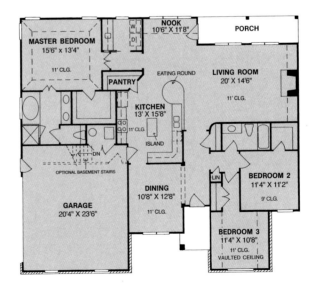

Starter Homes

Plan: HPK3200067

First Floor: 837 sq. ft.
Second Floor: 977 sq. ft.
Total: 1,814 sq. ft.
Bedrooms: 4

Bathrooms: 2 ½
Width: 58' - 4"
Depth: 41' - 4"

This traditional design features a garden room with twin skylights, a sloped ceiling, and two walls of windows. The kitchen provides plenty of counter space and easily serves the formal dining room, which opens through double doors to the garden room. A balcony overlooks the great room, which is warmed by a fireplace. All four bedrooms including the master suite with its full bath and plentiful storage space, are on the upper level.

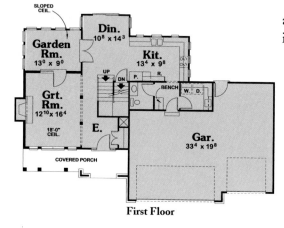

First Floor

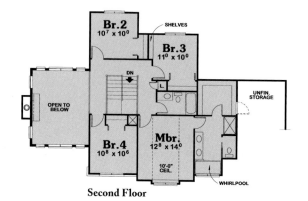

Second Floor

Plan: HPK3200068

First Floor: 972 sq. ft.
Second Floor: 843 sq. ft.
Total: 1,815 sq. ft.
Bonus Space: 180 sq. ft.
Bedrooms: 3

Bathrooms: 2 ½
Width: 45' - 0"
Depth: 37' - 0"
Foundation: Crawlspace

First Floor

Second Floor

A brick arch and a two-story bay window adorn the facade of this comfortable family home. Inside, the formal bayed living room and dining room combine to make entertaining a breeze. At the rear of the home, family life is easy with the open floor plan of the family room, breakfast nook, and efficient kitchen. A fireplace graces the family room, and sliding glass doors access the outdoors from the nook. Upstairs, three bedrooms include the master suite with a pampering bath. A full hall bath with twin vanities is shared by the family bedrooms. A bonus room is available for future development as a study, library, or fourth bedroom.

Starter Homes

©1999 Donald A. Gardner, Inc.

Plan: HPK3200069

Square Footage: 1,829	Bathrooms: 2
Bonus Space: 424 sq. ft.	Width: 54' - 11"
Bedrooms: 3	Depth: 58' - 7"

Similar elements are arranged asymmetrically to add interest to this brick cottage's exterior. Keystone arches and shutters accent small-pane windows. The floor plan is simple and practical. The great room, the heart of the home, includes a focal-point fireplace, built-in shelves, a cathedral ceiling, and access to a rear covered porch. The bumped-out dining room is elegant, octagonal in shape, and wrapped in windows to enhance mealtimes with natural sunlight or moonlight. A second porch leads into a sizable utility room off the kitchen.

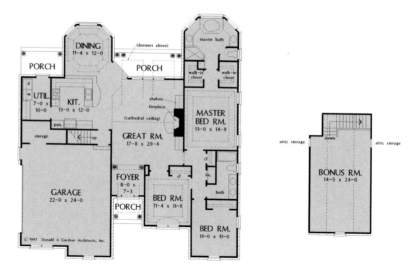

Plan: HPK3200070

Square Footage: 1,832
Bonus Space: 68 sq. ft.
Bedrooms: 3
Bathrooms: 2 ½
Width: 59' - 6"

Depth: 52' - 6"
Foundation: Crawlspace, Slab, Unfinished Walkout Basement

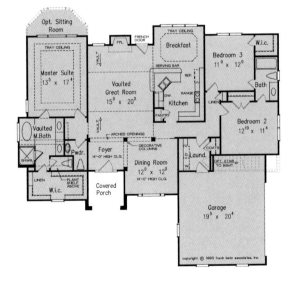

This compact one-story has plenty of living in it. The master suite features an optional sun-washed sitting area with views to the rear of the home. A vaulted great room with fireplace conveniently accesses the kitchen via a serving bar. Meals can also be taken in the cozy breakfast area. For formal occasions the dining room creates opulence with its decorative columns. Two family bedrooms flank the right of the home with a shared bath, linen storage, and easy access to laundry facilities.

Starter Homes

Plan: HPK3200071

First Floor: 972 sq. ft.
Second Floor: 860 sq. ft.
Total: 1,832 sq. ft.
Bedrooms: 3
Bathrooms: 2 ½

Width: 38' - 0"
Depth: 53' - 0"
Foundation: Unfinished
Basement, Block

There's lots of bang for your buck in this narrow-lot Colonial. The first floor incorporates an open plan that encompasses a great room, kitchen, and bayed casual dining nook. A bayed formal dining room, near the foyer and the kitchen, conveniently hosts guests for meals. A laundry and powder room are also located on the first floor. Upstairs, two family bedrooms and a full bath comprise the second floor, along with the master suite. This bedroom includes a double-vanity bath and a spacious walk-in closet.

First Floor

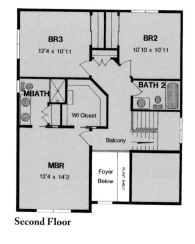

Second Floor

Corner quoins, French shutters, and rounded windows provide an Old World feel to this modern cottage design. A stunning brick facade hints at the exquisite beauty of the interior spaces. The great room is warmed by a fireplace and accesses the rear porch. The casual kitchen/ dinette area provides pantry space. The master suite offers a private bath and enormous walk-in closet. Two family bedrooms on the opposite side of the home share a full hall bath and linen storage. A double garage and laundry room are located nearby.

Plan: HPK3200072

Square Footage: 1,834	Width: 55′ - 0″
Bedrooms: 3	Depth: 60′ - 4″
Bathrooms: 2	Foundation: Slab

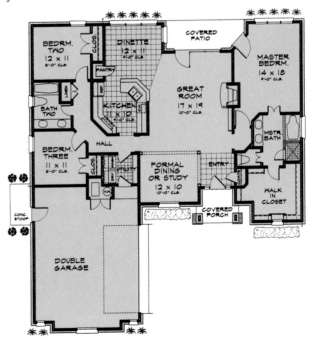

Starter Homes

Plan: HPK3200073

Square Footage: 1,835	Bathrooms: 2
Bonus Space: 866 sq. ft.	Width: 53' - 4"
Bedrooms: 3	Depth: 57' - 10"

Beaming with grandeur, this floor plan exhibits exceptional architectural detail in its fascinating exterior. The multiple gables and large dormer grant height, while elegant windows spark instant curb appeal. For added luxury, the large master suite features a lengthy walk-in closet and stylish tray ceiling. A built-in shower seat and linen closet add flair to the master bath. Adjacent to the master bedroom, the dining room is also accented with a ceiling treatment that grants altitude to the formal room. For entertaining or just enjoying family time, the vaulted great room includes a fireplace and built-in shelves for family knick-knacks. Accessing the rear porch and overlooking the front, the great room provides double oportunities for enjoying Mother Nature. The bonus room offers 866 square feet of additional flexible space.

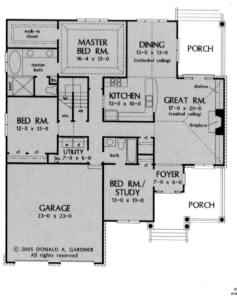

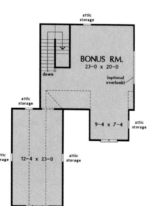

Plan: HPK3200074

First Floor: 1,022 sq. ft.	Bathrooms: 2 ½
Second Floor: 813 sq. ft.	Width: 36' - 0"
Total: 1,835 sq. ft.	Depth: 33' - 0"
Bedrooms: 3	Foundation: Slab

This home is quite appealing, with its steeply sloping rooflines and large sunburst and multipane windows. The plan not only accommodates a narrow lot, but it also fits a sloping site. The angled corner entry gives way to a two-story living room with a tiled hearth. The dining room shares an interesting angled space with this area and offers easy service from the efficient kitchen. Double doors in the family room lead to a refreshing balcony. A powder room and laundry room complete the main level. Upstairs, a vaulted master bedroom has a private bath; two other bedrooms share a bath.

First Floor

Second Floor

Starter Homes

© Sater Design Collection, Inc.

Plan: HPK3200075

First Floor: 1,342 sq. ft.
Second Floor: 511 sq. ft.
Total: 1,853 sq. ft.
Bedrooms: 3
Bathrooms: 2

Width: 44' - 0"
Depth: 40' - 0"
Foundation: Unfinished Basement

Matchstick details and a careful blend of stone and siding lend a special style and spirit to this stately retreat. Multipane windows take in the scenery and deck out the refined exterior of this cabin-style home, designed for a life of luxury. An open foyer shares its natural light with the great room—a bright reprieve filled with its own outdoor light. Dinner guests may wander from the coziness of the hearth space into the crisp night air through lovely French doors. The master retreat is an entire wing of the main level.

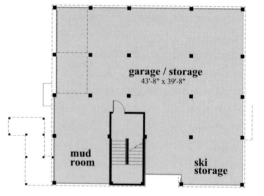

Second Floor

First Floor

Interesting rooflines in this European-influenced, tacked-stone-and-stucco home are just one of the many architectural details that make this plan special. Note the flared copper hood over the extended bay window. The first-floor master suite, featuring a large walk-in closet and private bath, serves as a private retreat away from the traffic flow. Stairs are conveniently placed in the breakfast area leading to the sleeping zone—which consists of two family bedrooms, a full hall bath and an optional bonus room. Don't miss the large laundry room located near the garage entrance.

Plan: HPK3200076

First Floor: 1,317 sq. ft.	Bathrooms: 2 ½
Second Floor: 537 sq. ft.	Width: 53' - 0"
Total: 1,854 sq. ft.	Depth: 52' - 0"
Bonus Space: 288 sq. ft.	Foundation: Unfinished Basement
Bedrooms: 3	

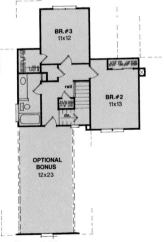

Second Floor

First Floor

Starter Homes

© 1991 Donald A. Gardner, Architects, Inc.

Plan: HPK3200077

First Floor: 1,416 sq. ft.
Second Floor: 445 sq. ft.
Total: 1,861 sq. ft.
Bonus Space: 284 sq. ft.

Bedrooms: 3
Bathrooms: 2 ½
Width: 58' - 3"
Depth: 68' - 6"

Arched windows and triple gables provide a touch of elegance to this traditional home. An entrance supported by columns welcomes family and guests inside. On the main level, the dining room offers round columns at the entrance. The great room boasts a cathedral ceiling, a fireplace, and an arched window over the doors to the deck. The kitchen features an island cooktop and an adjoining breakfast nook for informal dining. The master suite offers twin walk-in closets and a lavish bath that includes a whirlpool tub and a double-basin vanity.

©1991 Donald A. Gardner Architects, Inc.

First Floor

Second Floor

First Floor

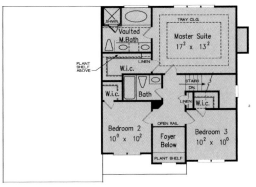

Second Floor

Plan: HPK3200078

First Floor: 1,103 sq. ft.
Second Floor: 759 sq. ft.
Total: 1,862 sq. ft.
Bonus Space: 342 sq. ft.
Bedrooms: 4
Bathrooms: 3

Width: 50' - 4"
Depth: 35' - 0"
Foundation: Crawlspace,
Slab, Unfinished Walkout
Basement

This charming country home speaks well of an American vernacular style, with classic clapboard siding, shutters, and sash windows—all dressed up for 21st-Century living. A flex room on the first floor can be a study, playroom, or fourth bedroom. The casual living space includes a fireplace, wide views of the rear property, and a French door to the outside. Upstairs, the master suite features a vaulted bath with separate shower, dual vanity, and walk-in closet with linen storage.

Starter Homes

Plan: HPK3200079

Square Footage: 1,869	Depth: 60' - 6"
Bedrooms: 3	Foundation: Crawlspace,
Bathrooms: 2	Slab, Unfinished Walkout
Width: 54' - 0"	Basement

This quaint design is picture perfect for any neighborhood setting. Inside, a foyer opens to the formal dining room. The living room is warmed by a fireplace. The kitchen easily serves the bayed breakfast nook, which accesses the rear patio/deck. The master bedroom is located to the right side of the plan and features an elegant master bath with a walk-in closet. A laundry room accesses the two-car garage. Bedrooms 2 and 3 share a hall bath. Upstairs, the bonus room is great for a private home office, guest suite, or attic space.

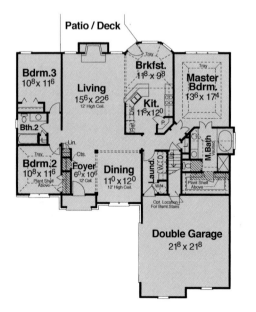

This spacious plan announces a well-planned interior with an elevation that mixes European elements with a ranch-house feeling. On the outside, stone and brick combine to create the look of an English manor. Inside, the main living area boasts a single level filled with ontemporary amenities, such as a spa-style tub with a mitered window in the master suite and an island kitchen overlooking a bayed breakfast nook.

Plan: HPK3200080

Square Footage: 1,871
Bonus Space: 390 sq. ft.
Bedrooms: 3
Bathrooms: 2
Width: 73' - 4"

Depth: 51' - 8"
Foundation: Crawlspace, Slab, Unfinished Basement

Starter Homes

Plan: HPK3200081

First Floor: 870 sq. ft.
Second Floor: 1,007 sq. ft.
Total: 1,877 sq. ft.
Bonus Space: 263 sq. ft.
Bedrooms: 4

Bathrooms: 2 ½
Width: 40' - 0"
Depth: 49' - 0"
Foundation: Crawlspace

This early American home is Colonial in appearance, but features traditional Neoclassic and transitional accents. Inside, the first floor offers formal areas, as well as an island kitchen with a nook and a casual family room with a fireplace. A garage and powder room are located nearby. Upstairs, the vaulted master bedroom provides a private bath and walk-in closet. The three additional family bedrooms share the full hall bath. Bonus space is reserved for storage, a home office, guest suite or exercise room.

NOOK
8/0 X 10/2
(9' CLG.)

FAMILY
13/0 X 14/2
(9' CLG.)

DINING
11/4 X 9/0
(9' CLG.)

PAN.

GARAGE
19/6 X 27/0

LIVING
11/4 X 11/0
(9' CLG.)

UP

First Floor

VAULTED
MASTER
13/8 X 12/2

BR. 4
11/10 X 10/0

BR. 2
11/8 X 10/0

BONUS
19/6 X 10/8

BR. 3
11/8 X 10/0

Second Floor

© 1999 Donald A. Gardner, Inc.

An arched window in a center front-facing gable lends style and beauty to the facade of this three-bedroom home. An open common area features a great room with a cathedral ceiling, a formal dining room with a tray ceiling, a functional kitchen, and an informal breakfast area that separates the master suite from the secondary bedrooms for privacy. The master suite provides a dramatic vaulted ceiling, access to the back porch, and abundant closet space. Access to a versatile bonus room is near the master bedroom.

Plan: HPK3200082

Square Footage: 1,882	Bathrooms: 2 ½
Bonus Space: 363 sq. ft.	Width: 61' - 4"
Bedrooms: 3	Depth: 55' - 0"

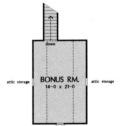

BONUS RM.
14-0 x 21-0
attic storage   attic storage

The Big Book of Traditional House Plans   **61**

Starter Homes

Plan: HPK3200083

First Floor: 1,347 sq. ft.	Bathrooms: 2 ½
Second Floor: 537 sq. ft.	Width: 32' - 10"
Total: 1,884 sq. ft.	Depth: 70' - 10"
Bedrooms: 3	Foundation: Crawlspace

This old-fashioned townhouse design features an attractive two-story floor plan. Two front covered porches enhance the traditional facade. Inside, the foyer introduces an island kitchen that overlooks the dining room. A formal two-story living room, located at the rear of the plan, is warmed by a fireplace. The first-floor master suite features a private bath and huge walk-in closet. A powder room, laundry room, and two-car garage complete the first floor. Upstairs, two secondary bedrooms—one with a walk-in closet—share a full hall bath. Bedroom 3 features a private balcony overlooking the front property. Optional storage is available on this floor, as well.

Second Floor

First Floor

Plan: HPK3200084

First Floor: 1,408 sq. ft.
Second Floor: 476 sq. ft.
Total: 1,884 sq. ft.
Bedrooms: 3

Bathrooms: 2 ½
Width: 41' - 8"
Depth: 56' - 4"

If there's a narrow-lot home that provides a lot of living for its square footage, this is it. While a front-entry garage provides convenience, a spacious patio encourages outdoor relaxation. With a central hall dividing the common rooms from the sleeping quarters, the floor plan marries openness with privacy. Both the foyer and great room have two-story ceilings, which expand visual space; a bay window with a seat extends the breakfast nook. The dining room is topped by a cathedral ceiling. In the master suite, a tray ceiling crowns the bedroom. The master bath includes a double vanity, garden tub, shower with seat, and a compartmented toilet.

First Floor

Second Floor

Starter Homes

Plan: HPK3200085

Square Footage: 1,890
Bedrooms: 3
Bathrooms: 2
Width: 65' - 10"

Depth: 53' - 5"
Foundation: Crawlspace, Slab

This classic home exudes elegance and style and offers sophisticated amenities in a compact size. Ten-foot ceilings throughout the plan lend an aura of spacious hospitality. A generous living room with a sloped ceiling, built-in bookcases, and a centerpiece fireplace offers views as well as access to the rear yard. The nearby breakfast room shares an informal eating counter with the ample kitchen, which serves the coffer-ceilinged dining room through French doors. Three bedrooms include a sumptuous master suite with windowed whirlpool tub and walk-in closet, and two family bedrooms that share a full bath.

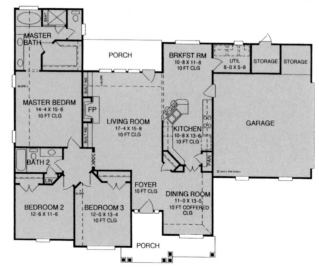

Plan: HPK3200086

First Floor: 830 sq. ft.
Second Floor: 1,060 sq. ft.
Total: 1,890 sq. ft.
Bedrooms: 3
Bathrooms: 2 ½

Width: 41' - 0"
Depth: 40' - 6"
Foundation: Walkout
Basement

First Floor

DECK

BREAKFAST
10'-0" x 7'-0"

GREAT ROOM
18'-6" x 15'-6"

KITCHEN
12'-0" x 10'-10"

UP

DN

FOYER

DINING
9'-6" x 12'-10"

POWDER

TWO-CAR GARAGE
20'-0" x 21'-0"

PORCH

© Stephen Fuller, Inc.

Second Floor

MASTER SUITE
14'-10" x 15'-8"

M. BATH

LAUN.
6'-0" x 5'-8"

W.I.C.

BEDROOM NO. 2
12'-0" X 14'-0"

BATH

BEDROOM No.3
10'-0" x 12'-10"

The pleasing character of this house does not stop behind its facade. The foyer opens to a great room with a fireplace and also to the eat-in kitchen. Stairs lead from the great room to the second floor, where a laundry room is conveniently placed near the bedrooms. The master suite spares none of the amenities: a full bath with a double vanity, shower, tub, and walk-in closet. Bedrooms 2 and 3 share a full bath.

Starter Homes

Plan: HPK3200087

Square Footage: 1,891
Bonus Space: 409 sq. ft.
Bedrooms: 3
Bathrooms: 2 ½
Width: 56' - 0"

Depth: 60' - 0"
Foundation: Crawlspace, Slab, Unfinished Walkout Basement

The stucco exterior and combination rooflines give a stately appearance to this traditional home. Inside, the well-lit foyer leads to an elegant living room with a vaulted ceiling, fireplace, radius window, and French door that opens to the rear property. Two family bedrooms share a full bath on the right side of the home; an impressive master suite resides to the left for privacy. A formal dining room and an open kitchen with plenty of counter space complete the plan.

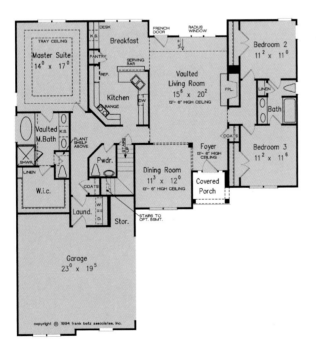

Plan: HPK3200088

First Floor: 1,334 sq. ft.
Second Floor: 562 sq. ft.
Total: 1,896 sq. ft.
Bedrooms: 3

Bathrooms: 2 ½
Width: 55' - 0"
Depth: 47' - 0"

First Floor

NOOK
11'4" X 11'8"
DESK
PORCH
GARAGE
19'8" X 19'6"
AC
D W
PANTRY
EATING BAR
KITCHEN
11'4" X 12'
NICHE
ARCH
DINING ROOM
11'4" X 10'6"
9' CLG.
PORCH
VAULTED CEILING
LIVING ROOM
18'10" X 16'6"
18' CLG.
OPEN TO ABOVE
OPTIONAL BASEMENT STAIRS
UP
DN
MASTER BEDROOM
15'4" X 12'8"
9' CLG.
WINDOW SEAT

Second Floor

ATTIC
AC
OPEN TO BELOW
DN
BEDROOM 2
11'4" X 11'6"
GAME ROOM
13'4" X 9'6"
BEDROOM 3
11'4" X 10'4"
VAULTED CEILING

Siding and a covered porch lend farmhouse flair to this traditional home. The foyer directs traffic ahead, past an archway with a decorative niche, to the living room. A vaulted ceiling and bright windows accentuate natural light, as a cozy fireplace warms the space. The master suite provides respite from daily stresses with a comforting bedroom and a soothing spa bath with a window seat. Secondary bedrooms are located upstairs, sharing a full bath and family game room.

Starter Homes

Plan: HPK3200089

Square Footage: 1,902	Width: 84' - 7"
Bedrooms: 3	Depth: 34' - 5"
Bathrooms: 2 ½	Foundation: Slab

Decidedly country, this estate is designed to take advantage of pastoral views front and back. Fine columns grace the covered front porch that creates an enjoyable extended living space. A tiled entry gives way to an open gallery that expertly guides you through the floor plan. To the left, the master wing houses the private master suite featuring a secluded patio, amentity-filled bath, and a spacious walk-in closet with built-ins. To the right, secondary bedrooms—one with a bay window—share a full bath. At the rear of the home, the oversized great room is a hub of warmth with its extended-hearth fireplace. Within steps, the country kitchen unfolds into an attractive workhorse meant for entertaining and cooking.

Plan: HPK3200090

Square Footage: 1,906
Bedrooms: 3
Bathrooms: 2 ½
Width: 72' - 0"

Depth: 44' - 8"
Foundation: Unfinished Basement

This hip-roofed ranch has an exterior that tastefully mixes brick and siding. The recessed entrance with arched transom and sidelights fills the formal entry with glowing light. The foyer opens to the large living room with high ceilings and a fireplace, the perfect spot for family gatherings. There is a large kitchen with ample cupboard space, and a roomy dining area, which leads to the backyard. The spacious master bedroom with sweeping windows overlooking the rear yard has a large walk-in closet. The private master bath amenities include a whirlpool tub, double vanity, and a large corner shower. Two additional bedrooms share a full bath and each have large closets. The laundry room is on the main level between the three-car garage and kitchen and has a large utility closet.

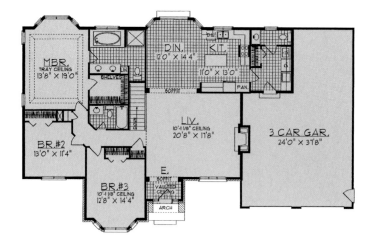

Starter Homes

Plan: HPK3200091

First Floor: 915 sq. ft.
Second Floor: 994 sq. ft.
Total: 1,909 sq. ft.
Bedrooms: 3
Bathrooms: 2 ½

Width: 38' - 0"
Depth: 38' - 0"
Foundation: Unfinished
Basement

The arches on the windows and above the front entrance, combined with keystone details, provide aesthetic appeal to this traditional design and invite you inside to explore a grand floor plan. Enter either into the foyer, with a practical home office directly to the right, or use the side entrance into the kitchen. Eat a casual meal at the island in the kitchen, or formalize the occasion in the dining room. The great room is set into the right side of the plan, which juts out slightly, providing a cozy family atmosphere. The second floor houses three bedrooms and two full baths.

First Floor

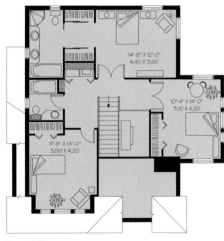

Second Floor

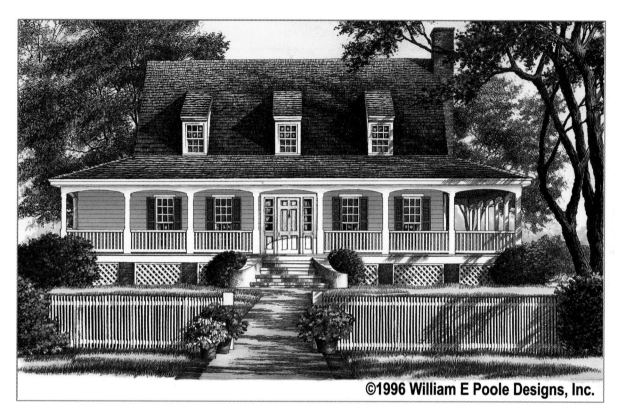

©1996 William E Poole Designs, Inc.

A wraparound porch that envelopes the plan on three sides adds an inviting presence to the facade. Enter through the front to the foyer, where visitors have a choice of destinations. Turn left to the full-depth living room with space for all. Go upstairs to reach two family bedrooms and a full bath. On the left, a powder room is convenient for guests. Straight ahead, a doorway leads to the C-shaped kitchen with stove-top peninsula snack bar. Another doorway, off the breakfast area, opens to the master suite, where a walk-in closet and private bath are sure to please.

Plan: HPK3200092

First Floor: 1,201 sq. ft.	Bathrooms: 2 ½
Second Floor: 708 sq. ft.	Width: 56' - 8"
Total: 1,909 sq. ft.	Depth: 39' - 8"
Bedrooms: 3	Foundation: Crawlspace

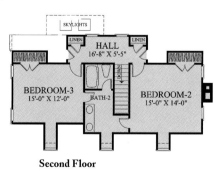

Second Floor

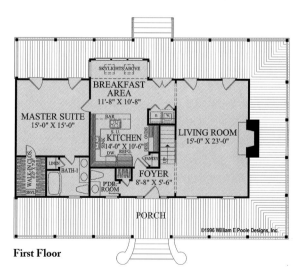

First Floor

Starter Homes

Plan: HPK3200093

Square Footage: 1,911   Width: 56' - 0"
Bedrooms: 3   Depth: 58' - 0"
Bathrooms: 2

This sophisticated ranch design shows off its facade with fanlights and elegant arches. Grace pervades the interior, starting with the formal dining room with a 12-foot coffered ceiling and an arched window. An extensive great room shares a see-through fireplace with a bayed hearth room. The well-planned kitchen features a spacious work area and a snack-bar pass-through to the breakfast area. The secluded master suite offers a coffered ceiling, corner windows, a whirlpool tub, and a skylight. On the opposite side of the plan, two family bedrooms—or one bedroom and a den—share a hall bath that has a skylight.

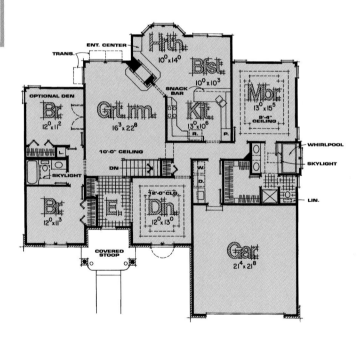

Plan: HPK3200094

Square Footage: 1,911	Width: 45' - 0"
Bedrooms: 3	Depth: 80' - 4"
Bathrooms: 2	Foundation: Crawlspace

Clean lines and an efficient floor plan make this striking home surprisingly economical to build. Stucco and decorative shutters create a welcoming facade as you enter from the covered stoop. Inside, the island kitchen is created for family get-togethers, with lots of space and an open design that encourages conversation from the naturally lit dining room. The gathering room has a dramatic vaulted ceiling and a warming fireplace. At the rear, the master suite accesses a covered lanai and enjoys a sumptuous bath. Two secondary bedrooms are on the far left, or make one a comfortable den.

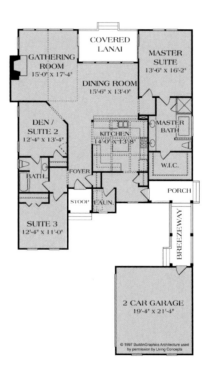

Starter Homes

Plan: HPK3200095

Square Footage: 1,915
Bedrooms: 3
Bathrooms: 2

Width: 47' - 10"
Depth: 62' - 6"
Foundation: Crawlspace

Choose three bedrooms or two bedrooms plus a den in this single-level contemporary design. The well-equipped kitchen is open to a large dining room that overlooks the deck just beyond. The gathering room with a sloped ceiling has a wall of windows across the back and a fireplace in the side wall. The master suite features twin basins and a walk-in closet. Two other bedrooms with an adjoining bath reside off the entry foyer. One of these bedrooms may be used as a den.

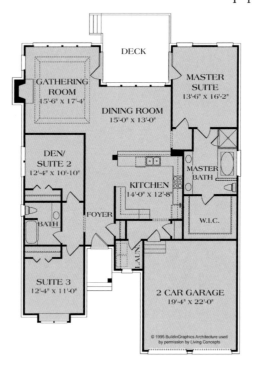

Plan: HPK3200096

Square Footage: 1,922	Width: 79' - 3"
Bedrooms: 3	Depth: 40' - 0"
Bathrooms: 2 ½	Foundation: Slab

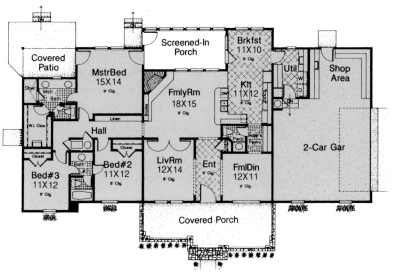

In the Craftsman tradition, this one-story home is enhanced by rubblework masonry and multipaned windows. The covered porch leads into the entry, flanked by the living room and formal dining room. The hearth-warmed family room offers views to the rear screened porch. The island kitchen provides plenty of counter space and close proximity to the breakfast nook. All bedrooms reside on the left side of the plan. The master bedroom boasts a private covered patio and lavish full bath, and two family bedrooms share a full bath. A unique shop area attached to the two-car garage completes the plan.

Starter Homes

Plan: HPK3200097

Square Footage: 1,925	Bathrooms: 2 ½
Bonus Space: 343 sq. ft.	Width: 70' - 0"
Bedrooms: 3	Depth: 49' - 8"

Decorative wood brackets enhance gables as columns and an arched entryway add drama to this lovely home. Inside, an open floor plan creates a natural traffic flow, and custom features like a fireplace, built-in cabinetry, kitchen pass-through, and columns add a personal touch. Tray ceilings highlight the dining room and master bedroom. The breakfast nook is surrounded by windows so early morning coffee can be enjoyed with the sun and outstanding views. Front and rear porches accommodate outdoor living. The master bedroom is located for privacy with a soothing bath. The secondary bedrooms are separated by a full bath. The powder room, laundry room, and bonus room are positioned for convenience. The two-car garage includes storage space.

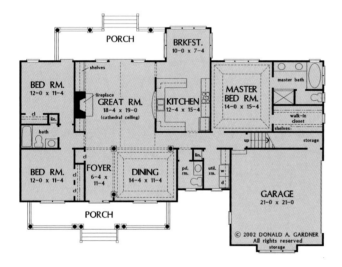

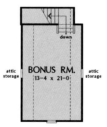

Beautiful brick accentuates arch accents on the entry, windows, and garage. Just off the foyer, the formal dining room, with 12-foot ceilings, features decorative columns. Casual eating space is found off the kitchen and connects to a bright cathedral-ceilinged sunroom. The great room provides a warming fireplace and built-ins. This split floor plan locates three secondary bedrooms, sharing a hall bath, to the right of the plan. The secluded master suite enjoys several windows, two walk-in closets, and a super bath.

Plan: HPK3200098

Square Footage: 1,926	Depth: 56' - 6"
Bedrooms: 4	Foundation: Crawlspace,
Bathrooms: 2	Slab, Unfinished
Width: 63' - 10"	Basement

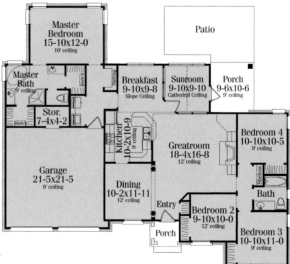

Starter Homes

Plan: HPK3200099

First Floor: 1,002 sq. ft.	Bedrooms: 3
Second Floor: 926 sq. ft.	Bathrooms: 2 ½
Total: 1,928 sq. ft.	Width: 46' - 0"
Bonus Space: 262 sq. ft.	Depth: 51' - 0"

Brick and siding combine over the exterior of this handsome traditional home. A spacious living room and hearth room share a see-through fireplace. Adjoining the kitchen and breakfast room is a convenient snack bar. Just around the corner is a powder room and laundry room. Upstairs, the master suite features a private bath with a whirlpool tub, separate shower, and walk-in closet. Two additional family bedrooms share a full hall bath that includes dual vanities. An unfinished bonus room is available above the two-car garage.

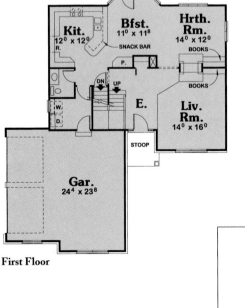

First Floor

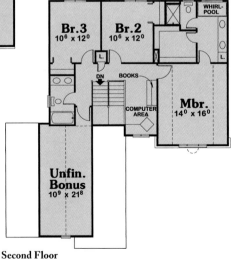

Second Floor

A stone-and-stucco facade invites everyone in to enjoy the outstanding comforts found inside this home. Most notable is the sense of spaciousness created by the free-flowing layout of the kitchen, dining room, breakfast nook, and grand room. The master suite is highlighted by a roomy walk-in wardrobe, twin vanities, and both a tub and shower. Two more bedrooms and a bath are located upstairs, along with a loft that would work well as a computer room.

Plan: HPK3200100

First Floor: 1,314 sq. ft.
Second Floor: 616 sq. ft.
Total: 1,930 sq. ft.
Bedrooms: 3
Bathrooms: 2 ½

Width: 40' - 0"
Depth: 54' - 6"
Foundation: Unfinished Walkout Basement

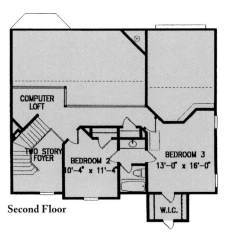

Second Floor

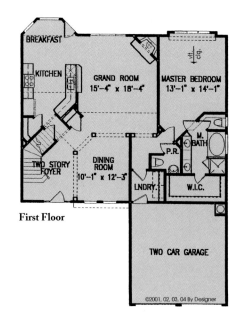

First Floor

Starter Homes

Plan: HPK3200101

Square Footage: 1,930	Width: 52' - 0"
Bedrooms: 4	Depth: 71' - 6"
Bathrooms: 2	Foundation: Crawlspace

This enchanting home incorporates the best floor planning all on one level. The great room, which is convenient for large family gatherings, is highlighted by the fireplace and a 9-foot boxed ceiling. Easy access from the kitchen to the dining room makes hosting a dinner party more convenient. Entertain family and friends during the summer out on the rear grilling porch. As evening approaches, retreat to your master bath complete with large walk-in closet, double vanities, and corner whirlpool tub.

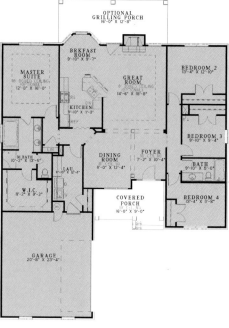

Enter this beautiful home through graceful archways and columns. The foyer, dining room, and living room are one open space defined by a creative room arrangement. The living room opens to the breakfast room and porch. The bedrooms are off a small hall reached through an archway. Two family bedrooms share a bath, and the master bedroom has a private bath with a double-bowl vanity. A garage with storage and a utility room completes the floor plan.

Plan: HPK3200102

Square Footage: 1,932
Bedrooms: 3
Bathrooms: 2
Width: 65' - 10"

Depth: 53' - 5"
Foundation: Crawlspace, Slab

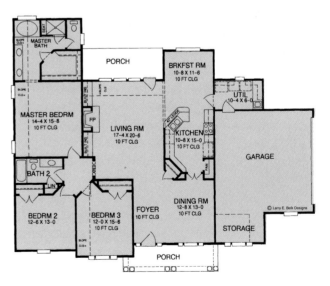

Starter Homes

© William E Poole Designs, Inc.

Plan: HPK3200103

Square Footage: 1,942
Bonus Space: 1,040 sq. ft.
Bedrooms: 3
Bathrooms: 2 ½

Width: 64' - 10"
Depth: 58' - 2"
Foundation: Crawlspace,
Unfinished Basement

Welcome to the perfect starter home. Classical elements lend an air of formality so you'll always feel comfortable welcoming visitors to this tidy cottage. A wealth of bonus space on the second floor invites expansion as your family grows and matures. All the basic elements are here: a formal dining room, a spacious great room, an open kitchen and nook, and a master suite with all the amenities. Elegant touches include paired columns supporting a pedimented porch roof, oculus windows in the great room and master suite, and a built-in bookcase beside the great room's fireplace. Two family bedrooms share a full bath on the first floor, but there is room for more upstairs; or, if you prefer, you can transform the extra space into a home office, an exercise room, or a game room.

First Floor

Second Floor

Plan: HPK3200104

Square Footage: 1,955	Depth: 65' - 0"
Bedrooms: 3	Foundation: Crawlspace,
Bathrooms: 2	Slab
Width: 60' - 10"	

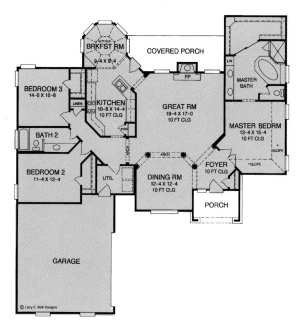

Decorative brick quoin details and oversized multipane windows give a stately look to this traditional home. The expanse of the great room encompasses a fireplace and visually continues to the covered patio via windows. The tiled kitchen is designed for gourmet meals with a door to the back porch and a lovely gazebo breakfast room. Two family bedrooms are split from the master bedroom to afford privacy and share a large hall bath. The master suite has an oversized walk-in closet and a twin-vanity bath.

Starter Homes

Plan: HPK3200105

Square Footage: 1,955
Bedrooms: 3
Bathrooms: 2
Width: 65' - 0"

Depth: 58' - 8"
Foundation: Crawlspace, Slab

First Floor

Plan: HPK3200532

First Floor: 978 sq. ft.
Second Floor: 984 sq. ft.
Total: 1,962 sq. ft.
Bedrooms: 2

Bathrooms: 2 ½
Width: 44' - 0"
Depth: 44' - 0"
Foundation: Crawlspace

Second Floor

This beautiful home, with its covered porch, stone facade, and many windows, is wonderful for a family to enjoy. The design features a study received by double doors, a great room with a cozy fireplace, and a spacious kitchen with a dinette area accessing the rear covered patio. Along with the floor plan is a master bedroom with double doors, a private bath, and access to the private patio. Completing this home is a family bedroom and a three-car garage.

Plan: HPK3200106

Square Footage: 1,966	Width: 85' - 0"
Bedrooms: 2	Depth: 46' - 4"
Bathrooms: 2 ½	Foundation: Slab

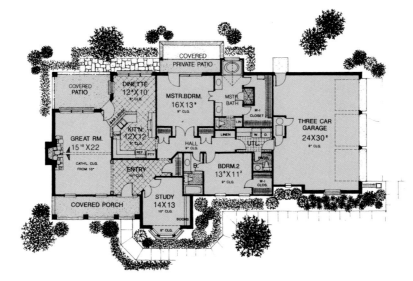

Starter Homes

Plan: HPK3200107

First Floor: 1,497 sq. ft.
Second Floor: 473 sq. ft.
Total: 1,970 sq. ft.
Bonus Space: 401 sq. ft.
Bedrooms: 3

Bathrooms: 2 ½
Width: 55' - 0"
Depth: 63' - 6"
Foundation: Unfinished
Basement

Here is a wonderful home with a delightful facade. Gables, dormers, a covered-porch entry, and a blending of horizontal siding and brick create interest to enhance any neighborhood. The hub of this design—the foyer, dining room, and great room—is expansive and open, lending itself well to entertaining on a grand scale. The U-shaped kitchen offers a sunny breakfast nook for less formal dining. The master bedroom suite is on the first floor for privacy, and the two family bedrooms are located on the second floor.

First Floor

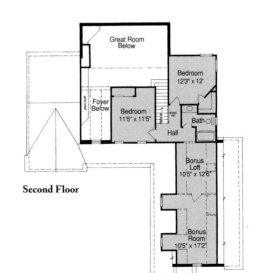

Second Floor

© 1996 Donald A. Gardner Architects, Inc.

Plan: HPK3200108

Square Footage: 1,972	Bathrooms: 2
Bonus Space: 398 sq. ft.	Width: 67' - 7"
Bedrooms: 3	Depth: 56' - 7"

This delightful country cottage elevation gives way to a modern floor plan. The formal dining room is set off from the expansive great room with decorative columns. Amenities in the nearby kitchen include an abundance of counter and cabinet space, a bilevel island with a snack bar, and a gazebo breakfast nook. The master suite is detailed with a tray ceiling and features a lush private bath with a large walk-in closet. Two additional bedrooms share a full hall bath. A bonus room over the garage can be finished as extra living space.

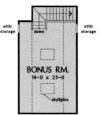

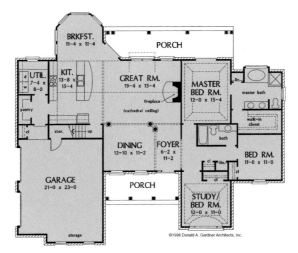

©1996 Donald A. Gardner Architects, Inc.

Starter Homes

© 1994 Donald A. Gardner Architects, Inc.

Plan: HPK3200109

Square Footage: 1,977
Bonus Space: 430 sq. ft.
Bedrooms: 3

Bathrooms: 2
Width: 69' - 8"
Depth: 59' - 6"

A two-story foyer with a Palladian window above sets the tone for this sunlit home. Columns mark the passage from the foyer to the great room, where a central fireplace and built-in cabinets stretch the length of one wall. A screened porch with four skylights above and a wet bar provides a pleasant place to start the day or wind down after work. The kitchen is flanked by the formal dining room and the breakfast room. Hidden quietly at the rear, the master suite includes a bath with dual vanities and skylights. Two family bedrooms (one an optional study) share a bath with twin sinks.

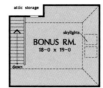

© 1994 Donald A. Gardner Architects, Inc.

© Sater Design Collection, Inc

First Floor

Second Floor

Plan: HPK3200110

First Floor: 1,383 sq. ft.	Width: 48' - 0"
Second Floor: 595 sq. ft.	Depth: 48' - 8"
Total: 1,978 sq. ft.	Foundation: Unfinished
Bedrooms: 3	Walkout Basement
Bathrooms: 2	

The stone facade and woodwork detail give this home a Craftsman appeal. The foyer opens to a staircase up to the vaulted great room, which features a fireplace flanked by built-ins and French-door access to the rear covered porch. The open dining room with a tray ceiling offers convenience to the spacious kitchen. Two family bedrooms share a bath and have private porches. An overlook to the great room below is a perfect introduction to the master suite. The second level spreads out the luxury of the master suite with a spacious walk-in closet, a private porch, and a glorious master bath with a garden tub, dual vanities, and a compartmented toilet.

Starter Homes

Plan: HPK3200111

Square Footage: 1,980
Bedrooms: 3
Bathrooms: 2

Width: 61' - 0"
Depth: 61' - 0"

As American as apple pie, this traditional design will appear long-established as soon as it is built. Enter from a covered porch to find living spaces crowned by 11-foot ceilings. The study and open dining room flank the foyer; archways announce the airy living room, warmed by a cozy hearth. The gourmet island kitchen easily serves the bayed breakfast nook. Two nearby bedrooms share a full bath. The master suite provides privacy with a bayed sitting area, luxurious bath, and ample closet space.

© W. L. Martin Designs

Built for corner or narrow lots, this two-story home offers lots of amenities within its compact space. The covered-porch entry leads to an open combination great room and dining room with access to a side deck. The efficient U-shaped kitchen offers plenty of counter space. A handy utility room and a powder room adjacent to the two-car garage complete the first floor. On the second floor, the master bedroom features a bay window, a walk-in closet, and a private bath with dual sinks. Two family bedrooms share a full bath. The family/recreation room, also located on the second floor, will become a favorite spot to share the day's events.

Plan: HPK3200112

First Floor: 720 sq. ft.	Bathrooms: 2 ½
Second Floor: 1,263 sq. ft.	Width: 44' - 0"
Total: 1,983 sq. ft.	Depth: 42' - 0"
Bedrooms: 3	Foundation: Crawlspace

First Floor

GARAGE 23⁶ x 23⁰

UTILITY

KIT 12⁶ x 11²

POWDER ROOM

REFG

RANGE

DINING 12⁶ x 11⁶

DECK

RAILING

GREAT RM 19⁰ x 12⁰

COVERED PORCH

RAILING

Second Floor

LINE OF CEILING CLG

FAMILY/ RECREATION 23⁶ x 23⁰

BEDRM 9⁴ x 10⁰

BEDRM 9⁴ x 10⁰

CLG CLG

CLG CLG

BATH

WALK-IN CLOSET

BATH

MASTER SUITE 13⁸ x 13⁴

SLOPED CLG

ROOF OF PORCH BELOW

Starter Homes

Plan: HPK3200113

Square Footage: 1,989	Bathrooms: 2
Bonus Space: 469 sq. ft.	Width: 69' - 8"
Bedrooms: 3	Depth: 59' - 6"

Equipped with dormers, arched windows, and skylights, this executive home is flooded with light and space. Designed for elegance and versatility, the bedroom/study, screened porch with wet bar, and bonus room are elements of a home that can meet different needs for any family. The great room—with its cathedral ceiling, fireplace and built-in cabinets—is a comfortable place for everyday life as well as entertaining. Copious closet and storage space add to the smart floor plan. The large master suite has access to the deck as well as a sizable walk-in closet. A garden tub, along with His and Her lavatories, creates a master bath with luxury and convenience.

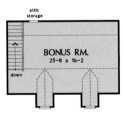

Beautiful boxed columns frame the regal dining room in this home. Enjoy the openness of the great room with a fireplace and access to the rear covered porch. When guests arrive, they will enjoy their own private suite with walk-in closet for ample storage. Mornings bring a new day and preparing breakfast will be enjoyable in the spacious kitchen with breakfast room. A beautiful tray ceiling adorns the master bedroom while the bathroom is complete with a huge walk-in closet, whirlpool tub, and a corner glass shower.

Plan: HPK3200114

Square Footage: 1,989	Depth: 49' - 0"
Bedrooms: 4	Foundation: Crawlspace,
Bathrooms: 3	Slab
Width: 64' - 2"	

Starter Homes

Plan: HPK3200115

Square Footage: 1,992
Bedrooms: 3
Bathrooms: 2 ½
Width: 63' - 0"

Depth: 57' - 2"
Foundation: Crawlspace, Slab, Unfinished Basement

This mid-sized ranch offers plentiful amenities all wrapped into a new compact design. The elegant brick exterior is accented by a Palladian window, multilevel trim, and an inviting front porch. The exquisite master suite, the three-car garage, and a large screened porch make this home irresistible. The exceptional master retreat provides direct access to the deck, a sitting area, a full-featured bath, and a spacious walk-in closet. A bay window brightens the breakfast room and kitchen. Vaulted or trayed ceilings adorn the living, family, and dining rooms, along with the master suite. Other rooms offer 9-foot ceilings. The secondary bedrooms provide walk-in closets and share a His and Hers bath.

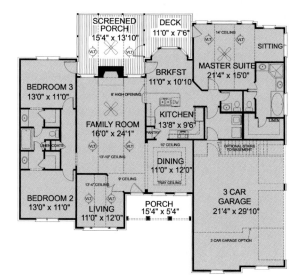

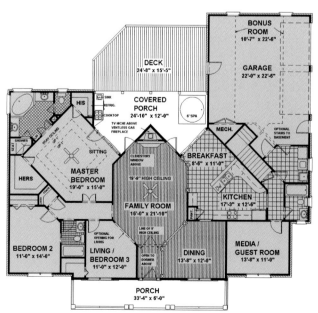

Plan: HPK3200116

Square Footage: 1,992	Width: 66' - 2"
Bonus Space: 247 sq. ft.	Depth: 62' - 0"
Bedrooms: 3	Foundation: Slab,
Bathrooms: 3	Unfinished Basement

This elegant country home is both classic and contemporary. From the inviting front porch to the screened rear porch and deck, this home provides dramatic spaces and true flexibility. The bonus room and optional basement provide areas for future expansion. Just beyond the porch, the entry is lit by a clerestory dormer. Directly ahead is a spacious diamond-shaped family room with a gas fireplace, entertainment center above, and arched clerestory window. French doors with transoms lead to the rear porch with a spa and outdoor kitchenette. The kitchen is spacious and provides a wonderful view of activities on the rear property and in the family room. The unusual master suite is loaded with amenities such as direct access to the screened porch, a sitting room, a luxurious bath, and His and Hers walk-in closets.

Starter Homes

Plan: HPK3200117

Square Footage: 1,993	Width: 66' - 10"
Bonus Space: 307 sq. ft.	Depth: 71' - 5"
Bedrooms: 3	Foundation: Crawlspace,
Bathrooms: 2	Slab

A gabled roof, flanked by attractive dormers, tops the welcoming covered front porch of this country charmer. Inside, a formal dining room opens directly off the foyer, announced by decorative columns. The nearby living room offers a warming fireplace and access to the rear covered porch. Angled counters in the kitchen contribute to easy food preparation, while a snack counter accommodates quick meals. Nestled in its own wing, the master suite opens through double doors from a private vestibule and offers a relaxing retreat for the homeowner. On the other side of the plan, two family bedrooms share a full hall bath.

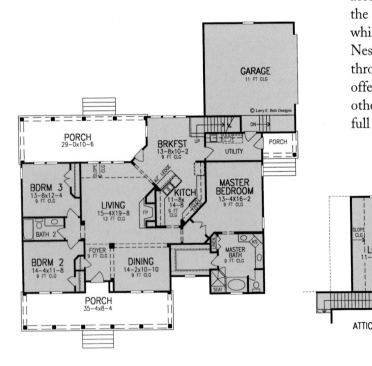

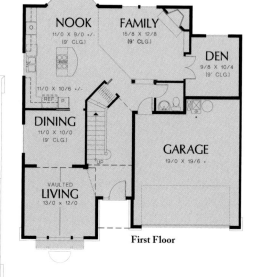

In just under 2,000 square feet, this traditional family home shines with Palladian windows and a brilliant floor plan. The entry leads to a vaulted living room bathed in light, or ahead to the family room warmed by a corner fireplace. The kitchen features an island cooktop with a serving bar and easy access to the bayed breakfast nook and the formal dining room. A private den makes a great home office or gym. Located on the upper level, two secondary bedrooms (one vaulted) share a full bath. The master suite revels in a vaulted bedroom, private spa bath, and large walk-in closet.

Plan: HPK3200118

First Floor: 1,112 sq. ft.
Second Floor: 882 sq. ft.
Total: 1,994 sq. ft.
Bedrooms: 3

Bathrooms: 2 ½
Width: 40' - 0"
Depth: 43' - 0"
Foundation: Crawlspace

Second Floor

First Floor

Starter Homes

Plan: HPK3200119

First Floor: 728 sq. ft.	Bathrooms: 2 ½
Second Floor: 1,268 sq. ft.	Width: 44' - 8"
Total: 1,996 sq. ft.	Depth: 42' - 4"
Bedrooms: 3	Foundation: Crawlspace

Immerse yourself in a traditional design loaded with amenities. The open layout between the great room and the dining room allows plenty of space for entertaining. Around the corner, the kitchen hides all of the prep work and is conveniently near a utility room, powder room, and rear entrance. A side deck allows for outdoor meals as well. Upstairs, a landing offers the choice of heading left to the sizable family/recreation room or right to the two family bedrooms, a full bath, and the master suite at the end of the hall. The suite is a pleasing place for homeowners, with a twin-vanity bath, bay window, and walk-in closet.

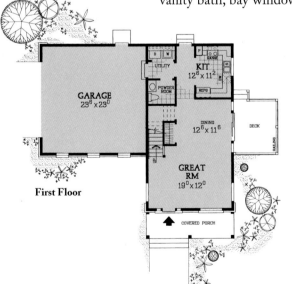

First Floor

Second Floor

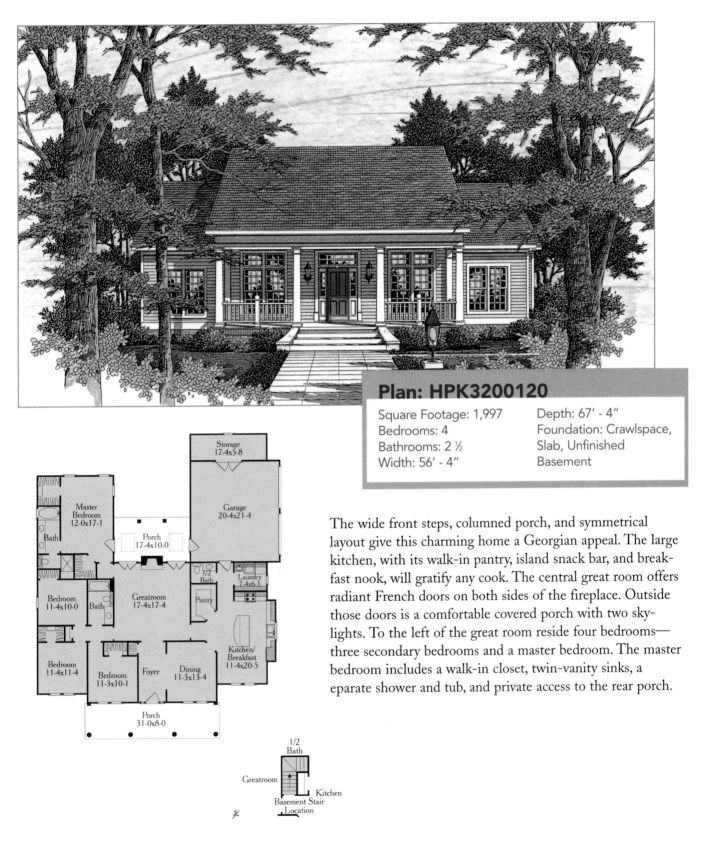

Plan: HPK3200120

Square Footage: 1,997
Bedrooms: 4
Bathrooms: 2 ½
Width: 56' - 4"

Depth: 67' - 4"
Foundation: Crawlspace, Slab, Unfinished Basement

The wide front steps, columned porch, and symmetrical layout give this charming home a Georgian appeal. The large kitchen, with its walk-in pantry, island snack bar, and breakfast nook, will gratify any cook. The central great room offers radiant French doors on both sides of the fireplace. Outside those doors is a comfortable covered porch with two skylights. To the left of the great room reside four bedrooms—three secondary bedrooms and a master bedroom. The master bedroom includes a walk-in closet, twin-vanity sinks, a eparate shower and tub, and private access to the rear porch.

Starter Homes

Plan: HPK3200121

First Floor: 1,078 sq. ft.
Second Floor: 921 sq. ft.
Total: 1,999 sq. ft.
Bedrooms: 3

Bathrooms: 3
Width: 24' - 11"
Depth: 73' - 10"
Foundation: Crawlspace

This charming clapboard home is loaded with character and is perfect for a narrow lot. Columns and connecting arches separate the great room and the dining room. The efficient U-shaped kitchen features a corner sink with a window view and a bayed breakfast area with access to the rear porch. A bedroom and a bath are conveniently located for guests on the first floor. Upstairs, the master suite features a vaulted ceiling and a luxurious bath with dual vanities, a whirlpool tub, and a separate shower. A secondary bedroom and a full bath are also located on the second floor with a large rear balcony completing this highly livable plan.

Second Floor

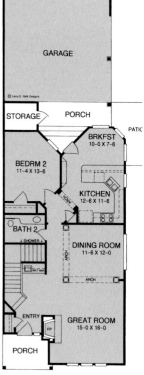

First Floor

Taking the Next Step

White columns support a front, covered porch, which lends itself to the traditional appeal of the home.

Familiar elements such as front-facing gables, a covered porch, shingled porch, and brick and siding set a warm, old-neighborhood tone on the outside. Palladian windows above a transomed entry create a focal point at the center of the exterior. Having the garage load at the side of the home preserves the look of the curbside elevation.

Inside, decorative columns help define an elegant dining room to the right of a large two-story foyer. Straight ahead lies the heart of the home: a vaulted family room with a radius window, French door to the rear property, and a fireplace visible from the foyer. Traditional mouldings and arched pass-throughs add formal touches to all three spaces.

At the left of the plan, a first-floor master suite features a private bath with a vaulted ceiling and a whirlpool tub set off with a radius window. Just beyond it, the tremendous walk-in closet is naturally lit by a front-facing window. More windows and a tray ceiling elevate the master bedroom.

The second floor boasts two bedrooms, each with a walk-in closet. The single bath is designed for comfortable sharing. The bedrooms are separated by an open hallway that overlooks the family room and foyer. Bonus space above the garage can be used for storage or easily converted into a game room or fifth bedroom.

Decorative columns and arches help define the formal dining room.

LEFT: A short hallway separates the family room from the foyer.

BELOW: Warm-toned cabinetry surrounds a serving bar perfect for grabbing a quick meal.

Move-Up Homes

Plan: HPK3200122

First Floor: 1,583 sq. ft.
Second Floor: 543 sq. ft.
Total: 2,126 sq. ft.
Bonus Space: 251 sq. ft.
Bedrooms: 4
Bathrooms: 3

Width: 53' - 0"
Depth: 47' - 0"
Foundation: Crawlspace, Slab, Unfinished Walkout Basement

An attractive stepped ceiling crowns the spacious master bedroom.

First Floor

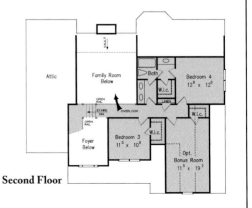

Second Floor

ABOVE: Windows frame the stacked-stone fireplace and carved mantel, brightening the vaulted family room.

LEFT: Let creativity run wild in the bonus room, which can convert to a comfortable game room.

Move-Up Homes

Plan: HPK3200123

Square Footage: 2,010
Bedrooms: 3
Bathrooms: 2

Width: 68' - 10"
Depth: 52' - 0"
Foundation: Slab

An arched entrance, a sunburst, and sidelights around the four-panel door provide a touch of class to this European-style home. An angled bar opens the kitchen and breakfast room to the living room with bookcases and a fireplace. The master suite boasts a sloped ceiling and private bath with a 5-foot turning radius, dual-sink vanity, and a separate tub and shower. Two family bedrooms provide ample closet space and share a full hall bath and linen closet. Don't miss the two-car garage located to the far right of the plan.

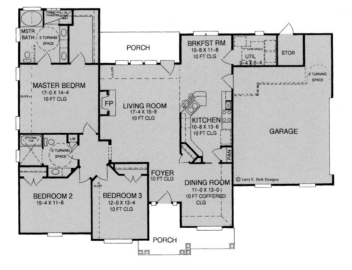

Move-Up Homes

First Floor

Second Floor

© 2004 Donald A. Gardner, Inc.

Plan: HPK3200124

First Floor: 1,507 sq. ft.
Second Floor: 523 sq. ft.
Total: 2,030 sq. ft.
Bedrooms: 3

Bathrooms: 2 ½
Width: 42' - 5"
Depth: 63' - 2"

Plan: HPK3200125

First Floor: 1,559 sq. ft.
Second Floor: 475 sq. ft.
Total: 2,034 sq. ft.
Bonus Space: 321 sq. ft.
Bedrooms: 4
Bathrooms: 3

Width: 50' - 0"
Depth: 56' - 4"
Foundation: Crawlspace,
Slab, Unfinished Walkout
Basement

First Floor

Second Floor

Move-Up Homes

First Floor

Second Floor

Photo courtesy of Drummond Designs, Inc. This home, as shown in the photography, may differ from the actual blueprints. For more detailed

Plan: HPK3200126

First Floor: 1,347 sq. ft.
Second Floor: 690 sq. ft.
Total: 2,037 sq. ft.
Bedrooms: 4
Bathrooms: 2

Width: 55' - 0"
Depth: 41' - 0"
Foundation: Unfinished Basement

Rear Exterior

Plan: HPK3200127

Square Footage: 2,046
Bedrooms: 3
Bathrooms: 2 ½
Width: 68' - 2"

Depth: 57' - 4"
Foundation: Crawlspace, Slab, Unfinished Basement

Order blueprints anytime at
eplans.com or 1-800-521-6797

Move-Up Homes

First Floor

Second Floor

Plan: HPK3200128

First Floor: 1,233 sq. ft.
Second Floor: 824 sq. ft.
Total: 2,057 sq. ft.
Bedrooms: 3

Bathrooms: 3
Width: 31' - 10"
Depth: 77' - 10"
Foundation: Crawlspace

Plan: HPK3200129

First Floor: 1,098 sq. ft.
Second Floor: 960 sq. ft.
Total: 2,058 sq. ft.
Bedrooms: 3
Bathrooms: 2 ½

Width: 50' - 0"
Depth: 36' - 0"
Foundation: Crawlspace,
Slab, Unfinished
Basement

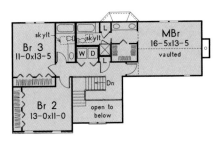

First Floor

Second Floor

Move-Up Homes

Plan: HPK3200130

Square Footage: 2,061
Bedrooms: 3
Bathrooms: 2 ½
Width: 60' - 0"

Depth: 57' - 1"
Foundation: Crawlspace, Slab

First Floor

Second Floor

Plan: HPK3200131

First Floor: 1,376 sq. ft.
Second Floor: 695 sq. ft.
Total: 2,071 sq. ft.
Bedrooms: 3
Bathrooms: 2 ½

Width: 47' - 0"
Depth: 49' - 8"
Foundation: Finished Walkout Basement

Move-Up Homes

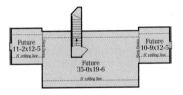

Plan: HPK3200132

Square Footage: 2,085
Bonus Space: 1,000 sq. ft.
Bedrooms: 3
Bathrooms: 2 ½

Width: 65' - 11"
Depth: 67' - 9"
Foundation: Crawlspace, Slab, Unfinished Basement

First Floor

Second Floor

Plan: HPK3200133

First Floor: 1,139 sq. ft.
Second Floor: 948 sq. ft.
Total: 2,087 sq. ft.
Bedrooms: 3
Bathrooms: 2 ½

Width: 32' - 0"
Depth: 59' - 4"
Foundation: Unfinished Basement

Move-Up Homes

© William E. Poole Designs, Inc.

Plan: HPK3200134

Square Footage: 2,096
Bonus Space: 374 sq. ft.
Bedrooms: 3
Bathrooms: 2

Width: 64' - 8"
Depth: 60' - 0"
Foundation: Crawlspace,
Unfinished Basement

First Floor

Second Floor

Plan: HPK3200533

First Floor: 1,296 sq. ft.
Second Floor: 819 sq. ft.
Total: 2,115 sq. ft.
Bedrooms: 3

Bathrooms: 3
Width: 42' - 0"
Depth: 68' - 0"
Foundation: Crawlspace

Move-Up Homes

Second Floor

First Floor

First Floor

Second Floor

Move-Up Homes

First Floor

Second Floor

Plan: HPK3200135

First Floor: 1,694 sq. ft.	Bedrooms: 4
Second Floor: 436 sq. ft.	Bathrooms: 3
Total: 2,130 sq. ft.	Width: 54' - 0"
Bonus Space: 345 sq. ft.	Depth: 53' - 8"

First Floor

Second Floor

Plan: HPK3200536

First Floor: 1,100 sq. ft.	Bathrooms: 2 ½
Second Floor: 1,054 sq. ft.	Width: 58' - 0"
Total: 2,157 sq. ft.	Depth: 40' - 0"
Bedrooms: 3	Foundation: Crawlspace

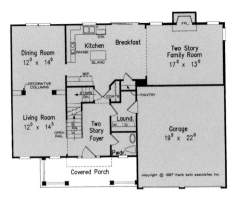

First Floor

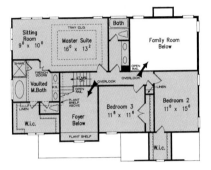

Second Floor

Plan: HPK3200136

First Floor: 1,092 sq. ft.
Second Floor: 1,059 sq. ft.
Total: 2,151 sq. ft.
Bedrooms: 3
Bathrooms: 2 ½

Width: 48' - 0"
Depth: 38' - 4"
Foundation: Crawlspace,
Unfinished Walkout
Basement

First Floor

Second Floor

Plan: HPK3200137

First Floor: 1,668 sq. ft.
Second Floor: 495 sq. ft.
Total: 2,163 sq. ft.
Bonus Space: 327 sq. ft.

Bedrooms: 4
Bathrooms: 3
Width: 52' - 7"
Depth: 50' - 11

Move-Up Homes

First Floor

Second Floor

Plan: HPK3200138

First Floor: 1,580 sq. ft.
Second Floor: 595 sq. ft.
Total: 2,175 sq. ft.
Bedrooms: 3
Bathrooms: 2 ½

Width: 50' - 2"
Depth: 70' - 11"
Foundation: Walkout Basement

Plan: HPK3200139

Square Footage: 2,176
Bedrooms: 2
Bathrooms: 2

Width: 70' - 8"
Depth: 68' - 8"

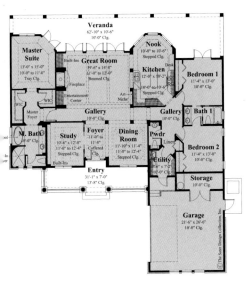

Plan: HPK3200140

Square Footage: 2,191
Bedrooms: 3
Bathrooms: 2 ½

Width: 62' - 10"
Depth: 73' - 6"
Foundation: Slab

Plan: HPK3200141

Square Footage: 2,197
Bedrooms: 3
Bathrooms: 2 ½

Width: 60' - 0"
Depth: 64' - 0"
Foundation: Crawlspace

Move-Up Homes

First Floor

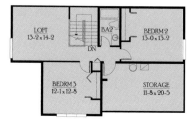

Second Floor

Plan: HPK3200537

First Floor: 1,460 sq. ft.
Second Floor: 753 sq. ft.
Total: 2,213 sq. ft.
Bonus Space: 249 sq. ft.
Bedrooms: 3

Bathrooms: 2 ½
Width: 50' - 0"
Depth: 45' - 0"
Foundation: Crawlspace

First Floor

Second Floor

Plan: HPK3200142

First Floor: 1,209 sq. ft.
Second Floor: 1,005 sq. ft.
Total: 2,214 sq. ft.
Bonus Space: 366 sq. ft.
Bedrooms: 3

Bathrooms: 2 ½
Width: 65' - 4"
Depth: 40' - 4"
Foundation: Crawlspace

Move-Up Homes

First Floor

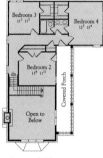

Second Floor

Plan: HPK3200143

First Floor: 1,369 sq. ft.
Second Floor: 856 sq. ft.
Total: 2,225 sq. ft.
Bedrooms: 4

Bathrooms: 2 ½
Width: 36' - 2"
Depth: 71' - 6"
Foundation: Slab

© 1998 Donald A. Gardner, Inc.

Plan: HPK3200144

First Floor: 1,701 sq. ft.
Second Floor: 534 sq. ft.
Total: 2,235 sq. ft.
Bonus Space: 274 sq. ft.

Bedrooms: 3
Bathrooms: 2 ½
Width: 65' - 11"
Depth: 43' - 5"

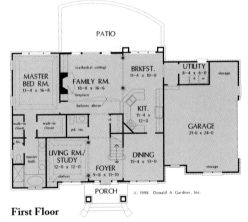

First Floor

Second Floor

Move-Up Homes

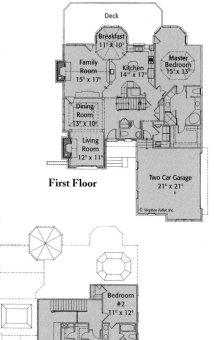

First Floor

Deck
Breakfast 11⁵ x 10⁵
Family Room 15⁵ x 17⁰
Kitchen 14¹⁰ x 17⁰
Master Bedroom 15⁴ x 13⁰
Dining Room 13° x 10°
Living Room 12° x 11⁶
Two Car Garage 21⁶ x 21⁶
© Stephen Fuller, Inc.

Second Floor

Bedroom #2 11° x 12⁶
Bedroom #3 11° x 12⁰

Plan: HPK3200145

First Floor: 1,732 sq. ft.
Second Floor: 504 sq. ft.
Total: 2,236 sq. ft.
Bedrooms: 3
Bathrooms: 2 ½

Width: 47' - 3"
Depth: 63' - 6"
Foundation: Unfinished
Walkout Basement

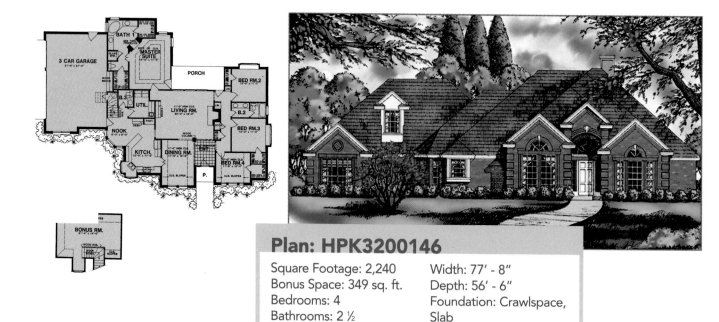

BONUS RM.

Plan: HPK3200146

Square Footage: 2,240
Bonus Space: 349 sq. ft.
Bedrooms: 4
Bathrooms: 2 ½

Width: 77' - 8"
Depth: 56' - 6"
Foundation: Crawlspace,
Slab

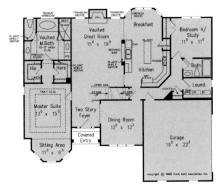

First Floor

Second Floor

Plan: HPK3200147

First Floor: 1,688 sq. ft.
Second Floor: 558 sq. ft.
Total: 2,246 sq. ft.
Bonus Space: 269 sq. ft.
Bedrooms: 4
Bathrooms: 3

Width: 54' - 0"
Depth: 48' - 0"
Foundation: Crawlspace,
Slab, Unfinished Walkout
Basement

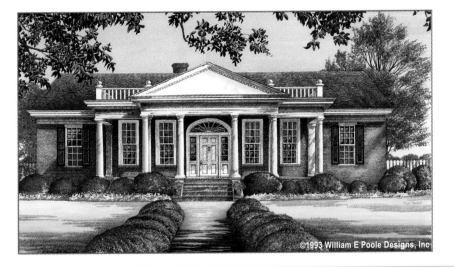

©1993 William E Poole Designs, Inc

Plan: HPK3200148

Square Footage: 2,249
Bedrooms: 3
Bathrooms: 2

Width: 72' - 6"
Depth: 76' - 8"
Foundation: Crawlspace

Move-Up Homes

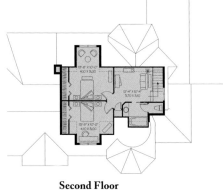

First Floor

Second Floor

Plan: HPK3200149

First Floor: 1,566 sq. ft.
Second Floor: 693 sq. ft.
Total: 2,259 sq. ft.
Bonus Space: 406 sq. ft.
Bedrooms: 3

Bathrooms: 2 ½
Width: 68' - 0"
Depth: 52' - 11"
Foundation: Unfinished
Basement

Plan: HPK3200150

Square Footage: 2,262
Bonus Space: 388 sq. ft.
Bedrooms: 4

Bathrooms: 2 ½
Width: 77' - 4"
Depth: 62' - 0"

Move-Up Homes

First Floor

GATHERING ROOM 13'-0" x 18'-4"

BREAKFAST 9'-2" x 7'-4"

KITCHEN 11'-4" x 11'-4"

DINING ROOM 11'-6" x 11'-4"

PDR.

PANT.

LIVING ROOM 12'-4" x 13'-6"

FOYER

GARAGE 20'-4" x 20'-8"

STOOP

© 1994 BuildenGraphics Architecture used by permission by Living Concepts

Second Floor

SUITE 3 10'-6" x 11'-4"

BATH

SUITE 2 10'-6" x 10'-4"

MASTER SUITE 18'-6" x 12'-8"

SUITE 4 12'-0" x 10'-2"

UTIL.

OPEN TO BELOW

MASTER BATH

W.I.C.

BONUS ROOM 10'-10" x 13'-8"

Plan: HPK3200151

First Floor: 1,118 sq. ft.
Second Floor: 1,144 sq. ft.
Total: 2,262 sq. ft.
Bedrooms: 4

Bathrooms: 2 ½
Width: 46' - 0"
Depth: 40' - 0"
Foundation: Crawlspace

Plan: HPK3200152

Square Footage: 2,267
Bedrooms: 4
Bathrooms: 2 ½
Width: 71' - 2"

Depth: 62' - 0"
Foundation: Crawlspace, Slab, Unfinished Basement

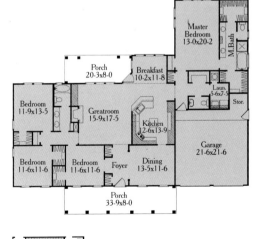

Master Bedroom 13-0x20-2

M.Bath

Porch 20-3x8-0

Breakfast 10-2x11-8

Laun. 5-6x7-5

Stor.

Bedroom 11-9x13-5

Greatroom 15-9x17-5

Kitchen 12-6x13-9

Bedroom 11-6x11-6

Bedroom 11-6x11-6

Foyer

Dining 13-5x11-6

Garage 21-6x21-6

Porch 33-9x8-0

Laun.

Basement Stair Location

Move-Up Homes

First Floor

Second Floor

Plan: HPK3200153

First Floor: 1,649 sq. ft.
Second Floor: 622 sq. ft.
Total: 2,271 sq. ft.
Bonus Space: 250 sq. ft.
Bedrooms: 3

Bathrooms: 2 ½
Width: 57' - 4"
Depth: 52' - 4"
Foundation: Unfinished
Walkout Basement

First Floor

Second Floor

Plan: HPK3200154

First Floor: 1,185 sq. ft.
Second Floor: 1,086 sq. ft.
Total: 2,271 sq. ft.
Bonus Space: 193 sq. ft.
Bedrooms: 3

Bathrooms: 2 ½
Width: 50' - 0"
Depth: 43' - 10"
Foundation: Unfinished
Basement

Move-Up Homes

First Floor

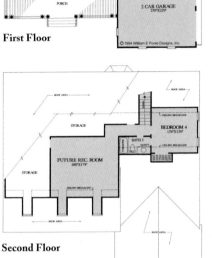

Second Floor

© 1994 William E Poole Designs, Inc.

Plan: HPK3200155

First Floor: 1,981 sq. ft.	Bathrooms: 3 ½
Second Floor: 291 sq. ft.	Width: 58' - 0"
Total: 2,272 sq. ft.	Depth: 53' - 0"
Bonus Space: 412 sq. ft.	Foundation: Crawlspace
Bedrooms: 4	

Plan: HPK3200156

First Floor: 1,290 sq. ft.	Width: 45' - 0"
Second Floor: 985 sq. ft.	Depth: 43' - 4"
Total: 2,275 sq. ft.	Foundation: Crawlspace,
Bonus Space: 186 sq. ft.	Slab, Unfinished Walkout
Bedrooms: 4	Basement
Bathrooms: 3	

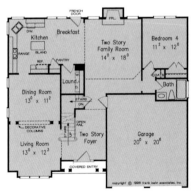

First Floor

Second Floor

Move-Up Homes

© William E. Poole Designs, Inc.

First Floor

Second Floor

Plan: HPK3200157

First Floor: 1,542 sq. ft.
Second Floor: 755 sq. ft.
Total: 2,297 sq. ft.
Bedrooms: 3
Bathrooms: 2 ½

Width: 48' - 4"
Depth: 39' - 6"
Foundation: Unfinished Walkout Basement

Plan: HPK3200158

Square Footage: 2,318
Bedrooms: 3
Bathrooms: 3

Width: 59' - 10"
Depth: 66' - 3"
Foundation: Slab

Order blueprints anytime at
eplans.com or 1-800-521-6797

Move-Up Homes

First Floor

Second Floor

© William E. Poole Designs, Inc.

Plan: HPK3200159

First Floor: 1,688 sq. ft.	Bathrooms: 3 ½
Second Floor: 630 sq. ft.	Width: 44' - 4"
Total: 2,318 sq. ft.	Depth: 62' - 4"
Bonus Space: 506 sq. ft.	Foundation: Crawlspace
Bedrooms: 3	

Plan: HPK3200160

Square Footage: 2,322	Depth: 61' - 0"
Bedrooms: 3	Foundation: Crawlspace,
Bathrooms: 2 ½	Slab, Unfinished Walkout
Width: 62' - 0"	Basement

Move-Up Homes

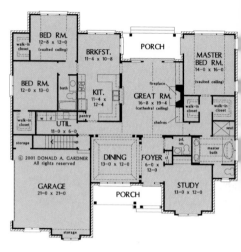

Plan: HPK3200161

Square Footage: 2,330	Bathrooms: 2 ½
Bonus Space: 364 sq. ft.	Width: 62' - 3"
Bedrooms: 3	Depth: 60' - 6"

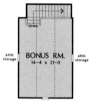

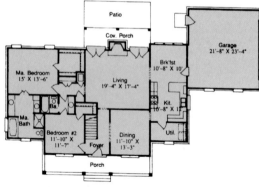

First Floor

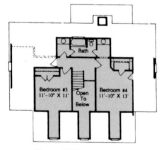

Second Floor

Plan: HPK3200162

First Floor: 1,685 sq. ft.	Width: 77' - 0"
Second Floor: 648 sq. ft.	Depth: 50' - 10"
Total: 2,333 sq. ft.	Foundation: Crawlspace,
Bedrooms: 4	Slab
Bathrooms: 3	

Order blueprints anytime at
eplans.com or 1-800-521-6797

First Floor

Second Floor

© 1994 Donald A. Gardner Architects, Inc.

Plan: HPK3200163

First Floor: 1,715 sq. ft.   Bedrooms: 3
Second Floor: 620 sq. ft.   Bathrooms: 2 ½
Total: 2,335 sq. ft.   Width: 58' - 6"
Bonus Space: 265 sq. ft.   Depth: 50' - 3"

First Floor   **Second Floor**

Plan: HPK3200164

First Floor: 1,237 sq. ft.   Bathrooms: 2 ½
Second Floor: 1,098 sq. ft.   Width: 29' - 4"
Total: 2,335 sq. ft.   Depth: 73' - 0"
Bedrooms: 3   Foundation: Slab

Move-Up Homes

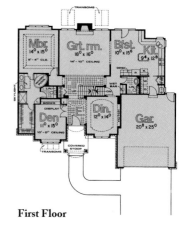

First Floor

Second Floor

Plan: HPK3200165

First Floor: 1,701 sq. ft.
Second Floor: 639 sq. ft.
Total: 2,340 sq. ft.
Bedrooms: 4

Bathrooms: 2 ½
Width: 56' - 8"
Depth: 48' - 0"

First Floor

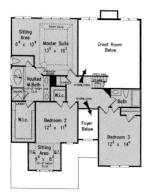

Second Floor

Plan: HPK3200166

First Floor: 1,208 sq. ft.
Second Floor: 1,137 sq. ft.
Total: 2,345 sq. ft.
Bedrooms: 3
Bathrooms: 3

Width: 38' - 6"
Depth: 51' - 4"
Foundation: Crawlspace,
Unfinished Walkout
Basement

Move-Up Homes

photography, may differ from the actual blueprints. For more detailed information, please check the floor plans carefully.

First Floor

Second Floor

Plan: HPK3200167

First Floor: 1,205 sq. ft.
Second Floor: 1,160 sq. ft.
Total: 2,365 sq. ft.
Bonus Space: 350 sq. ft.
Bedrooms: 3

Bathrooms: 2 ½
Width: 52' - 6"
Depth: 43' - 6"
Foundation: Walkout Basement

Plan: HPK3200168

Square Footage: 2,377
Bedrooms: 3
Bathrooms: 2
Width: 69' - 0"

Depth: 49' - 6"
Foundation: Walkout Basement

Move-Up Homes

First Floor

Second Floor

Plan: HPK3200169

First Floor: 1,291 sq. ft.
Second Floor: 1,087 sq. ft.
Total: 2,378 sq. ft.
Bonus Space: 366 sq. ft.
Bedrooms: 3

Bathrooms: 2 ½
Width: 65' - 4"
Depth: 40' - 0"
Foundation: Crawlspace

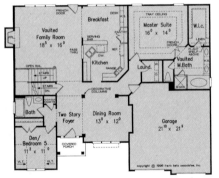

First Floor

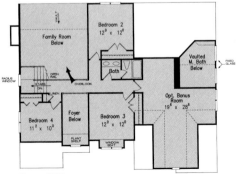

Second Floor

Plan: HPK3200170

First Floor: 1,687 sq. ft.
Second Floor: 694 sq. ft.
Total: 2,381 sq. ft.
Bonus Space: 407 sq. ft.
Bedrooms: 5
Bathrooms: 3

Width: 55' - 10"
Depth: 44' - 6"
Foundation: Crawlspace,
Unfinished Walkout
Basement

Move-Up Homes

First Floor

Second Floor

Plan: HPK3200171

First Floor: 1,223 sq. ft.
Second Floor: 1,163 sq. ft.
Total: 2,386 sq. ft.
Bonus Space: 204 sq. ft.
Bedrooms: 4
Bathrooms: 2 ½

Width: 50' - 0"
Depth: 48' - 0"
Foundation: Crawlspace,
Unfinished Walkout
Basement

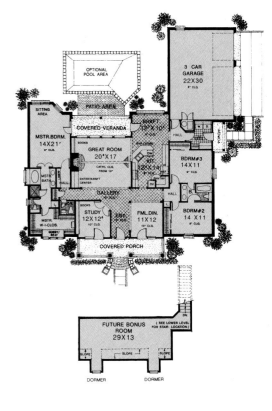

Plan: HPK3200172

Square Footage: 2,387
Bonus Space: 377 sq. ft.
Bedrooms: 3
Bathrooms: 2 ½

Width: 69' - 6"
Depth: 68' - 11"
Foundation: Crawlspace,
Slab

Move-Up Homes

© 1999 Donald A. Gardner, Inc.

First Floor

Second Floor

Plan: HPK3200173

First Floor: 1,918 sq. ft.
Second Floor: 469 sq. ft.
Total: 2,387 sq. ft.
Bonus Space: 374 sq. ft.

Bedrooms: 4
Bathrooms: 3
Width: 73' - 3"
Depth: 43' - 6"

First Floor

Second Floor

Plan: HPK3200174

First Floor: 1,847 sq. ft.
Second Floor: 548 sq. ft.
Total: 2,395 sq. ft.
Bonus Space: 395 sq. ft.
Bedrooms: 3
Bathrooms: 2 ½

Width: 60' - 0"
Depth: 66' - 4"
Foundation: Crawlspace,
Unfinished Walkout
Basement

First Floor

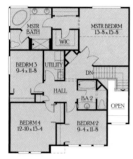

Second Floor

Plan: HPK3200538

First Floor: 1,239 sq. ft.
Second Floor: 1,168 sq. ft.
Total: 2,407 sq. ft.
Bedrooms: 4

Bathrooms: 2 ½
Width: 50' - 0"
Depth: 40' - 0"
Foundation: Crawlspace

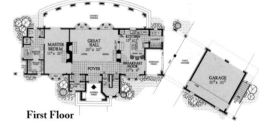

First Floor

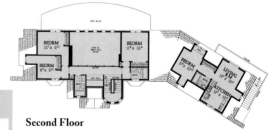

Second Floor

Plan: HPK3200175

First Floor: 1,566 sq. ft.
Second Floor: 837 sq. ft.
Total: 2,403 sq. ft.
Bedrooms: 5
Bathrooms: 4 ½

Width: 116' - 3"
Depth: 55' - 1"
Foundation: Unfinished
Basement

Move-Up Homes

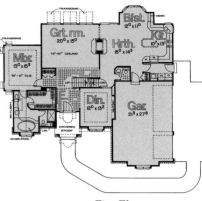

First Floor

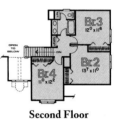

Second Floor

Plan: HPK3200176

First Floor: 1,733 sq. ft.
Second Floor: 672 sq. ft.
Total: 2,405 sq. ft.
Bedrooms: 4

Bathrooms: 2 ½
Width: 60' - 0"
Depth: 55' - 4"

First Floor

Second Floor

Plan: HPK3200177

First Floor: 1,447 sq. ft.
Second Floor: 958 sq. ft.
Total: 2,405 sq. ft.
Bedrooms: 3
Bathrooms: 2 ½

Width: 66' - 4"
Depth: 48' - 0"
Foundation: Unfinished
Basement

Move-Up Homes

First Floor

Two Car Garage 21'2" x 21'1"

Patio

Porch

Storage

Master Bedroom 15'x 15'

WIC

Breakfast 13'8"x 10'7"

Living 19'4"x 17'1"

Kitchen 10'8"x 12'3"

Bedroom 12'x 11'7"

Dining 12'x 13'6"

Utility

Porch

Second Floor

Open to Below

Bath Balcony

Bedroom 12'x 11'7"

Bedroom 12'x 13'

Plan: HPK3200178

First Floor: 1,796 sq. ft.
Second Floor: 610 sq. ft.
Total: 2,406 sq. ft.
Bedrooms: 4
Bathrooms: 3 ½

Width: 65' - 9"
Depth: 64' - 9"
Foundation: Crawlspace, Slab

© William E. Poole Designs, Inc.

Plan: HPK3200179

First Floor: 1,627 sq. ft.
Second Floor: 783 sq. ft.
Total: 2,410 sq. ft.
Bonus Space: 418 sq. ft.
Bedrooms: 4

Bathrooms: 2 ½
Width: 46' - 0"
Depth: 58' - 0"
Foundation: Crawlspace

First Floor

TERRACE/DECK AREA

BREAKFAST 12'-8" X 7'-8"

KITCHEN 12'-6" X 12'-6"

FAMILY ROOM 15'-6" X 16'-4" 2 STORY CEILING

MASTER BEDROOM 17'-6" X 12'-10"

DINING ROOM 11'-10" X 12'-6"

UTILITY

MASTER BATH

LIVING ROOM 15'-6" X 13'-0"

FOYER

2 CAR GARAGE 20'-8" X 23'-4"

PORCH

© William E. Poole Designs

Second Floor

ROOF AREA

BEDROOM 3 12'-2" X 11'-0"

OPEN TO BELOW

BATH 2

BEDROOM 2 11'-8" X 14'-0"

BALCONY

BEDROOM 4 12'-2" X 11'-0"

FUTURE REC. ROOM 16'-4" X 23'-4"

ROOF AREA

Move-Up Homes

First Floor

Second Floor

Plan: HPK3200180

First Floor: 1,314 sq. ft.
Second Floor: 1,106 sq. ft.
Total: 2,420 sq. ft.
Bedrooms: 4
Bathrooms: 2 ½

Width: 54' - 0"
Depth: 36' - 0"
Foundation: Unfinished Basement

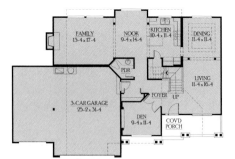

First Floor

Second Floor

Plan: HPK3200539

First Floor: 1,230 sq. ft.
Second Floor: 1,190 sq. ft.
Total: 2,420 sq. ft.
Bedrooms: 4

Bathrooms: 2 ½
Width: 62' - 0"
Depth: 42' - 0"
Foundation: Crawlspace

Move-Up Homes

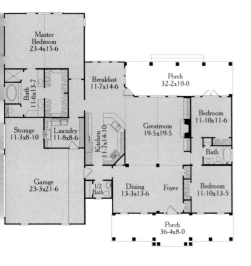

Plan: HPK3200181

Square Footage: 2,424
Bedrooms: 3
Bathrooms: 2 ½
Width: 68' - 2"

Depth: 67' - 6"
Foundation: Crawlspace,
Slab, Unfinished Basement

© 2004 Donald A. Gardner, Inc.

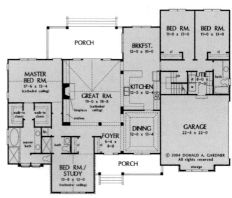

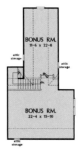

Plan: HPK3200182

Square Footage: 2,426
Bedrooms: 4
Bathrooms: 3

Width: 73' - 2"
Depth: 58' - 0"

Move-Up Homes

Plan: HPK3200183

Square Footage: 2,428
Bonus Space: 860 sq. ft.
Bedrooms: 3
Bathrooms: 2 ½

Width: 70' - 10"
Depth: 65' - 4"
Foundation: Crawlspace,
Slab, Unfinished Basement

First Floor

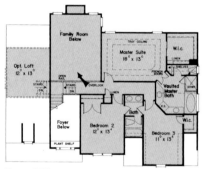

Second Floor

Plan: HPK3200184

First Floor: 1,415 sq. ft.
Second Floor: 1,015 sq. ft.
Total: 2,430 sq. ft.
Bonus Space: 169 sq. ft.
Bedrooms: 4
Bathrooms: 3 ½

Width: 54' - 0"
Depth: 43' - 4"
Foundation: Crawlspace,
Unfinished Walkout
Basement

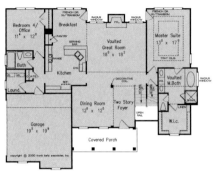

First Floor

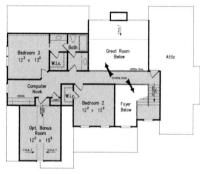

Second Floor

Plan: HPK3200185

First Floor: 1,720 sq. ft.
Second Floor: 724 sq. ft.
Total: 2,444 sq. ft.
Bonus Space: 212 sq. ft.
Bedrooms: 4
Bathrooms: 3

Width: 58' - 0"
Depth: 47' - 0"
Foundation: Crawlspace,
Unfinished Walkout
Basement

Plan: HPK3200186

Square Footage: 2,444
Bedrooms: 3
Bathrooms: 2 ½
Width: 67' - 0"

Depth: 66' - 0"
Foundation: Crawlspace,
Slab

photography, may differ from the actual blueprints. For more detailed information, please check the floor plans carefully.

Move-Up Homes

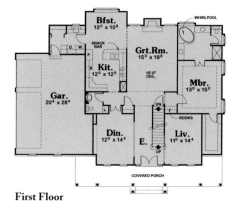

First Floor

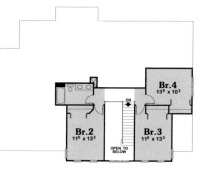

Second Floor

Plan: HPK3200187

First Floor: 1,755 sq. ft.
Second Floor: 693 sq. ft.
Total: 2,448 sq. ft.
Bedrooms: 4

Bathrooms: 2 ½
Width: 62' - 0"
Depth: 44' - 4"

First Floor

Second Floor

Plan: HPK3200540

First Floor: 1,365 sq. ft.
Second Floor: 1,155 sq. ft.
Total: 2,520 sq. ft.
Bedrooms: 3

Bathrooms: 2 ½
Width: 40' - 0"
Depth: 52' - 0"
Foundation: Crawlspace

Move-Up Homes

Enjoy an exciting floor plan that flows exceptionally well for lots of entertainment possibilities. High-volume ceilings throughout accentuate this open plan. A large gathering room off the full kitchen includes a magnificent Palladian window. An octagonal tray ceiling reflects the bay-window shape in the dining room. The master suite, located away from the other bedrooms for enhanced privacy, features its own private sitting area and morning bar, along with huge dual walk-in closets. The master retreat and gathering room are connected by a covered lanai complete with a skylight. A private deck is located off Suite 2.

Plan: HPK3200188

Square Footage: 2,452
Bonus Space: 427 sq. ft.
Bedrooms: 3
Bathrooms: 2 ½

Width: 58' - 0"
Depth: 76' - 0"
Foundation: Crawlspace, Unfinished Basement

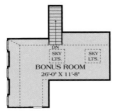

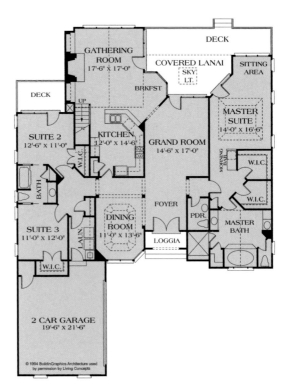

© The Sater Design Collection, Inc.

Plan: HPK3200189

Square Footage: 2,454
Bonus Space: 256 sq. ft.
Bedrooms: 3
Bathrooms: 2

Width: 80' - 6"
Depth: 66' - 0"
Foundation: Crawlspace

This traditional home offers a wide variety of modern amenities. The spacious foyer opens to the great room, which boasts built-in bookshelves, a wall of double doors to the rear porch, and a double-sided fireplace shared with the study. To the far left, the master suite is enhanced by a bay window, His and Hers walk-in closets, and a luxury whirlpool bath. The island cooktop kitchen serves the dining area with ease. Two additional family bedrooms share a hall bath. The bonus room above the garage is perfect for a home office or guest suite.

Move-Up Homes

Plan: HPK3200190

First Floor: 1,447 sq. ft.
Second Floor: 1,008 sq. ft.
Total: 2,455 sq. ft.
Bonus Space: 352 sq. ft.
Bedrooms: 3

Bathrooms: 2 ½
Width: 65' - 0"
Depth: 37' - 11"
Foundation: Crawlspace, Slab, Unfinished Basement

This home is unique because of its farmhouse styling and the multitude of windows—Palladian, decorative, and sunburst—that grace the exterior of the plan. A large front porch and flower box add even more charm. A rounded formal dining room looks out through windows to the front porch. The kitchen, with an island, leads to the dining area, which offers access to the patio. Upstairs, the master bedroom boasts a vaulted ceiling and a private sitting area, as well as a full bath and walk-in closet. Bedrooms 2 and 3 share a full bath.

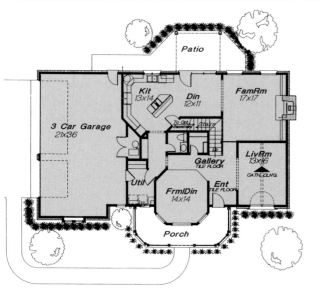

First Floor

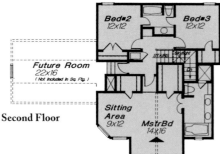

Second Floor

© 2001 Donald A. Gardner, Inc.

Plan: HPK3200191

Square Footage: 2,461	Bathrooms: 2
Bonus Space: 397 sq. ft.	Width: 71' - 2"
Bedrooms: 4	Depth: 67' - 2"

Turret-style bay windows, an arched entryway, and an elegant balustrade add timeless appeal to a remarkable facade; yet, this refined exterior encompasses a very practical layout. Separated from the kitchen by an angled island, the great room features built-in shelves on both sides of the fireplace as well as French doors leading to the rear porch with a wet bar. Custom-style details include tray ceilings in the dining room and study/bedroom as well as columns in the foyer and master bath.

Move-Up Homes

© 2005 Donald A. Gardner, Inc.

VATHAUER STUDIO

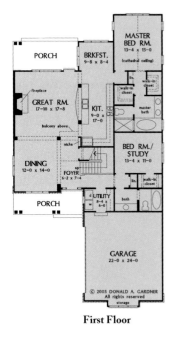

First Floor

Second Floor

Plan: HPK3200192

First Floor: 1,820 sq. ft.	Bedrooms: 4
Second Floor: 645 sq. ft.	Bathrooms: 3
Total: 2,465 sq. ft.	Width: 42' - 4"
Bonus Space: 456 sq. ft.	Depth: 79' - 10"

Possessing radiant curb appeal, this design's stone and siding facade stylishly blends with triple gable peaks, columns, and decorative windows to showcase a truly unique exterior. A grand staircase immediately greets guests in the formal foyer, while an adjacent art niche adds flair. The open dining and great rooms permit a natural traffic flow and embrace the home's open layout. The breakfast room overlooks a rear porch. Completing the first level is a spacious master suite and study/bedroom with nearby full bath. Featuring a private privy, dual vanities, separate shower, and tub, the master bath's details fuse functionality with modern living.

Move-Up Homes

Plan: HPK3200193

Square Footage: 2,471	Width: 62' - 10"
Bedrooms: 4	Depth: 75' - 3"
Bathrooms: 2 ½	Foundation: Slab

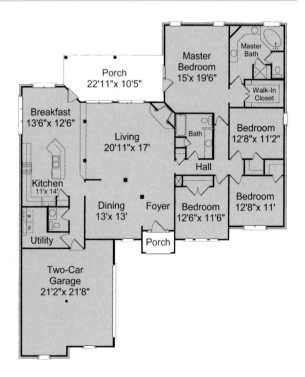

This modern home is definitely an eye-catcher with its tall entrance and ribbon of windows. Just to the left of the foyer is the dining room, which leads to the island kitchen. The kitchen enjoys close proximity to the well-lit breakfast room and a convenient utility room. The hearth-warmed living room looks to a rear porch. The right side of the plan is devoted to the sleeping quarters. The master bedroom is situated at the rear and boasts a private bath with many amenities. Three family bedrooms and another full bath complete this plan.

Plan: HPK3200194

First Floor: 2,112 sq. ft.
Second Floor: 361 sq. ft.
Total: 2,473 sq. ft.
Bedrooms: 4
Bathrooms: 3 ½

Width: 59' - 5"
Depth: 69' - 5"
Foundation: Crawlspace, Slab

This exciting contemporary design is enhanced by distinctively European details. Just inside, the foyer is flanked by family bedrooms and a formal dining room. Straight ahead, the formal two-story living room is warmed by a cozy fireplace. The kitchen is open to the casual breakfast room. The master suite is located to the left and includes a roomy walk-in closet, private bath, and rear-porch/patio access. On the opposite side of the home, two additional family bedrooms share a hall bath. A utility room, powder room, and two-car garage complete the first floor. Upstairs, an additional bedroom features a private bath and walk-in closet—perfect for a guest suite.

First Floor

Second Floor

Move-Up Homes

Plan: HPK3200195

First Floor: 1,160 sq. ft.
Second Floor: 1,316 sq. ft.
Total: 2,476 sq. ft.
Bedrooms: 4
Bathrooms: 2 ½

Width: 52' - 0"
Depth: 44' - 0"
Foundation: Unfinished
Walkout Basement

Brick detailing, shingles, and siding come together to create a refined exterior on this country farmhouse. The foyer is flanked by a dining room and a living room. At the rear of the house is the two-story family room, which is graced with a central fireplace and rear-door access to a sun deck. The kitchen blends into the breakfast area and is provided with backyard views. Storage space, a powder room, and a computer station complete the first floor of this plan. The sleeping quarters upstairs include a lavish master suite—with a full bath and sitting area—three vaulted family bedrooms, another full bath, and a laundry area.

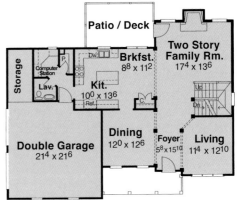

First Floor

Second Floor

This plan offers a well-designed, compact home ideal for a growing family with hopes of future expansion. Upstairs houses an optional game room, and a study on the first floor doubles as an optional bedroom. The open kitchen layout serves the adjoining breakfast nook, and an eating bar backs the living room. A rear screen porch makes outdoor dining a possibility. The spacious master suite sits on the first floor. A second first-floor bedroom equipped with a full bath could serve as a guest suite. Two additional family bedrooms sharing a full bath are on the second floor.

Plan: HPK3200196

First Floor: 2,019 sq. ft.	Bedrooms: 4
Second Floor: 468 sq. ft.	Bathrooms: 3
Total: 2,487 sq. ft.	Width: 59' - 0"
Bonus Space: 286 sq. ft.	Depth: 58' - 0"

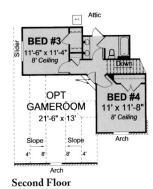

Second Floor

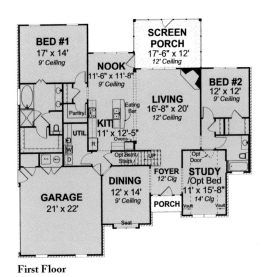

First Floor

Move-Up Homes

Plan: HPK3200197

First Floor: 1,436 sq. ft.
Second Floor: 1,069 sq. ft.
Total: 2,505 sq. ft.
Bedrooms: 3
Bathrooms: 2 ½

Width: 70' - 0"
Depth: 40' - 0"
Foundation: Crawlspace,
Unfinished Basement

The brick quoins draw attention to the cabin feeling of this home's facade, making it a perfect home for wooded areas. The covered front porch extends to the middle of the home, allowing for plenty of space to lounge outside. The open family room features a fireplace and connects to the breakfast nook where French doors lead to the rear patio. Upstairs, a deluxe raised tub and an immense walk-in closet grace the master suite.

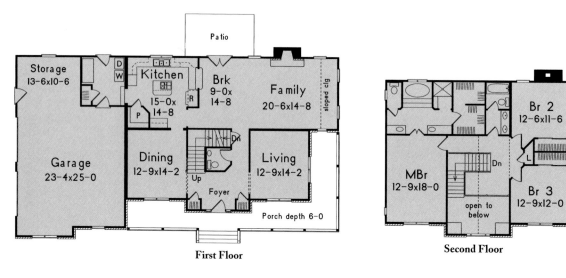

First Floor

Second Floor

A porch full of columns gives a relaxing emphasis to this country home. To the right of the foyer, the dining area resides conveniently near the efficient kitchen. The kitchen island, walk-in pantry, and serving bar add plenty of work space to the food-preparation zone. Natural light fills the breakfast nook through a ribbon of windows. Escape to the relaxing master suite featuring a private sunroom/retreat and a luxurious bath set between His and Hers walk-in closets. The great room features a warming fireplace and built-ins.

Plan: HPK3200198

Square Footage: 2,506
Bedrooms: 4
Bathrooms: 2 ½
Width: 72' - 2"

Depth: 66' - 4"
Foundation: Crawlspace, Slab, Unfinished Basement

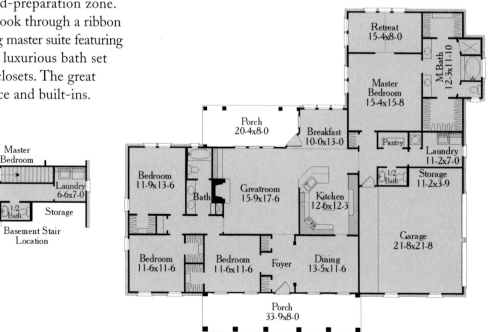

Move-Up Homes

Plan: HPK3200199

First Floor: 1,228 sq. ft.
Second Floor: 1,285 sq. ft.
Total: 2,513 sq. ft.
Bedrooms: 4
Bathrooms: 2 ½

Width: 36' - 8"
Depth: 66' - 2"
Foundation: Unfinished
Basement

Amenities in this four-bedroom home include fireplaces in the family room and master bedroom, a covered porch that opens to the patio, and access from the master bedroom to an upper-level covered porch. From the tiled foyer, enter the open living room/dining room or the kitchen with its planning desk and angled snack bar. Kitchen space flows into the breakfast nook and from there to the family room. A powder room and laundry room, with garage access, complete the first floor. Upstairs, the master suite includes a study area with a built-in desk and shelves, a walk-in closet and a luxurious bath with separate vanities. Three family bedrooms and a bath with a double-bowl vanity complete the second floor.

First Floor

Second Floor

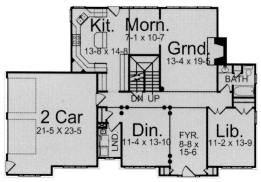

First Floor

Second Floor

Plan: HPK3200200

First Floor: 1,380 sq. ft.
Second Floor: 1,140 sq. ft.
Total: 2,520 sq. ft.
Bedrooms: 3
Bathrooms: 3

Width: 59' - 6"
Depth: 39' - 0"
Foundation: Crawlspace,
Unfinished Basement

An imposing yet graceful hipped roofline tops myriad windowpanes in this stately design. Fanlight and oxeye windows over a casement door light the two-story foyer that leads to the U-shaped staircase. Columns decorate the formal dining hall. The kitchen leads to a butler's pantry and includes a corner sink and a bar. The morning room adjoins the two-story grand salon through an elegant archway, which dramatizes the height of that room's ceiling. A full bath serves a guest room that has double doors and windows to the front. The master suite upstairs features double doors, an octagonal tray ceiling, and closets in both the bedroom and the bath. The bath also offers a corner tub, shower seat, and twin vanities. Two additional bedrooms on this floor share a full bath that includes private vanities.

Move-Up Homes

Plan: HPK3200201

Square Footage: 2,542	Width: 80' - 0"
Bedrooms: 4	Depth: 64' - 0"
Bathrooms: 3 ½	Foundation: Slab

Five gables and a stepped roofline create a stunning exterior for this sprawling traditional home. An enchanting entry leads to the long gallery and gracious formal dining area with vaulted ceiling. Wide windows frame the brick fireplace and hearth in the living room. The master suite features a vaulted ceiling and a French door leading to a covered patio. Relax in the private bath with a skylight in the sloped ceiling. Three additional bedrooms, each with its own walk-in closet and bath, complete this wonderful home.

© 2000 Donald A. Gardner, Inc.

Refined elegance characterizes this stunning home with a dynamic open floor plan. Elegant columns separate the large great room with cathedral ceiling from the smart, angled kitchen with skylit breakfast area. Tucked away for privacy, the master suite is a grand getaway with a well-appointed bath that includes a corner tub, separate shower, and spacious vanity. The semi-private privy is also a plus. Stunning tray ceilings enhance the bedroom/study and the dining room. The dining room is also distinguished by two stately columns gracing the hallway to the kitchen and foyer. As for plenty of closet and storage space, this home has it, plus an additional bonus room above the garage.

Plan: HPK3200202

Square Footage: 2,544	Bathrooms: 2 ½
Bonus Space: 394 sq. ft.	Width: 62' - 8"
Bedrooms: 4	Depth: 82' - 1"

Move-Up Homes

©1993 William E Poole Designs, Inc.

Plan: HPK3200203

First Floor: 1,884 sq. ft.
Second Floor: 661 sq. ft.
Total: 2,545 sq. ft.
Bonus Space: 489 sq. ft.
Bedrooms: 3

Bathrooms: 2 ½
Width: 71' - 4"
Depth: 62' - 2"
Foundation: Crawlspace

The Colonial architecture of Williamsburg, Virginia, inspired this design. Dormers top a side-gabled roof that breaks to provide a covered stoop for the front entrance. Inside, a traditional layout reigns, with the great room on the left and the dining room, kitchen, and breakfast area on the right. Toward the back of the home lies the master suite with spacious bedroom, luxury bath, and walk-in closet. The room's location buffers it from any front or side street noise. A private doorway accesses the screened porch. Upstairs, two family bedrooms, a full hall bath, and a bonus room complete the plan.

First Floor

Second Floor

© 1996 Donald A. Gardner Architects, Inc

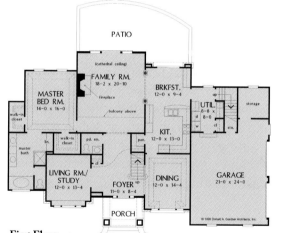

First Floor

Second Floor

Plan: HPK3200204

First Floor: 1,904 sq. ft.	Bedrooms: 3
Second Floor: 645 sq. ft.	Bathrooms: 2 ½
Total: 2,549 sq. ft.	Width: 71' - 2"
Bonus Space: 434 sq. ft.	Depth: 45' - 8"

This stucco home contrasts gently curved arches with gables and uses large multipane windows to illuminate the interior with natural light. Square pillars form an impressive entry, leading to a two-story foyer. The living room is set apart from the informal area of the house and could serve as a cozy study instead. The back patio can be reached from both the breakfast nook and the family room, which features a cathedral ceiling and a fireplace. The master suite offers two walk-in closets and a bath with twin vanities, a garden tub, and separate shower.

Move-Up Homes

Plan: HPK3200205

First Floor: 1,972 sq. ft.
Second Floor: 579 sq. ft.
Total: 2,551 sq. ft.
Bonus Space: 256 sq. ft.
Bedrooms: 3
Bathrooms: 2 ½

Width: 57' - 4"
Depth: 51' - 2"
Foundation: Crawlspace, Slab, Unfinished Walkout Basement

A beautiful one-story turret is accompanied by arched windows and a stucco facade. A terrific casual combination of kitchen, breakfast area, and vaulted keeping room provides space for family gatherings. Both the keeping room and great room sport cheerful fireplaces. The master suite is secluded on the first floor. This relaxing retreat offers a sitting room, His and Hers walk-in closets, dual vanities, and a compartmented toilet. Two family bedrooms share a full bath on the second floor. An optional bonus room can be used as a game room or home office.

First Floor

Second Floor

Plan: HPK3200541

First Floor: 1,235 sq. ft.	Bathrooms: 2 ½
Second Floor: 1,325 sq. ft.	Width: 62' - 0"
Total: 2,560 sq. ft.	Depth: 41' - 0"
Bedrooms: 3	Foundation: Crawlspace

A gambrel roof and Craftsman trim create a stunning facade for this popular family home. Step inside from the covered porch and a foyer opens to four equally enticing options. To the right sits the living and dining rooms. To the left, the den, or home office, awaits. Veer around the corner and a perfectly placed powder rooms sits adjacent to the welcoming breakfast nook. The adjoining kitchen and family room expand the space. The fourth option leads upstairs where the sleeping quarters are housed. The master suite enjoys a lovely view from the rear of the home. Two additional family bedrooms face the front of the home and are flanked by a spacious bonus room, ideal for a game or media room.

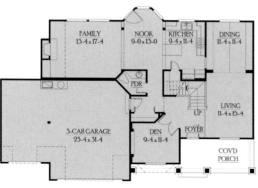

First Floor

Second Floor

Move-Up Homes

Plan: HPK3200206

First Floor: 1,784 sq. ft.
Second Floor: 777 sq. ft.
Total: 2,561 sq. ft.
Bonus Space: 232 sq. ft.
Bedrooms: 4

Bathrooms: 2 ½
Width: 60' - 0"
Depth: 51' - 0"
Foundation: Crawlspace

This traditional home is a perfect semblance of old-fashioned style and modern features. Triple dormers and a front covered porch add country accents to the facade. A dining room and study flank the foyer, providing a formal greeting to guests. Ahead, vaulted ceilings enhance the great room and the breakfast nook on the left; an island kitchen serves both. The first-floor master bedroom is complete with two closets—one a walk-in—and a private, double-vanity bath. Three additional bedrooms and a bonus room reside upstairs.

First Floor

Second Floor

Beyond the entry of this attractive two-story home, 15-foot arched openings frame the great room. French doors in the breakfast room open to a versatile office with a sloping 10-foot ceiling. A convenient utility area off the kitchen features access to the garage, a half-bath, and a generous laundry room complete with a folding table. A private entrance into the master suite reveals a pleasing interior. On the second floor, three large secondary bedrooms share a bath with dual sinks.

Plan: HPK3200207

First Floor: 1,875 sq. ft.	Bathrooms: 2 ½
Second Floor: 687 sq. ft.	Width: 60' - 0"
Total: 2,562 sq. ft.	Depth: 59' - 4"
Bedrooms: 4	

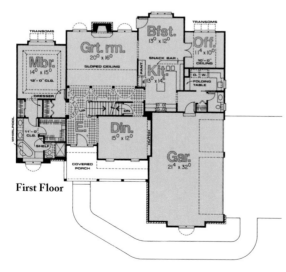

First Floor

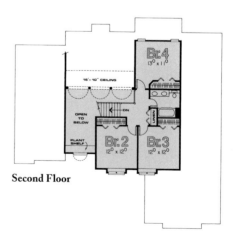

Second Floor

Move-Up Homes

Plan: HPK3200208

First Floor: 1,387 sq. ft.
Second Floor: 1,175 sq. ft.
Total: 2,562 sq. ft.
Bonus Space: 362 sq. ft.
Bedrooms: 3

Bathrooms: 2 ½
Width: 55' - 0"
Depth: 78' - 6"
Foundation: Crawlspace

Graceful arches adorn the large front porch, welcoming visitors to this charming home. A mixture of materials, including shake, stone, and clapboard, lend a rustic yet sophisticated appeal. Step inside to the foyer, which is open to the living room and dining room. Stepped, beamed, and coffered ceilings lend elegance to the living spaces of this home. At the left side of the plan, a sizable kitchen opens directly to the living room and a bowed breakfast nook with generous windows. A rear porch with outdoor grill is perfect for entertaining. Upstairs a master suite with sitting room and luxurious bath occupies the entire right side of the plan. Two additional bedrooms and a computer loft overlooking the foyer below complete this level.

Second Floor

First Floor

Move-Up Homes

©1995 William E. Poole Designs, Inc.

First Floor

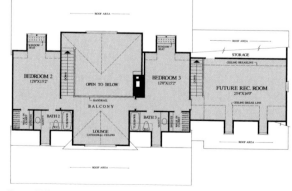

Second Floor

Plan: HPK3200209

First Floor: 1,694 sq. ft.
Second Floor: 874 sq. ft.
Total: 2,568 sq. ft.
Bonus Space: 440 sq. ft.
Bedrooms: 3

Bathrooms: 3 ½
Width: 74' - 2"
Depth: 46' - 8"
Foundation: Crawlspace,
Unfinished Basement

A welcoming front porch lined by graceful columns introduces this fine farmhouse. Inside, the foyer leads through an elegant arch to the spacious great room, which features a fireplace and built-ins. The formal dining room and sunny breakfast room flank a highly efficient kitchen, complete with a pantry and a serving bar. Located on the first floor for privacy, the master suite is filled with pampering amenities. Upstairs, two large bedrooms have private baths and walk-in closets.

Move-Up Homes

Plan: HPK3200210

First Floor: 1,502 sq. ft.
Second Floor: 1,073 sq. ft.
Total: 2,575 sq. ft.
Bonus Space: 373 sq. ft.
Bedrooms: 3

Bathrooms: 2 ½
Width: 60' - 0"
Depth: 44' - 0"
Foundation: Crawlspace

Timber frames support the covered front porch of a country gem. From the foyer, double doors lead to the den on the left, and a pass-through announces the living room on the right. Take the stairs straight ahead to find two secondary bedrooms, a full bath, and a bonus room. The second-floor master suite includes a spa bath and enormous walk-in closet. Downstairs, a kitchen and nook lie between the dining room and family room for formal and casual occasions.

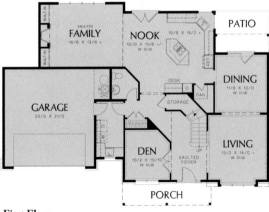

First Floor

Second Floor

Move-Up Homes

Plan: HPK3200211

First Floor: 1,894 sq. ft.
Second Floor: 683 sq. ft.
Total: 2,577 sq. ft.
Bonus Space: 210 sq. ft.
Bedrooms: 4
Bathrooms: 3

Width: 57' - 0"
Depth: 53' - 6"
Foundation: Crawlspace,
Unfinished Walkout
Basement

First Floor

Second Floor

Perfectly proportionate and definitely distinctive, this country home offers an open floor plan, abundant natural light, and plenty of space to kick back and relax. The plan begins with a two-story foyer that leads ahead to a family room lit by second-floor radius windows. Decorative columns define the nearby dining room, and a freestanding pantry is all that separates the family room from the welcoming island kitchen. The breakfast nook flows easily into the vaulted keeping room, surrounded by sparkling windows. Two bedrooms reside on this level, including a secondary bedroom with a box-bay window and a master suite with a sitting bay and a vaulted bath. Upstairs, two bedrooms enjoy privacy and share a full bath and a loft. Optional bonus space is available to expand as your family's needs change.

Move-Up Homes

Plan: HPK3200212

Square Footage: 2,585
Bonus Space: 519 sq. ft.
Bedrooms: 3
Bathrooms: 2 ½

Width: 62' - 6"
Depth: 83' - 10"
Foundation: Crawlspace

Designed to take full advantage of panoramic rear vistas, this home possesses some great visual effects of its own. Its unusual and creative use of space includes an angled gathering room, expansive grand room, and continuous covered lanai. High ceilings throughout create an air of spaciousness. A tray ceiling reflects the pentagonal shape of the open dining room. The master retreat features a sitting area and a bath that includes both His and Hers vanities and walk-in closets. A private staircase leads to a large bonus room.

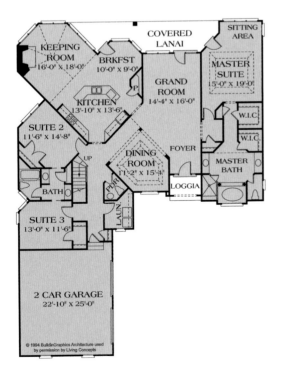

Plan: HPK3200213

Square Footage: 2,585	Width: 72' - 0"
Bonus Space: 160 sq. ft.	Depth: 69' - 10"
Bedrooms: 4	Foundation: Crawlspace,
Bathrooms: 3	Slab, Unfinished Basement

This luxurious, sprawling, brick home features elegantly zoned living spaces for everyone in your family. With its arched transom window, sidelights, and a stepped ceiling, the entry makes a strong statement to arriving guests. Flanking the foyer, the formal living and dining rooms boast pillar-framed entrances and stepped ceilings. A fireplace warms the living room, while the dining room's proximity to the kitchen makes dinner parties easy. The island kitchen includes a walk-in pantry, plus an angled, combination snack and serving counter that extends to the great room and breakfast area. The dramatic great room contains a fireplace, access to the rear porch, and built-ins for a media center. The sensational master suite enjoys a bayed sitting area, a walk-in closet, and a large private bath with two vanities and a windowed spa tub. An adjacent office accesses a side porch. Plans for an unfinished attic are included in the blueprints.

Move-Up Homes

Plan: HPK3200214

First Floor: 1,790 sq. ft.
Second Floor: 797 sq. ft.
Total: 2,587 sq. ft.
Bedrooms: 4
Bathrooms: 3 ½

Width: 64' - 4"
Depth: 50' - 0"
Foundation: Unfinished Basement

A brick-and-stone facade with arched windows, a covered porch, and shingle siding, decorate the exterior of this exciting home. The foyer showcases an angled staircase and opens generously to the great room, which enjoys a spectacular rear view. The spacious kitchen serves the breakfast alcove and dining room with equal ease and enjoys a bar with seating, a window above the sink, and a walk-in pantry. The master suite boasts a sitting area and a deluxe dressing area. The whirlpool tub, double-bowl vanity, and walk-in closet offer a luxurious retreat. Three bedrooms, one with a private bath, reside upstairs.

First Floor

Second Floor

First Floor

Second Floor

Plan: HPK3200215

First Floor: 1,809 sq. ft.
Second Floor: 785 sq. ft.
Total: 2,594 sq. ft.
Bonus Space: 353 sq. ft.
Bedrooms: 5
Bathrooms: 4

Width: 72' - 7"
Depth: 51' - 5"
Foundation: Crawlspace,
Slab, Unfinished Walkout
Basement

With elements of country style, this unique Colonial-inspired home presents a rustic attitude blended with the delicate features that make this design one of a kind. Upon entry, a second-story arched window lights the foyer. Straight ahead, the family room soars with a two-story vault balanced by a cozy fireplace. A pass-through from the island kitchen keeps conversation going as the family chef whips up delectable feasts for the formal dining room or bayed breakfast nook. A bedroom at the rear provides plenty of privacy for guests, or as a home office. The master suite takes up the entire right wing, hosting a bayed sitting area and marvelous vaulted bath. Upstairs, three bedrooms access a versatile bonus room, limited only by your imagination.

Move-Up Homes

Plan: HPK3200216

Square Footage: 2,606
Bonus Space: 751 sq. ft.
Bedrooms: 4
Bathrooms: 2 ½

Width: 67' - 6"
Depth: 73' - 10"
Foundation: Crawlspace, Slab, Unfinished Basement

An open floor plan is just one of the many highlights in this European-style home. The study/bedroom to the left of the foyer accesses a private patio. A single column, defining the dining room, is the only obstruction to traffic patterns between the dining room, great room, kitchen, and hearth room. French doors in the great room open to the rear grilling porch—the hearth room and the master bedroom also have porch access. Twin walk-in closets house homeowners' wardrobes, while a corner tub and corner shower soothe and relax. Two more bedrooms are nestled in the upper right corner of the plan.

Classic lines define the statuesque look of this four-bedroom home. The formal rooms flank the foyer and provide views to the front. An angled snack bar in the kitchen serves the breakfast area that is bathed in natural light. Connecting the spacious family room and living room is a wet bar that has the option of being used as a computer den. Upstairs, Bedrooms 3 and 4 share a bath; Bedroom 2 offers a private bath, making it a fine guest suite. The master bedroom is sure to please with His and Hers walk-in closets, a whirlpool tub, and a tray ceiling. Completing this level is a large bonus room available for future expansion.

Plan: HPK3200217

First Floor: 1,333 sq. ft.	Bathrooms: 3 ½
Second Floor: 1,280 sq. ft.	Width: 58' - 0"
Total: 2,613 sq. ft.	Depth: 44' - 4"
Bonus Space: 294 sq. ft.	
Bedrooms: 4	

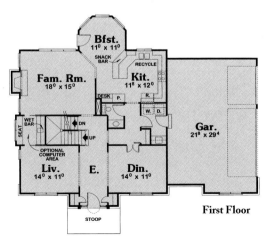

First Floor

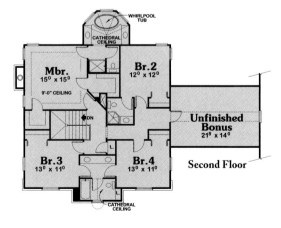

Second Floor

Move-Up Homes

Plan: HPK3200218

Square Footage: 2,696	Width: 80' - 0"
Bedrooms: 4	Depth: 64' - 1"
Bathrooms: 3 ½	Foundation: Slab

A brick archway covers the front porch of this European-influenced home, creating a truly grand entrance. Situated beyond the entry, the living room takes center stage with a fireplace flanked by tall windows. To the right is a bayed eating area and an efficient kitchen. Steps away is the formal dining room. Skillful planning creates flexibility for the master suite. If you wish, use Bedroom 2 as a secondary bedroom or guest room, with the adjacent study accessible to everyone. Or, if you prefer, combine the master suite with the study and use it as a private retreat with Bedroom 2 as a nursery, creating a wing that provides total privacy. Completing this clever plan are two family bedrooms, a powder room, and a utility room.

First Floor

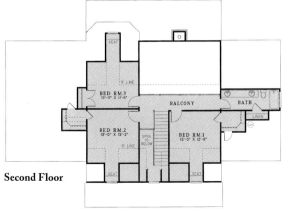

Second Floor

Plan: HPK3200219

First Floor: 1,813 sq. ft.
Second Floor: 885 sq. ft.
Total: 2,698 sq. ft.
Bedrooms: 5
Bathrooms: 3

Width: 70' - 2"
Depth: 51' - 4"
Foundation: Crawlspace,
Slab, Unfinished
Basement

Four graceful columns support a long covered porch topped by three attractive dormers. The two-story foyer is flanked by a formal dining room and a cozy study—or make it a guest suite with the full bath nearby. The island kitchen is sure to please with a walk-in pantry and easy access to the breakfast area. A spacious great room has a balcony overlook from the second floor and a fireplace. The master suite boasts two walk-in closets, a whirlpool tub, and a separate shower. Upstairs, three bedrooms—all with window seats—share a full hall bath.

Move-Up Homes

Plan: HPK3200220

First Floor: 1,365 sq. ft.
Second Floor: 1,336 sq. ft.
Total: 2,701 sq. ft.
Bedrooms: 3
Bathrooms: 3 ½

Width: 82' - 0"
Depth: 44' - 0"
Foundation: Unfinished
Basement

This impressive Colonial design sings of timeless elegance and modern amenities. A front covered porch adds a country accent to the exterior. Inside, a formal dining room and a study warmed by a fireplace flank the entry. The island snack-bar kitchen is open to both the breakfast nook and family room. A three-season porch is attached at the rear of the plan. A three-car garage and laundry room complete the first floor. Upstairs, the master bedroom features a private bath and walk-in closet. Bedrooms 2 and 3 boast their own walk-in closets and private baths. The bonus room is great for a family recreation room or home office.

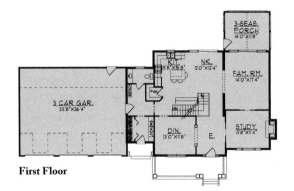

First Floor

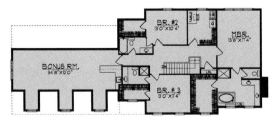

Second Floor

Plan: HPK3200221

First Floor: 1,650 sq. ft.	Width: 53' - 0"
Second Floor: 1,060 sq. ft.	Depth: 68' - 2"
Total: 2,710 sq. ft.	Foundation: Walkout
Bedrooms: 4	Basement
Bathrooms: 3 ½	

This home features keystone arches that frame the arched front door and windows. Inside, the foyer opens directly to the large great room with a fireplace and French doors that lead outside. Just off the foyer, the dining room is defined by columns. Adjacent to the breakfast room is the keeping room, which includes a corner fireplace and more French doors to the large rear porch. The master suite has dual vanities and a spacious walk-in closet. Upstairs, two family bedrooms enjoy separate access to a shared bath; down the hall, a fourth bedroom includes a private bath.

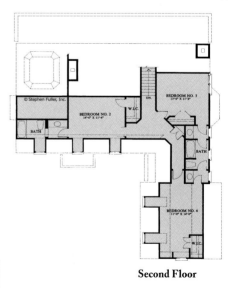

Second Floor

First Floor

Move-Up Homes

Plan: HPK3200222

First Floor: 2,117 sq. ft.
Second Floor: 620 sq. ft.
Total: 2,737 sq. ft.
Bedrooms: 3

Bathrooms: 3 ½
Width: 56' - 0"
Depth: 60' - 0"
Foundation: Crawlspace

An eye-catching exterior and well-designed interior make this home worthy of a second look. An attractive stone entryway leads into the casual foyer that immediately opens to the rest of the home. A built-in entertainment center and central fireplace make this room ideal for family gatherings. The open design is perfect for entertaining. A guest suite is a comfortable retreat for visitors. Upstairs houses a third bedroom complete with full bath and a game room with wet bar.

First Floor

Second Floor

A European feel is shown on the exterior facade of this exciting two-story home and hints at the exquisite grace of the interior. The sensational view at the foyer includes high windows across the rear wall, a fireplace, open stairs with rich wood trim, and volume ceilings. The formal dining room offers dimension to the entry and is conveniently located for serving from the kitchen. The spacious breakfast room, wraparound bar in the kitchen, and open hearth room offer a cozy gathering place for family members. The deluxe master bedroom suite boasts an 11-foot ceiling, a sitting area, and a garden bath. The second-floor balcony leads to a bedroom suite with a private bath, and two additional bedrooms with large closets and private access to a shared bath.

Plan: HPK3200223

First Floor: 1,915 sq. ft.
Second Floor: 823 sq. ft.
Total: 2,738 sq. ft.
Bedrooms: 4
Bathrooms: 3 ½

Width: 63' - 4"
Depth: 48' - 0"
Foundation: Unfinished Basement

First Floor

Second Floor

Move-Up Homes

Plan: HPK3200224

First Floor: 1,915 sq. ft.
Second Floor: 823 sq. ft.
Total: 2,738 sq. ft.
Bedrooms: 4
Bathrooms: 3 ½

Width: 63' - 4"
Depth: 48' - 0"
Foundation: Unfinished Basement

A luxuriously styled exterior with wood and stone accents, a boxed window, and an octagonal tower combine with a functional floor plan to create a home that will excite the most discriminating buyer. The spectacular view offered at the foyer includes high windows across the rear wall, a fireplace, open stairs with rich wood trim, and a volume ceiling. The formal dining room adds dimension to the entry. The spacious breakfast room opens to the hearth room, offering a comfortable gathering place. The first-floor master suite boasts a sitting alcove and a deluxe bath. The second-floor balcony leads to three family bedrooms.

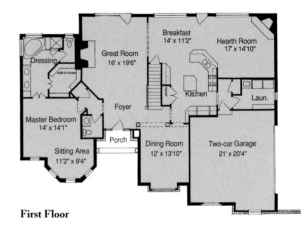

First Floor

Second Floor

Plan: HPK3200225

First Floor: 1,932 sq. ft.
Second Floor: 807 sq. ft.
Total: 2,739 sq. ft.
Bedrooms: 4
Bathrooms: 2 ½

Width: 63' - 0"
Depth: 51' - 6"
Foundation: Walkout
Basement

First Floor

Second Floor

This sensational country Colonial exterior is set off by a cozy covered porch, just right for enjoying cool evenings outside. A two-story foyer opens to a quiet study with a centered fireplace, and to the formal dining room with views to the front property. The gourmet kitchen features an island cooktop counter and a charming bayed breakfast nook. The great room soars two stories high but is made cozy with an extended-hearth fireplace. Two walk-in closets, a garden tub, and a separate shower highlight the master bath; a coffered ceiling decorates the master bedroom. Three family bedrooms, each with a walk-in closet, share a full bath upstairs.

Move-Up Homes

Plan: HPK3200226

Square Footage: 2,745	Depth: 76' - 8"
Bedrooms: 4	Foundation: Crawlspace,
Bathrooms: 2 ½	Slab, Unfinished Basement
Width: 69' - 6"	

A gentle European charm flavors the facade of this ultra-modern layout. The foyer opens to a formal dining room, which leads to the kitchen through privacy doors. Here, a center cooktop island complements wrapping counter space, a walk-in pantry, and a snack counter. Casual living space shares a through-fireplace with the formal living room and provides its own access to the rear porch. Clustered sleeping quarters include a well-appointed master suite, two family bedrooms, and an additional bedroom that could double as a study.

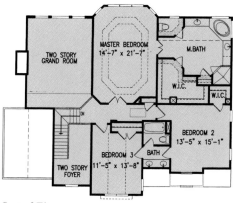

First Floor

TWO STORY GRAND ROOM 15'-0" x 20'-1"
BREAKFAST 14'-9" x 10'-6"
W.I.C.
STUDY/ BEDROOM 4 11'-1" x 10'-11"
BATH
KITCHEN 11'-6" x 14'-5"
LAUNDRY
LIVING ROOM 11'-1" x 15'-5"
DN
TWO CAR GARAGE 19'-7" x 19'-7"
DINING 11'-5" x 14'-2"
TWO STORY FOYER

Second Floor

TWO STORY GRAND ROOM
MASTER BEDROOM 14'-7" x 21'-7"
M.BATH
W.I.C.
W.I.C.
DN
BEDROOM 2 13'-5" x 15'-1"
BEDROOM 3 11'-5" x 13'-8"
BATH
TWO STORY FOYER

Plan: HPK3200227

First Floor: 1,486 sq. ft.
Second Floor: 1,265 sq. ft.
Total: 2,751 sq. ft.
Bedrooms: 4
Bathrooms: 3

Width: 52' - 0"
Depth: 40' - 0"
Foundation: Unfinished Walkout Basement

A two-story foyer, flanked by formal living and dining areas, welcomes visitors into this Colonial home. Once inside, the grand room sits at the heart of the home and opens to the kitchen and breakfast nook. Flex space adjacent to the laundry room can be used as a study or guest suite. Upstairs houses the spacious master suite, and two family bedrooms sharing a full bath. A two-car garage completes this plan—customize it to load from the front or the side!

Move-Up Homes

Plan: HPK3200228

First Floor: 2,061 sq. ft.
Second Floor: 701 sq. ft.
Total: 2,762 sq. ft.
Bonus Space: 405 sq. ft.
Bedrooms: 3

Bathrooms: 2 ½
Width: 60' - 10"
Depth: 64' - 0"
Foundation: Crawlspace

A perfect selection for a golf or lake setting, this transitional house offers a great open floor plan with plenty of large windows in back. The foyer, two-story living room, dining room, and sunroom create one continuous space. A wet bar in the dining room is a great addition for entertaining. The large, full kitchen offers an island cooktop and the convenience of a walk-in pantry. A sumptuous master suite provides an oversized walk-in closet and a garden tub with bay window. Two more suites and a bath are upstairs, along with an extra large bonus room over the courtyard garage.

First Floor

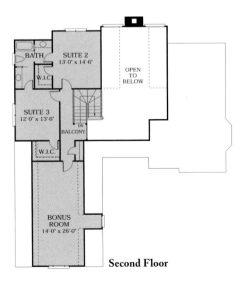

Second Floor

Move-Up Homes

Plan: HPK3200229

Square Footage: 2,774
Bonus Space: 367 sq. ft.
Bedrooms: 3
Bathrooms: 3 ½

Width: 66' - 10"
Depth: 84' - 9"
Foundation: Crawlspace

Interesting room orientation distinguishes this unusual floor plan. The grand room's octagonal tray ceiling demonstrates that this is an elegant home inhabited by hospitable people. Beyond the grand room, a partially covered lanai offers options for outdoor entertaining. The bay-shaped breakfast nook and gathering room play off the kitchen's angled countertops, creating an integrated, informal space. Note how the offset fireplace in the gathering room will ease furniture arrangement. The right wing of the home houses two bedroom suites, one with a private lanai, and a stair to the bonus room above the two-car garage. The master retreat occupies the left wing. More elegant ceiling treatments and a posh bath will make everyday living feel like a fantasy vacation!

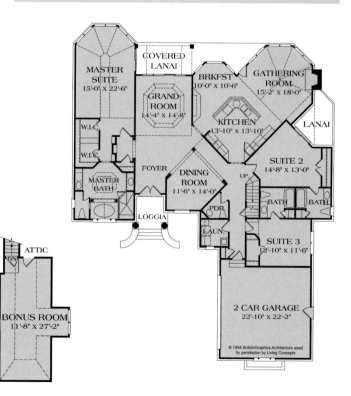

Move-Up Homes

Plan: HPK3200230

First Floor: 1,279 sq. ft.
Second Floor: 1,499 sq. ft.
Total: 2,778 sq. ft.
Bonus Space: 240 sq. ft.
Bedrooms: 4
Bathrooms: 2 ½

Width: 53' - 0"
Depth: 46' - 6"
Foundation: Crawlspace,
Unfinished Walkout
Basement

Variety abounds across the facade of this classic Colonial design. The pedimented entry gives way to the two-story foyer that opens to the living room, dining room, and engaging two-story family room. The kitchen overlooks the bayed breakfast room. A walk-in pantry is placed next to the entry to the three-car garage. The second floor holds the master suite along with three bedrooms and a shared full bath. The vaulted master bath is a luxurious retreat for the homeowners and extends into an enormous walk-in closet.

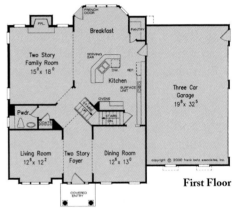

First Floor

Optional Layout

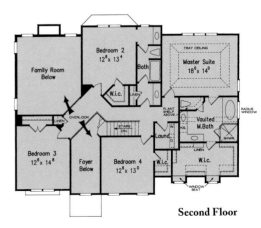

Second Floor

Plan: HPK3200231

Square Footage: 2,781	Depth: 76' - 9"
Bedrooms: 4	Foundation: Crawlspace,
Bathrooms: 3	Slab
Width: 64' - 10"	

A multifaceted facade and classic arches blend with an intricate hipped roof design, dressing this home with a sheer sense of elegance. The dining and living rooms meld with the breakfast nook creating an expansive common area that spills out onto the rear covered porch. The four bedrooms are split with two on each side of the plan—the master suite on the left boasts a lavish master bath and twin walk-in closets. The unfinished game room easily converts to a home office or attic storage.

Move-Up Homes

©2005 William E Poole Designs, Inc.

Plan: HPK3200232

First Floor: 1,816 sq. ft.	Bathrooms: 3 ½
Second Floor: 968 sq. ft.	Width: 54' - 6"
Total: 2,784 sq. ft.	Depth: 52' - 5"
Bedrooms: 4	Foundation: Crawlspace

Pediments and lintels adorn the front of this brick Colonial home. In true Fedral fashion, symmetry guides the main part of the home. Inset dormers decorate the roofline while increasing floor space in two of the three upstairs bedrooms. A traditional layout separates the front rooms with partial walls and columns while contemporary design keeps the kitchen and breakfast area open to the two-story family room. The master bedroom, in the left section of the plan, awaits homeowners with a bay window, amenity-filled bath, and long walk-in closet. The two-bay garage can be customized to suit your lot.

First Floor

Second Floor

Move-Up Homes

This dream home features dormers, multipane windows, and a pediment supported by columns at the entry to accent its brick-and-siding facade. To the right of the entry the dining room accesses both the covered front porch and the angled kitchen. The adjoining breakfast nook offers expansive views to the rear while the spacious family room to the left creates a friendly atmosphere with a warming fireplace. For more formal entertaining, the living room resides to the left of the foyer. Upstairs, three bedrooms share a full bath. The extravagant master suite includes a sunny sitting area and an enormous walk-in closet.

Plan: HPK3200233

First Floor: 1,332 sq. ft.
Second Floor: 1,457 sq. ft.
Total: 2,789 sq. ft.
Bedrooms: 4
Bathrooms: 2 ½

Width: 58' - 0"
Depth: 46' - 6"
Foundation: Crawlspace, Unfinished Walkout Basement

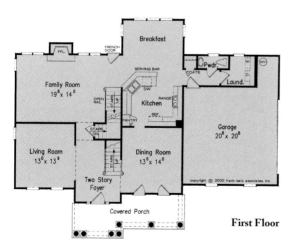

First Floor

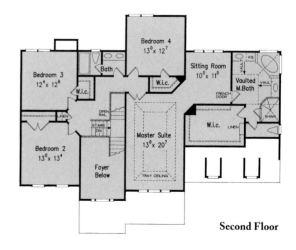

Second Floor

Move-Up Homes

©1993 William E Poole Designs, Inc.

Plan: HPK3200234

First Floor: 1,927 sq. ft.
Second Floor: 879 sq. ft.
Total: 2,806 sq. ft.
Bonus Space: 459 sq. ft.
Bedrooms: 4

Bathrooms: 3 ½
Width: 71' - 0"
Depth: 53' - 0"
Foundation: Crawlspace

This charming southern plantation home packs quite a punch in 2,800 square feet! The elegant foyer is flanked by the formal dining room and the living room. To the rear, the family room has a fireplace and an expansive view of the outdoors. An archway leads to the breakfast area and on to the island kitchen. The luxurious master suite is tucked away for privacy behind the two-car garage. Three additional bedrooms rest on the second floor where they share two full baths. Space above the garage is available for future development.

First Floor

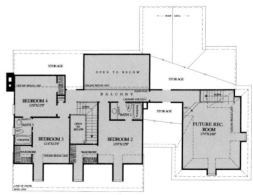

Second Floor

Plan: HPK3200235

First Floor: 1,383 sq. ft.	Bathrooms: 3 ½
Second Floor: 1,437 sq. ft.	Width: 42' - 0"
Total: 2,820 sq. ft.	Depth: 53' - 0"
Bedrooms: 4	Foundation: Crawlspace

Bold lines modernize this home's traditional facade and give it stand-out appeal. An open floor plan facilitates movement between the living room, dining area, and kitchen with accent columns, bumped-out bays, and a butler's pantry. The kitchen combines with an eating nook—with double French doors to the rear—and the two-story great room with fireplace and built-in storage. Upstairs, three large family bedrooms—one with a private bath—and a vaulted master suite provide comfortable family space.

First Floor

Second Floor

Move-Up Homes

Plan: HPK3200236

First Floor: 1,438 sq. ft.
Second Floor: 1,395 sq. ft.
Total: 2,833 sq. ft.
Bedrooms: 5

Bathrooms: 3
Width: 54' - 6"
Depth: 40' - 6"

After a day away, it will be a pleasure to come home to this four- or five-bedroom home. The two-story foyer, which is flanked by the formal dining and living rooms, leads straight ahead to the two-story family room. This room features a fireplace and decorative columns, which separate the family room from the kitchen and breakfast nook. The lavish master suite and the remaining three bedrooms are on the second floor. A private rear study on the first floor can be used for a fifth bedroom with its own full bath.

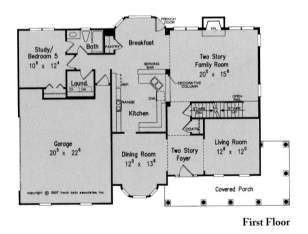

First Floor

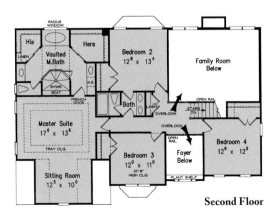

Second Floor

Plan: HPK3200237

First Floor: 1,604 sq. ft.	Bathrooms: 2 ½
Second Floor: 1,230 sq. ft.	Width: 60' - 0"
Total: 2,834 sq. ft.	Depth: 52' - 0"
Bonus Space: 284 sq. ft.	Foundation: Crawlspace
Bedrooms: 3	

The combination of stone and siding gives the facade of this traditional home an inviting feel. Inside, the first floor is a study in family togetherness. The expansive kitchen invites friends and family to share in the cooking experience, be it by conversing from the adjoining nook or adjacent family room, or actually getting their hands dirty at the convenient island counter. The dining room and nearby living room with a fireplace are perfect for formal entertaining. Completing this level are a den, a half-bath, and the three-car garage. Bedrooms dominate the second level, including a vaulted master suite and pampering master bath, along with bonus space to finish as you please.

First Floor

Second Floor

Move-Up Homes

Plan: HPK3200238

First Floor: 2,143 sq. ft.
Second Floor: 694 sq. ft.
Total: 2,837 sq. ft.
Bedrooms: 4

Bathrooms: 3
Width: 52' - 0"
Depth: 72' - 0"

Brick homes have the unique advantage of appearing well-established, even when brand new—this distinctive design is no exception. Inside, elegant ceiling treatments and a thoughtful floor plan create a home that values both style and privacy. Enter through a two-story foyer; the living room receives guests on the left and features a tall vault. The dining room includes a built-in china cabinet. Ahead, a volume ceiling in the family room is balanced by a cozy hearth. The kitchen hosts an eating bar for easy service to the sunny nook. The master suite is tucked to the rear with a pampering resort-style bath. A secondary bedroom is sheltered from street noise and accesses a semi-private bath. Upstairs, two bedrooms with private vanities share a full bath and a game room.

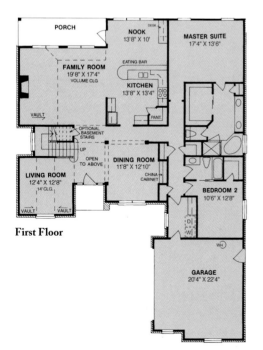

First Floor

Second Floor

Move-Up Homes

Plan: HPK3200239

Square Footage: 2,846
Bedrooms: 4
Bathrooms: 2 ½
Width: 84' - 6"

Depth: 64' - 2"
Foundation: Crawlspace,
Slab

This Southern Colonial home is distinguished by its columned porch and double dormers. Inside, columns and connecting arches define the angled foyer. The master suite is located away from the other bedrooms for privacy and includes a large master bath and a walk-in closet. Three additional bedrooms are located adjacent to the family room. The kitchen, breakfast area, and family room are open—perfect for informal entertaining and family gatherings. The foyer, living room, and dining room have 12-foot ceilings. Ten-foot ceilings are used in the family room, kitchen, breakfast area, and master suite to give this home an open, spacious feeling.

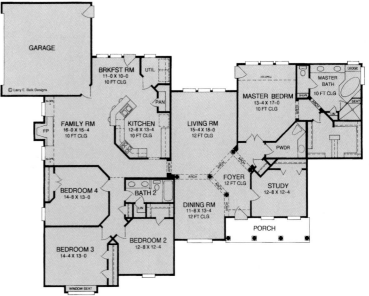

Move-Up Homes

© THE SATER DESIGN COLLECTION

Plan: HPK3200240

First Floor: 1,642 sq. ft.
Second Floor: 1,205 sq. ft.
Total: 2,847 sq. ft.
Bonus Space: 340 sq. ft.
Bedrooms: 3

Bathrooms: 3 ½
Width: 53' - 7"
Depth: 72' - 6"
Foundation: Crawlspace

Stone accents complement the siding facade and add a touch of warmth and personality. Once inside, upgraded ceiling treatments are found throughout, adding presence. A fireplace in the leisure room is accentuated by built-in bookcases. Double French doors open to a rear porch, extending the living space outdoors. The island kitchen opens to the adjoining breakfast nook. Upstairs houses the sleeping quarters, including the luxurious master suite complete with private deck access, a makeup station, a whirlpool tub, and His and Hers amenities. Two secondary bedrooms share a Jack-and-Jill bath. Equipped with a full bath and a walk-in closet, the bonus room over the garage could serve as a guest suite or a future media room.

First Floor

Second Floor

Asymmetrical gables and a graceful arched entry supported by square columns complement a careful mix of stone and siding with this magnificent facade. Inside, the foyer opens to a spacious living room that offers views of the front property. The gourmet kitchen leads to the formal dining room through a servery area, which can facilitate planned events. Built-in shelves and a centered fireplace enhance the great room. French doors lead out to the rear deck—a perfect arrangement for entertaining. Upstairs, the master suite includes a double-sink lavatory, compartmented toilet, and oversized shower. Three secondary bedrooms share a gallery hall that leads to a future area.

Plan: HPK3200241

First Floor: 1,482 sq. ft.	Bathrooms: 3 ½
Second Floor: 1,373 sq. ft.	Width: 66' - 7"
Total: 2,855 sq. ft.	Depth: 41' - 6"
Bonus Space: 537 sq. ft.	Foundation: Unfinished
Bedrooms: 4	Basement

First Floor

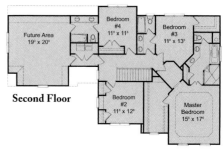

Second Floor

Move-Up Homes

Plan: HPK3200242

Square Footage: 2,863
Bedrooms: 4
Bathrooms: 3
Width: 73' - 8"

Depth: 97' - 9"
Foundation: Crawlspace, Slab, Unfinished Basement

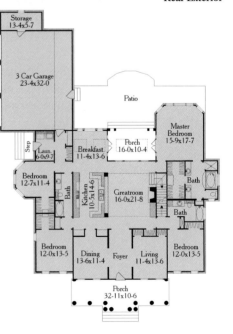

Rear Exterior

A pedimented front porch gives this Southern Colonial home a classic appeal. Inside, the living and dining rooms face each other across the foyer. At the center of the plan is the great room with a fireplace and built-ins. Skylights flood the covered porch and breakfast room with light. Escape the busy world in the master suite with a bay window and a luxurious bath. Two secondary bedrooms are placed on the opposite side of the home—one with a beautiful bay window—and a third is set in the front right corner.

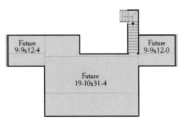

© Stephen Fuller, Inc.

Traditionalists will appreciate the classic styling of this Colonial home. The foyer opens to both a banquet-sized dining room and formal living room with a fireplace. Just beyond is the two-story great room. The entire right side of the main level is taken up by the enchanting master suite. The other side of the main level includes a large kitchen and a breakfast room just steps away from the detached garage. Upstairs, each bedroom features ample closet space and direct access to a bath. The detached garage features an unfinished office or studio on its second level.

Plan: HPK3200243

First Floor: 1,960 sq. ft.
Second Floor: 905 sq. ft.
Total: 2,865 sq. ft.
Bonus Space: 297 sq. ft.
Bedrooms: 4

Bathrooms: 3 ½
Width: 61' - 0"
Depth: 70' - 6"
Foundation: Walkout Basement

First Floor

Second Floor

Move-Up Homes

Plan: HPK3200244

First Floor: 2,249 sq. ft.	Bedrooms: 4
Second Floor: 620 sq. ft.	Bathrooms: 3 ½
Total: 2,869 sq. ft.	Width: 69' - 6"
Bonus Space: 308 sq. ft.	Depth: 52' - 0"

An impressive two-story entrance welcomes you to this stately home. Massive chimneys and pillars and varying rooflines add interest to the stucco exterior. The foyer, lit by a clerestory window, opens to the formal living and dining rooms. The living room—which could also serve as a study—features a fireplace, as does the family room. Both rooms access the patio. The L-shaped island kitchen opens to a bay-windowed breakfast nook, which is echoed by the sitting area in the master suite. A room next to the kitchen could serve as a bedroom or a home office. The second floor contains two family bedrooms plus a bonus room for future expansion.

First Floor

Second Floor

© William E. Poole Designs, Inc.

Plan: HPK3200245

Square Footage: 2,869	Width: 68' - 6"
Bedrooms: 3	Depth: 79' - 8"
Bathrooms: 3 ½	Foundation: Crawlspace

Here is a beautiful example of Colonial architecture complete with shuttered windows, lintels, and a column-supported pediment over the entry. Inside, the foyer opens to the living room and leads to the family room at the rear. Here, a panoramic view is complemented by an impressive fireplace framed by built-ins. To the left, the efficient island kitchen is situated between the sunny breakfast nook and the formal dining room. The right side of the plan holds two bedrooms and the lavish master suite.

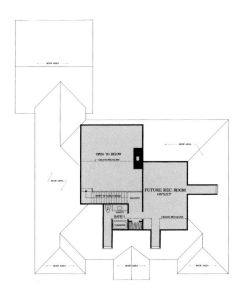

Move-Up Homes

Plan: HPK3200246

First Floor: 1,963 sq. ft.	Width: 58' - 0"
Second Floor: 907 sq. ft.	Depth: 51' - 6"
Total: 2,870 sq. ft.	Foundation: Unfinished
Bedrooms: 4	Basement
Bathrooms: 3 ½	

This elegant masterpiece is an amenity-filled retreat for any large family. Two-story ceilings enhance the foyer and the grand salon, which shares a see-through fireplace with the vaulted morning/keeping room. Columns define the dining room to the left of the foyer; to the right is a bayed library with an arched entrance. The spacious master suite includes two walk-in closets and a lavish private bath. Upstairs, three family bedrooms, one with a private bath, reside along a gallery hall that overlooks the foyer.

First Floor

Second Floor

Classic symmetry and four elegant columns make this home a gem in any neighborhood. Inside, luxury is evident by the dimensions of each room. The foyer is flanked by a large yet cozy library to the right and a gracefully formal living room to the left. It's just a couple of steps up into the formal dining room here, making this area perfect for entertaining. Toward the rear of the home, casual living takes place, with a huge family room connecting to a sunny breakfast room and near an efficient kitchen. The bedrooms are upstairs, including the deluxe master suite with a sumptuous private bath.

Plan: HPK3200247

First Floor: 1,482 sq. ft.
Second Floor: 1,460 sq. ft.
Total: 2,942 sq. ft.
Bedrooms: 4
Bathrooms: 3 ½

Width: 48' - 0"
Depth: 52' - 0"
Foundation: Unfinished Basement

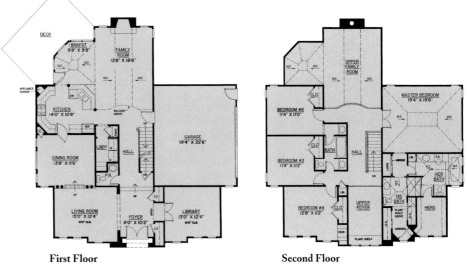

First Floor   Second Floor

Move-Up Homes

Plan: HPK3200248

Square Footage: 2,946	Width: 94' - 1"
Bedrooms: 4	Depth: 67' - 4"
Bathrooms: 3	Foundation: Slab

This home's varying hipped-roof planes make a strong statement. Exquisite classical detailing includes delightfully proportioned columns below a modified pedimented gable and masses of brick punctuated by corner quoins. The central foyer, with its high ceiling, leads to interesting traffic patterns. This extremely functional floor plan fosters flexible living. There are formal and informal areas, which are well defined by the living and family rooms. The sunken family room, wonderfully spacious with its high, sloping ceiling, contains a complete media-center wall and a fireplace flanked by doors to the entertainment patio. Occupying the isolated end of the floor plan, the master suite includes an adjacent office/den with a private porch.

First Floor

Second Floor

Plan: HPK3200249

First Floor: 1,463 sq. ft.
Second Floor: 1,490 sq. ft.
Total: 2,953 sq. ft.
Bedrooms: 5
Bathrooms: 4 ½

Width: 54' - 0"
Depth: 51' - 6"
Foundation: Crawlspace,
Slab, Unfinished Walkout
Basement

The nearly octagonal shape of the kitchen, with its long work island, will please the family's gourmet cook. The breakfast room, which opens to the back through a French door, flows into the two-story family room; to one side there's a butler's pantry leading to the dining room. The formal living room is on the other side of the two-story foyer. A bedroom with a private bath and walk-in closet could be an in-law suite, study, or home office. The other four bedrooms are upstairs off a balcony overlooking the family room. The laundry room is also on this floor. The master suite includes a sitting room, a walk-in closet, and a luxurious bath.

Move-Up Homes

Plan: HPK3200250

First Floor: 2,270 sq. ft.	Bedrooms: 3
Second Floor: 685 sq. ft.	Bathrooms: 2 ½
Total: 2,955 sq. ft.	Width: 75' - 1"
Bonus Space: 563 sq. ft.	Depth: 53' - 6"

Hipped rooflines, sunburst windows, and French-style shutters are the defining elements of this home's exterior. Inside, the foyer is flanked by the dining room and the study. Further on, the lavish great room can be entered by walking between two stately columns and is complete with a fireplace, built-in shelves, a vaulted ceiling, and views to the rear patio. The island kitchen easily accesses a pantry and a desk and flows into the bayed breakfast area. The first-floor master bedroom boasts a fireplace, two walk-in closets, and an amenity-filled private bath. Two additional bedrooms reside upstairs, along with a sizable bonus room.

First Floor

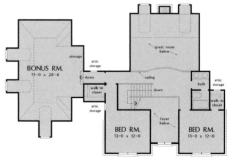

Second Floor

Order blueprints anytime at
eplans.com or 1-800-521-6797

Move-Up Homes

The delightful farmhouse holds two family bedrooms, each with twin closets, and a master suite with a vaulted ceiling and a gorgeous arch-top window. The covered porch announces the entry that presents the stunning staircase. To the left, the spacious formal dining room accommodates large gatherings. A swinging door quiets the distractions of the adjoining island kitchen. A sunny bay, to the right, enlivens the breakfast nook which leads to the family room. To the right of the foyer, the living room opens to the family room via an elegant archway. Upstairs, the master suite includes twin walk-in closets and a study.

Plan: HPK3200251

First Floor: 1,450 sq. ft.	Width: 69' - 0"
Second Floor: 1,517 sq. ft.	Depth: 37' - 0"
Total: 2,967 sq. ft.	Foundation: Unfinished
Bedrooms: 4	Basement
Bathrooms: 3 ½	

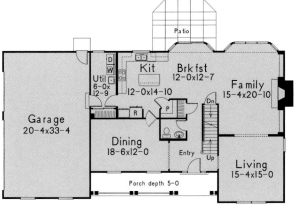

First Floor

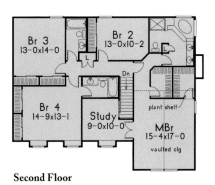

Second Floor

Move-Up Homes

Plan: HPK3200252

First Floor: 2,101 sq. ft.
Second Floor: 877 sq. ft.
Total: 2,978 sq. ft.
Bedrooms: 4

Bathrooms: 3
Width: 66' - 0"
Depth: 51' - 0"

The centerpiece of this home's facade is its imposing arch. Inside, the foyer is flanked by a dining room and living room, and the spacious family room—with a porch out back—is straight ahead. Bedroom 2 and the master suite occupy the left wing. An ample playroom/study complements the two bedrooms upstairs.

First Floor

Second Floor

©The Sater Design Collection, Inc.

Plan: HPK3200253

First Floor: 2,096 sq. ft.
Second Floor: 892 sq. ft.
Total: 2,988 sq. ft.
Bedrooms: 3
Bathrooms: 3 ½

Width: 56' - 0"
Depth: 54' - 0"
Foundation: Unfinished
Walkout Basement

Siding and shingles give this home a Craftsman look while columns and gables suggest a more traditional style. The foyer opens to a short flight of stairs that leads to the great room, which features a lovely coffered ceiling, a fireplace, built-ins, and French doors to the rear veranda. To the left, the open island kitchen has a pass-through to the great room and easy service to the dining bay.

The secluded master suite features two walk-in closets, a luxurious bath, and veranda access. Upstairs, two family bedrooms have their own full baths and share a loft area.

First Floor

Second Floor

Move-Up Homes

Plan: HPK3200254

Square Footage: 2,990	Width: 80' - 0"
Bedrooms: 4	Depth: 68' - 0"
Bathrooms: 3 ½	Foundation: Slab

A brick exterior, cast-stone trim, and corner quoins make up this attractive single-level design. The entry introduces a formal dining room to the right and a living room with a wall of windows to the left. The hearth-warmed family room opens to the kitchen/dinette, both with 10-foot ceilings. A large bay window enhances the dinette with a full glass door to the covered patio. A large master suite with vaulted ceilings features a bayed sitting area, a luxurious bath with double sinks, and an oversized walk-in closet.

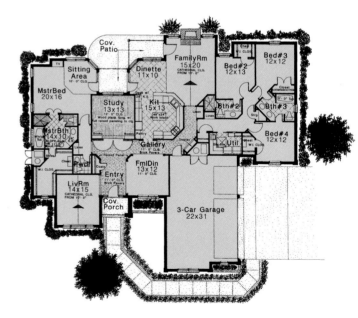

Move-Up Homes

Classical details and a stately brick exterior accentuate the grace and timeless elegance of this home. Inside, the foyer opens to a large banquet-sized dining room and an adjacent formal living room. Just beyond, the two-story great room awaits, featuring a wet bar and warming fireplace. A large covered porch off the kitchen completes the family center. Upstairs, the master suite features an unusual bay-window design, private sundeck, garden tub, His and Hers vanities and walk-in closets, and a compartmented toilet. Two bedrooms with a connecting bath complete the second floor.

First Floor

Second Floor

Plan: HPK3200255

First Floor: 1,581 sq. ft.
Second Floor: 1,415 sq. ft.
Total: 2,996 sq. ft.
Bedrooms: 4
Bathrooms: 3

Width: 55' - 0"
Depth: 52' - 0"
Foundation: Walkout Basement

blueprints. For more detailed information, please check the floor plans carefully.

Altogether Now

The facade of this 3,700-square-foot design comprises a mix of brick, stone, and cedar siding that accentuates the various forms of the home's exterior. Prominent front-facing gables rise above a wide porch with Craftsman-style supports.

The spacious foyer showcases the home's formal spaces and long sight lines. Framed views of the rear property through the great room's exquisite windows make a dramatic impression on visitors. The elegant dining room and library hit similar notes of refinement.

The two-story great room opens onto the hearth room/breakfast area, both rooms offering grand views to the rear yard. The combined space forms the home's entertaining area, suitable for all family occasions and smaller gatherings; larger affairs can expand onto the rear deck.

Nearby, the modern-minded kitchen takes a central role in everyday life. Large surfaces and plenty of storage attend the cook, as does the spacious butler's pantry. Despite its location in the middle of the plan, the kitchen also offers views through the breakfast room's windows.

Private quarters are designed for full comfort. The master suite, set off from the rest of the home by a brief hallway, dominates the left side of the plan. The deluxe bath includes all conveniences: separate vanities, garden tub, compartmented toilet, steam shower, and decorative ceilings. The accompanying walk-in closet is a must-have.

Upstairs, three individual bedrooms share two baths with ease. Reach-in closets provide room for each family member's wardrobe, and a shared computer loft acts as an office or media center.

ABOVE: Shuttered windows and a covered porch are quaint touches to this expansive home.

LEFT: Built-ins around the fireplace create space to display art and collectibles.

Family Homes

RIGHT: An open design joins the hearth room with the breakfast nook and kitchen.

BELOW: Tall, stacked windows draw eyes up toward the cathedral ceiling in the great room.

Arched pass-throughs provide elegant
entries to the formal dining room.

**LEFT: The master bath is
large enough to include a
corner shower, window-
side tub, dual vanity sinks,
linen cupboard, and an
immense walk-in closet.**

A wall of expertly-crafted built-in shelves is the focus of this library, a room that could also be used as a den or home office.

First Floor

Second Floor

Plan: HPK3200256

First Floor: 2,665 sq. ft.
Second Floor: 1,081 sq. ft.
Total: 3,746 sq. ft.
Bedrooms: 4
Bathrooms: 3 ½

Width: 88' - 0"
Depth: 52' - 6"
Foundation: Unfinished Walkout Basement

© William E. Poole Designs, Inc.

This unique design presents an open yet cozy floor plan. A built-in entertainment center and a cathedral ceiling create a spacious great room that leads to the breakfast area and island kitchen. The terrace is accessible from the breakfast area. Privacy is afforded to the master bedroom, placed to the far right of the design; it's complemented by a master bath built for two and a walk-in closet with a window seat. At the top of the stairs, a balcony and a hall lead to a future recreation room. Three bedrooms, each with a full bath, are also available on the second floor.

Plan: HPK3200257

First Floor: 1,904 sq. ft.	Bathrooms: 4 ½
Second Floor: 1,098 sq. ft.	Width: 88' - 2"
Total: 3,002 sq. ft.	Depth: 54' - 0"
Bonus Space: 522 sq. ft.	Foundation: Crawlspace,
Bedrooms: 4	Unfinished Basement

Second Floor

First Floor

Family Homes

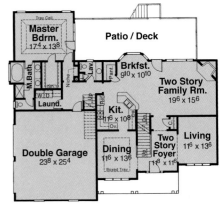

First Floor

Second Floor

Plan: HPK3200258

First Floor: 1,771 sq. ft.
Second Floor: 1,235 sq. ft.
Total: 3,006 sq. ft.
Bedrooms: 4
Bathrooms: 3 ½

Width: 61' - 4"
Depth: 54' - 0"
Foundation: Crawlspace,
Slab, Unfinished Walkout
Basement

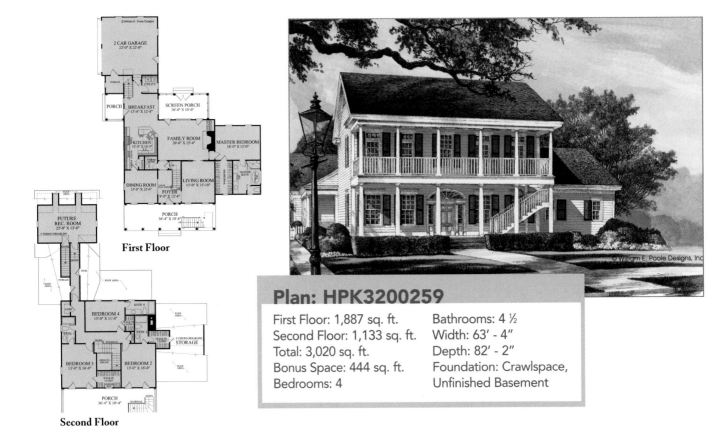

First Floor

Second Floor

Plan: HPK3200259

First Floor: 1,887 sq. ft.
Second Floor: 1,133 sq. ft.
Total: 3,020 sq. ft.
Bonus Space: 444 sq. ft.
Bedrooms: 4

Bathrooms: 4 ½
Width: 63' - 4"
Depth: 82' - 2"
Foundation: Crawlspace,
Unfinished Basement

First Floor

Second Floor

Plan: HPK3200260

First Floor: 2,081 sq. ft.
Second Floor: 940 sq. ft.
Total: 3,021 sq. ft.
Bedrooms: 4
Bathrooms: 3 ½

Width: 69' - 9"
Depth: 65' - 0"
Foundation: Walkout
Basement

First Floor

Second Floor

Plan: HPK3200261

First Floor: 2,014 sq. ft.
Second Floor: 1,026 sq. ft.
Total: 3,040 sq. ft.
Bedrooms: 4

Bathrooms: 3 ½
Width: 67' - 0"
Depth: 84' - 8"
Foundation: Crawlspace

Family Homes

First Floor

Second Floor

Plan: HPK3200262

First Floor: 2,121 sq. ft.
Second Floor: 920 sq. ft.
Total: 3,041 sq. ft.
Bedrooms: 4
Bathrooms: 3

Width: 63' - 0"
Depth: 63' - 0"
Foundation: Crawlspace, Slab

First Floor

Second Floor

Plan: HPK3200263

First Floor: 1,370 sq. ft.
Second Floor: 1,673 sq. ft.
Total: 3,043 sq. ft.
Bedrooms: 4
Bathrooms: 3 ½

Width: 73' - 6"
Depth: 49' - 0"
Foundation: Walkout Basement

First Floor

Second Floor

Plan: HPK3200264

First Floor: 1,415 sq. ft.
Second Floor: 1,632 sq. ft.
Total: 3,047 sq. ft.
Bedrooms: 4
Bathrooms: 3 ½

Width: 56' - 0"
Depth: 47' - 6"
Foundation: Crawlspace,
Unfinished Walkout
Basement

First Floor

Second Floor

Plan: HPK3200265

First Floor: 2,398 sq. ft.
Second Floor: 657 sq. ft.
Total: 3,055 sq. ft.
Bonus Space: 374 sq. ft.
Bedrooms: 4

Bathrooms: 3 ½
Width: 72' - 8"
Depth: 69' - 1"
Foundation: Crawlspace,
Unfinished Basement

Family Homes

First Floor

Second Floor

Plan: HPK3200266

First Floor: 2,167 sq. ft.	Bathrooms: 3
Second Floor: 891 sq. ft.	Width: 64' - 10"
Total: 3,058 sq. ft.	Depth: 74' - 0"
Bonus Space: 252 sq. ft.	Foundation: Crawlspace
Bedrooms: 4	

First Floor

Plan: HPK3200267

First Floor: 2,115 sq. ft.	Bathrooms: 3 ½
Second Floor: 947 sq. ft.	Width: 68' - 10"
Total: 3,062 sq. ft.	Depth: 58' - 1"
Bonus Space: 216 sq. ft.	Foundation: Crawlspace,
Bedrooms: 4	Slab, Unfinished Basement

Second Floor

Family Homes

Plan: HPK3200268

Square Footage: 3,063
Bedrooms: 3
Bathrooms: 3 ½
Width: 68' - 0"

Depth: 80' - 0"
Foundation: Walkout Basement

First Floor

Second Floor

Plan: HPK3200269

First Floor: 2,440 sq. ft.
Second Floor: 626 sq. ft.
Total: 3,066 sq. ft.
Bonus Space: 302 sq. ft.
Bedrooms: 3

Bathrooms: 2 ½
Width: 83' - 0"
Depth: 77' - 0"
Foundation: Crawlspace

Family Homes

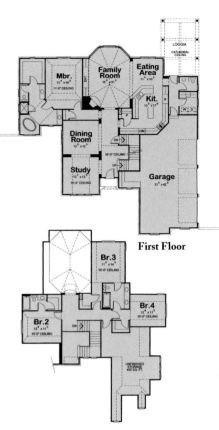

First Floor

Second Floor

Plan: HPK3200270

First Floor: 2,155 sq. ft.
Second Floor: 912 sq. ft.
Total: 3,067 sq. ft.
Bonus Space: 455 sq. ft.

Bedrooms: 4
Bathrooms: 3 ½
Width: 65' - 4"
Depth: 76' - 8"

First Floor

Second Floor

Plan: HPK3200271

First Floor: 1,262 sq. ft.
Second Floor: 1,816 sq. ft.
Total: 3,078 sq. ft.
Bedrooms: 4
Bathrooms: 2 ½

Width: 62' - 0"
Depth: 48' - 4"
Foundation: Unfinished Basement

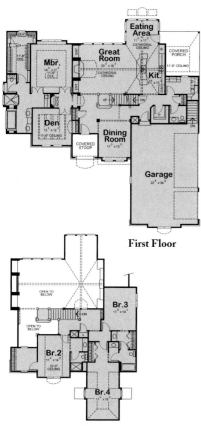

First Floor

Second Floor

Plan: HPK3200272

First Floor: 2,059 sq. ft.
Second Floor: 1,021 sq. ft.
Total: 3,080 sq. ft.
Bedrooms: 4

Bathrooms: 3 ½
Width: 67' - 0"
Depth: 69' - 0"

© 2005 Donald A. Gardner, Inc.

Plan: HPK3200273

Square Footage: 3,080
Bonus Space: 498 sq. ft.
Bedrooms: 4

Bathrooms: 4 ½
Width: 75' - 7"
Depth: 72' - 3"

Family Homes

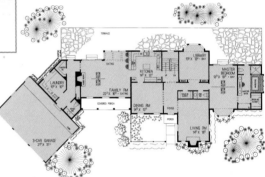

Plan: HPK3200274

First Floor: 2,465 sq. ft.
Second Floor: 617 sq. ft.
Total: 3,082 sq. ft.
Bedrooms: 3
Bathrooms: 2 ½ + ½

Baths
Width: 120' - 10"
Depth: 52' - 4"
Foundation: Unfinished Basement

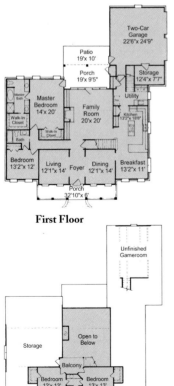

First Floor

Second Floor

Plan: HPK3200275

First Floor: 2,439 sq. ft.
Second Floor: 646 sq. ft.
Total: 3,085 sq. ft.
Bonus Space: 626 sq. ft.
Bedrooms: 4

Bathrooms: 3
Width: 66' - 10"
Depth: 79' - 2"
Foundation: Crawlspace, Slab

First Floor

Second Floor

Plan: HPK3200276

First Floor: 2,200 sq. ft.
Second Floor: 889 sq. ft.
Total: 3,089 sq. ft.
Bedrooms: 4
Bathrooms: 3

Width: 60' - 6"
Depth: 68' - 0"
Foundation: Crawlspace, Slab

First Floor

Second Floor

Plan: HPK3200277

First Floor: 1,495 sq. ft.
Second Floor: 1,600 sq. ft.
Total: 3,095 sq. ft.
Bedrooms: 4
Bathrooms: 3 ½

Width: 49' - 0"
Depth: 57' - 0"
Foundation: Walkout Basement

Family Homes

First Floor

Second Floor

Plan: HPK3200278

First Floor: 1,846 sq. ft.
Second Floor: 1,249 sq. ft.
Total: 3,095 sq. ft.
Bonus Space: 394 sq. ft.
Bedrooms: 4

Bathrooms: 3 ½
Width: 52' - 2"
Depth: 66' - 2"
Foundation: Crawlspace

First Floor

Second Floor

Plan: HPK3200279

First Floor: 1,936 sq. ft.
Second Floor: 1,159 sq. ft.
Total: 3,095 sq. ft.
Bedrooms: 4

Bathrooms: 3 ½
Width: 73' - 10"
Depth: 61' - 1"
Foundation: Crawlspace

Family Homes

First Floor

Second Floor

© Stephen Fuller, Inc.

Plan: HPK3200280

First Floor: 1,455 sq. ft.
Second Floor: 1,649 sq. ft.
Total: 3,104 sq. ft.
Bedrooms: 4
Bathrooms: 3 ½

Width: 54' - 4"
Depth: 46' - 0"
Foundation: Walkout Basement

First Floor

© Larry E. Belk Designs

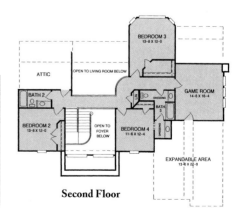

Second Floor

Plan: HPK3200281

First Floor: 1,919 sq. ft.
Second Floor: 1,190 sq. ft.
Total: 3,109 sq. ft.
Bonus Space: 286 sq. ft.
Bedrooms: 4

Bathrooms: 3 ½
Width: 64' - 6"
Depth: 55' - 10"
Foundation: Crawlspace, Slab, Unfinished Basement

Family Homes

© 2003 Donald A. Gardner, Inc.

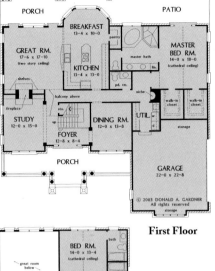

First Floor

Second Floor

Plan: HPK3200282

First Floor: 2,160 sq. ft.
Second Floor: 951 sq. ft.
Total: 3,111 sq. ft.
Bonus Space: 491 sq. ft.
Bedrooms: 4

Bathrooms: 3 ½
Width: 61' - 11"
Depth: 63' - 11"

First Floor

Second Floor

Plan: HPK3200283

First Floor: 1,652 sq. ft.
Second Floor: 1,460 sq. ft.
Total: 3,112 sq. ft.
Bonus Space: 256 sq. ft.
Bedrooms: 4

Bathrooms: 3 ½
Width: 48' - 0"
Depth: 78' - 4"
Foundation: Walkout
Basement

Order blueprints anytime at
eplans.com or 1-800-521-6797

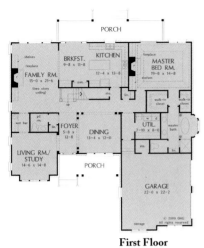

First Floor

Second Floor

© 2000 Donald A. Gardner, Inc.

Plan: HPK3200284

First Floor: 2,188 sq. ft.	Bedrooms: 4
Second Floor: 932 sq. ft.	Bathrooms: 2 ½
Total: 3,120 sq. ft.	Width: 60' - 8"
Bonus Space: 488 sq. ft.	Depth: 66' - 4"

First Floor

© William E. Poole Designs, Inc.

Plan: HPK3200285

First Floor: 2,357 sq. ft.	Bathrooms: 3
Second Floor: 772 sq. ft.	Width: 69' - 4"
Total: 3,129 sq. ft.	Depth: 67' - 4"
Bonus Space: 450 sq. ft.	Foundation: Crawlspace
Bedrooms: 4	

Second Floor

Family Homes

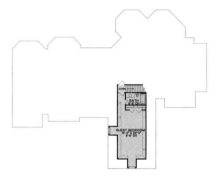

Plan: HPK3200286

Square Footage: 3,132
Bonus Space: 455 sq. ft.
Bedrooms: 3

Bathrooms: 2 ½
Width: 93' - 11"
Depth: 72' - 3"

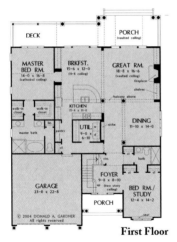

First Floor

Second Floor

© 2004 Donald A. Gardner, Inc.

Plan: HPK3200287

First Floor: 2,172 sq. ft.
Second Floor: 962 sq. ft.
Total: 3,134 sq. ft.
Bedrooms: 4

Bathrooms: 3
Width: 50' - 0"
Depth: 67' - 6"

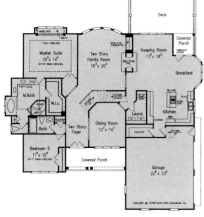

First Floor

Second Floor

Plan: HPK3200288

First Floor: 2,233 sq. ft.
Second Floor: 902 sq. ft.
Total: 3,135 sq. ft.
Bonus Space: 319 sq. ft.
Bedrooms: 5
Bathrooms: 4

Width: 66' - 0"
Depth: 59' - 0"
Foundation: Crawlspace,
Unfinished Walkout
Basement

First Floor

Second Floor

Plan: HPK3200289

First Floor: 2,092 sq. ft.
Second Floor: 1,045 sq. ft.
Total: 3,137 sq. ft.
Bonus Space: 546 sq. ft.
Bedrooms: 4

Bathrooms: 3 ½
Width: 77' - 0"
Depth: 56' - 4"
Foundation: Crawlspace

Family Homes

Patio / Deck

First Floor

Second Floor

Plan: HPK3200290

First Floor: 1,553 sq. ft.
Second Floor: 1,587 sq. ft.
Total: 3,140 sq. ft.
Bedrooms: 5
Bathrooms: 4

Width: 58' - 0"
Depth: 40' - 4"
Foundation: Unfinished
Walkout Basement

First Floor

Second Floor

Plan: HPK3200291

First Floor: 2,302 sq. ft.
Second Floor: 845 sq. ft.
Total: 3,147 sq. ft.
Bonus Space: 247 sq. ft.
Bedrooms: 4
Bathrooms: 3 ½

Width: 64' - 0"
Depth: 59' - 4"
Foundation: Crawlspace,
Slab, Unfinished Walkout
Basement

Family Homes

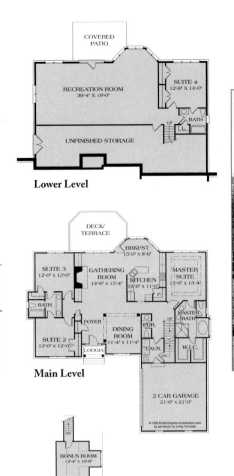

Lower Level

Main Level

Plan: HPK3200292

Main Level: 1,947 sq. ft.
Lower Level: 1,200 sq. ft.
Total: 3,147 sq. ft.
Bonus Space: 255 sq. ft.
Bedrooms: 4

Bathrooms: 3 ½
Width: 59' - 4"
Depth: 62' - 2"
Foundation: Finished Basement

Plan: HPK3200293

First Floor: 2,033 sq. ft.
Second Floor: 1,116 sq. ft.
Total: 3,149 sq. ft.
Bedrooms: 4
Bathrooms: 3 ½

Width: 71' - 0"
Depth: 56' - 0"
Foundation: Crawlspace, Slab

First Floor

Second Floor

Family Homes

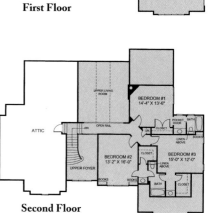

First Floor

Second Floor

Plan: HPK3200294

First Floor: 2,161 sq. ft.
Second Floor: 991 sq. ft.
Total: 3,152 sq. ft.
Bedrooms: 4
Bathrooms: 3 ½

Width: 67' - 6"
Depth: 53' - 6"
Foundation: Unfinished Basement

First Floor

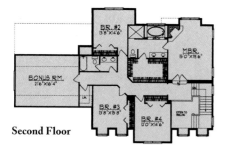

Second Floor

Plan: HPK3200295

First Floor: 1,700 sq. ft.
Second Floor: 1,454 sq. ft.
Total: 3,154 sq. ft.
Bonus Space: 351 sq. ft.
Bedrooms: 4

Bathrooms: 2 ½
Width: 67' - 0"
Depth: 53' - 0"
Foundation: Unfinished Basement

First Floor

Second Floor

Plan: HPK3200296

First Floor: 2,294 sq. ft.
Second Floor: 869 sq. ft.
Total: 3,163 sq. ft.
Bonus Space: 309 sq. ft.
Bedrooms: 4
Bathrooms: 3 ½

Width: 63' - 6"
Depth: 63' - 0"
Foundation: Crawlspace, Unfinished Walkout Basement

Donald A. Gardner Architects, Inc. This home, as shown in the photography, may differ from the actual blueprints. For more detailed information, please check the floor plans carefully.

First Floor

Second Floor

Plan: HPK3200297

First Floor: 2,086 sq. ft.
Second Floor: 1,077 sq. ft.
Total: 3,163 sq. ft.
Bonus Space: 403 sq. ft.

Bedrooms: 4
Bathrooms: 3 ½
Width: 81' - 10"
Depth: 51' - 8"

Family Homes

First Floor

Second Floor

Plan: HPK3200298

First Floor: 2,194 sq. ft.　　Bedrooms: 5
Second Floor: 971 sq. ft.　　Bathrooms: 3 ½
Total: 3,165 sq. ft.　　　　　Width: 82' - 7"
Bonus Space: 462 sq. ft.　　Depth: 51' - 1"

First Floor

Second Floor

Plan: HPK3200299

First Floor: 2,194 sq. ft.　　Bedrooms: 4
Second Floor: 973 sq. ft.　　Bathrooms: 3 ½
Total: 3,167 sq. ft.　　　　　Width: 71' - 11"
Bonus Space: 281 sq. ft.　　Depth: 54' - 4"

First Floor

Second Floor

Plan: HPK3200300

First Floor: 2,155 sq. ft.
Second Floor: 1,020 sq. ft.
Total: 3,175 sq. ft.
Bedrooms: 4
Bathrooms: 3 ½

Width: 62' - 0"
Depth: 63' - 0"
Foundation: Walkout Basement

Plan: HPK3200301

First Floor: 2,061 sq. ft.
Second Floor: 1,135 sq. ft.
Total: 3,196 sq. ft.
Bonus Space: 332 sq. ft.
Bedrooms: 4

Bathrooms: 3 ½
Width: 55' - 0"
Depth: 61' - 8"
Foundation: Crawlspace

First Floor

Second Floor

Family Homes

First Floor

Second Floor

Plan: HPK3200302

First Floor: 2,193 sq. ft.
Second Floor: 1,004 sq. ft.
Total: 3,197 sq. ft.
Bedrooms: 4

Bathrooms: 4 ½
Width: 67' - 0"
Depth: 74' - 4"
Foundation: Crawlspace

First Floor

© Stephen Fuller, Inc.

Second Floor

© Stephen Fuller, Inc.

Plan: HPK3200303

First Floor: 1,570 sq. ft.
Second Floor: 1,630 sq. ft.
Total: 3,200 sq. ft.
Bedrooms: 4
Bathrooms: 3 ½

Width: 59' - 10"
Depth: 43' - 4"
Foundation: Walkout Basement

First Floor

Second Floor

Plan: HPK3200304

First Floor: 2,200 sq. ft.
Second Floor: 1,001 sq. ft.
Total: 3,201 sq. ft.
Bonus Space: 674 sq. ft.
Bedrooms: 4

Bathrooms: 3 ½
Width: 70' - 4"
Depth: 74' - 4"
Foundation: Crawlspace

First Floor

Second Floor

Plan: HPK3200305

First Floor: 1,554 sq. ft.
Second Floor: 1,648 sq. ft.
Total: 3,202 sq. ft.
Bedrooms: 4
Bathrooms: 3 ½

Width: 60' - 0"
Depth: 43' - 0"
Foundation: Walkout Basement

Family Homes

First Floor

Second Floor

Plan: HPK3200306

First Floor: 1,548 sq. ft.
Second Floor: 1,666 sq. ft.
Total: 3,214 sq. ft.
Bedrooms: 5
Bathrooms: 4

Width: 55' - 4"
Depth: 54' - 0"
Foundation: Crawlspace,
Unfinished Walkout
Basement

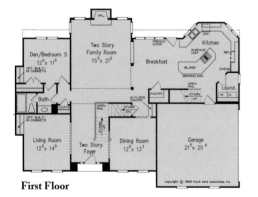

First Floor

Second Floor

Plan: HPK3200307

First Floor: 1,665 sq. ft.
Second Floor: 1,554 sq. ft.
Total: 3,219 sq. ft.
Bedrooms: 5
Bathrooms: 4

Width: 58' - 6"
Depth: 44' - 10"
Foundation: Crawlspace,
Unfinished Walkout
Basement

First Floor

Second Floor

Plan: HPK3200308

First Floor: 1,570 sq. ft.
Second Floor: 1,650 sq. ft.
Total: 3,220 sq. ft.
Bedrooms: 5
Bathrooms: 4

Width: 55' - 6"
Depth: 60' - 0"
Foundation: Crawlspace, Unfinished Walkout Basement

First Floor

Plan: HPK3200309

First Floor: 2,284 sq. ft.
Second Floor: 940 sq. ft.
Total: 3,224 sq. ft.
Bonus Space: 545 sq. ft.
Bedrooms: 4
Bathrooms: 3 ½

Width: 55' - 0"
Depth: 85' - 0"
Foundation: Crawlspace, Unfinished Walkout Basement

Second Floor

Family Homes

First Floor

Second Floor

Plan: HPK3200310

First Floor: 2,198 sq. ft.
Second Floor: 1,028 sq. ft.
Total: 3,226 sq. ft.
Bonus Space: 466 sq. ft.
Bedrooms: 4

Bathrooms: 3 ½
Width: 72' - 8"
Depth: 56' - 6"
Foundation: Crawlspace

First Floor

Second Floor

Plan: HPK3200311

First Floor: 2,101 sq. ft.
Second Floor: 1,127 sq. ft.
Total: 3,228 sq. ft.
Bedrooms: 5
Bathrooms: 3 ½

Width: 58' - 4"
Depth: 58' - 0"
Foundation: Finished Basement

Family Homes

First Floor

Second Floor

© William E. Poole Designs, Inc.

Plan: HPK3200312

First Floor: 2,307 sq. ft.
Second Floor: 926 sq. ft.
Total: 3,233 sq. ft.
Bonus Space: 334 sq. ft.
Bedrooms: 4

Bathrooms: 3 ½
Width: 69' - 4"
Depth: 65' - 0"
Foundation: Crawlspace,
Unfinished Basement

photography, may differ from the actual blueprints. For more detailed information, please check the floor plans carefully.

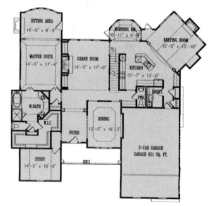

First Floor

Second Floor

Plan: HPK3200313

First Floor: 2,450 sq. ft.
Second Floor: 787 sq. ft.
Total: 3,237 sq. ft.
Bedrooms: 4
Bathrooms: 3 ½

Width: 68' - 11"
Depth: 65' - 7"
Foundation: Crawlspace,
Unfinished Basement

Family Homes

First Floor

Second Floor

Plan: HPK3200314

First Floor: 2,274 sq. ft.
Second Floor: 972 sq. ft.
Total: 3,246 sq. ft.
Bedrooms: 4
Bathrooms: 3 ½

Width: 66' - 0"
Depth: 89' - 10"
Foundation: Unfinished Basement

First Floor

Second Floor

Plan: HPK3200315

First Floor: 2,351 sq. ft.
Second Floor: 899 sq. ft.
Total: 3,250 sq. ft.
Bonus Space: 676 sq. ft.

Bedrooms: 4
Bathrooms: 3 ½ + ½
Width: 66' - 8"
Depth: 76' - 0"

Family Homes

First Floor

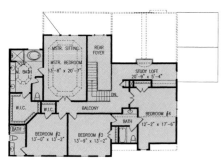

Second Floor

Plan: HPK3200316

First Floor: 1,649 sq. ft.
Second Floor: 1,604 sq. ft.
Total: 3,253 sq. ft.
Bedrooms: 4
Bathrooms: 3 ½

Width: 69' - 6"
Depth: 45' - 8"
Foundation: Slab,
Unfinished Walkout
Basement

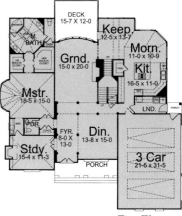

First Floor

Plan: HPK3200317

First Floor: 2,253 sq. ft.
Second Floor: 1,002 sq. ft.
Total: 3,255 sq. ft.
Bedrooms: 4
Bathrooms: 3 ½

Width: 61' - 6"
Depth: 64' - 0"
Foundation: Finished
Basement

Second Floor

Family Homes

First Floor

Second Floor

Plan: HPK3200318

First Floor: 1,418 sq. ft.
Second Floor: 1,844 sq. ft.
Total: 3,262 sq. ft.
Bedrooms: 4
Bathrooms: 3 ½

Width: 63' - 0"
Depth: 41' - 0"
Foundation: Crawlspace, Slab, Unfinished Walkout Basement

First Floor

Second Floor

Plan: HPK3200319

First Floor: 2,335 sq. ft.
Second Floor: 936 sq. ft.
Total: 3,271 sq. ft.
Bonus Space: 958 sq. ft.
Bedrooms: 3

Bathrooms: 3 ½
Width: 91' - 4"
Depth: 54' - 6"
Foundation: Unfinished Walkout Basement

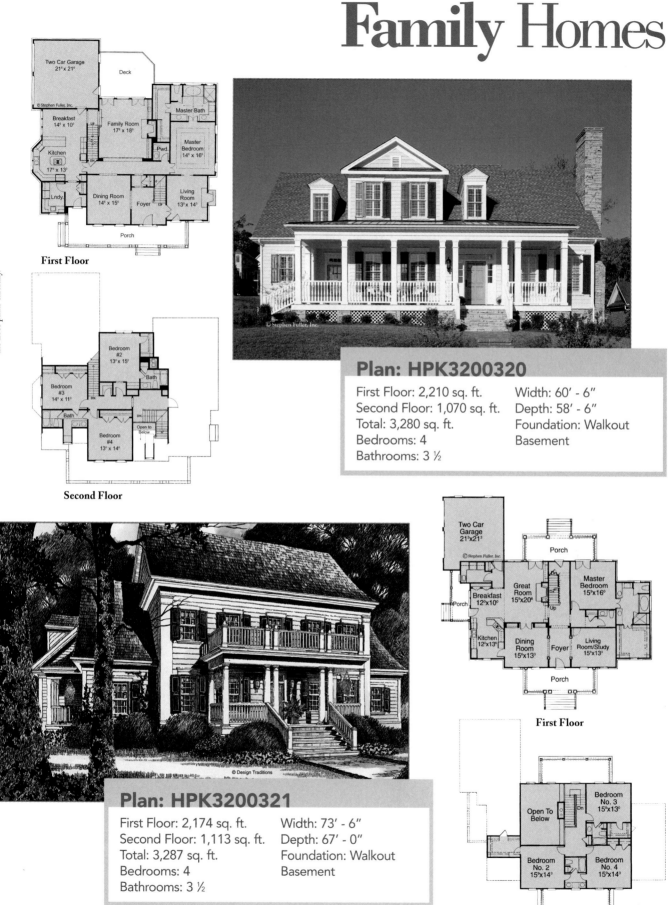

differ from the actual blueprints. For more detailed information, please check the floor plans carefully.

First Floor

Two Car Garage 21⁶ x 21⁶

© Stephen Fuller, Inc.

Deck

Breakfast 14⁶ x 10⁰

Family Room 17⁶ x 18⁵

Master Bath

Master Bedroom 14⁰ x 16⁰

Kitchen 17⁰ x 13⁵

Pwd.

Lndry.

Dining Room 14⁶ x 15⁰

Foyer

Living Room 13⁰ x 14³

Porch

Second Floor

Bedroom #2 13⁰ x 15⁰

Bath

Bedroom #3 14⁰ x 11⁰

Bath

Bedroom #4 13⁰ x 14⁰

Open to Below

© Stephen Fuller, Inc.

Plan: HPK3200320

First Floor: 2,210 sq. ft.
Second Floor: 1,070 sq. ft.
Total: 3,280 sq. ft.
Bedrooms: 4
Bathrooms: 3 ½

Width: 60' - 6"
Depth: 58' - 6"
Foundation: Walkout Basement

© Design Traditions

Plan: HPK3200321

First Floor: 2,174 sq. ft.
Second Floor: 1,113 sq. ft.
Total: 3,287 sq. ft.
Bedrooms: 4
Bathrooms: 3 ½

Width: 73' - 6"
Depth: 67' - 0"
Foundation: Walkout Basement

First Floor

Two Car Garage 21³ x 21³

© Stephen Fuller, Inc.

Porch

Breakfast 12⁶ x 10⁰

Great Room 15⁰ x 20⁶

Master Bedroom 15⁰ x 16⁰

Porch

Kitchen 12⁶ x 13⁰

Dining Room 15⁰ x 13³

Foyer

Living Room/Study 15⁰ x 13³

Up

Porch

Second Floor

Open To Below

Dn

Bedroom No. 3 15⁰ x 13⁰

Bedroom No. 2 15⁰ x 14³

Bedroom No. 4 15⁰ x 14³

Family Homes

First Floor

Second Floor

Plan: HPK3200322

First Floor: 1,847 sq. ft.
Second Floor: 1,453 sq. ft.
Total: 3,300 sq. ft.
Bedrooms: 4
Bathrooms: 3

Width: 63' - 3"
Depth: 47' - 0"
Foundation: Walkout Basement

First Floor

Second Floor

Plan: HPK3200323

First Floor: 2,187 sq. ft.
Second Floor: 1,118 sq. ft.
Total: 3,305 sq. ft.
Bonus Space: 328 sq. ft.
Bedrooms: 4

Bathrooms: 3 ½
Width: 81' - 2"
Depth: 41' - 2"
Foundation: Crawlspace

Plan: HPK3200324

First Floor: 2,292 sq. ft.	Width: 68' - 0"
Second Floor: 1,028 sq. ft.	Depth: 56' - 6"
Total: 3,320 sq. ft.	Foundation: Unfinished
Bedrooms: 5	Basement
Bathrooms: 3 ½ + ½	

This majestic brick home fits new traditional neighborhoods perfectly, with an inviting front porch and a side-loading garage. Formal and flex rooms accommodate modern lifestyles and allow space for surfing online or even a home office. The foyer opens to the dining room and a study—or make it a guest bedroom. The gourmet kitchen boasts an island counter and opens to an old-fashioned keeping room that features a fireplace. The breakfast room offers a bay window to let the sunlight in and opens to an expansive deck. The master suite sports a tray ceiling and a bath that provides more than just a touch of luxury. Upstairs, two family bedrooms share a full bath; a guest bedroom features a private bath.

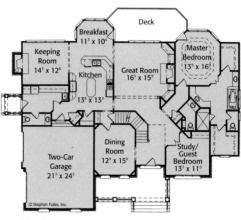

First Floor

Second Floor

Family Homes

Plan: HPK3200325

First Floor: 2,117 sq. ft.
Second Floor: 1,206 sq. ft.
Total: 3,323 sq. ft.
Bedrooms: 4

Bathrooms: 3 ½
Width: 83' - 11"
Depth: 56' - 11"

This elegant luxury home begins with a two-story turret and a formal entry lit by a gothic-style window. The family room and breakfast nook accommodate bright bays, which flood the island-cooktop kitchen with natural light. Ample counter space here makes it simple to serve the gracious dining room. The master suite aims to please with a rear ribbon of windows and a spectacular spa bath. The upper level houses three ample bedrooms, a game room, and a sun deck. Extra storage space in the three-car garage is a thoughtful touch.

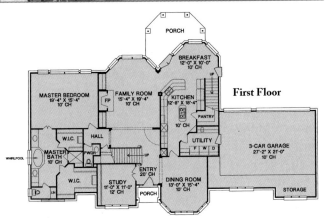

First Floor

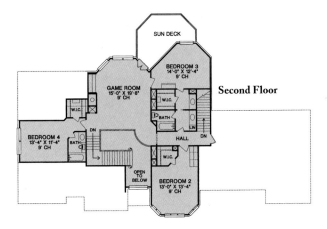

Second Floor

Optional Layout

© 1993 William E Poole Designs, Inc.

Sturdy columns on a spacious, welcoming front porch lend a Greek Revival feel to this design, and three dormer windows provide a relaxed country look. The living and dining rooms, each with a fireplace, flank the two-story foyer; the family room also includes a fireplace, as well as built-in shelves and a wall of windows. The L-shaped kitchen, conveniently near the breakfast area, features a work island and a large pantry. Two walk-in closets highlight the lavish master suite, which offers a private bath with a soothing whirlpool tub. Three family bedrooms—all with dormer alcoves and two with walk-in closets—sit upstairs, along with a future recreation room.

Plan: HPK3200326

First Floor: 2,320 sq. ft.	Bathrooms: 3 ½
Second Floor: 1,009 sq. ft.	Width: 80' - 4"
Total: 3,329 sq. ft.	Depth: 58' - 0"
Bonus Space: 521 sq. ft.	Foundation: Crawlspace
Bedrooms: 4	

First Floor

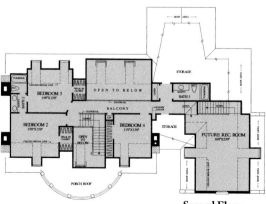

Second Floor

Family Homes

Plan: HPK3200327

First Floor: 2,298 sq. ft.	Bathrooms: 3 ½
Second Floor: 1,039 sq. ft.	Width: 65' - 0"
Total: 3,337 sq. ft.	Depth: 56' - 10"
Bedrooms: 4	Foundation: Crawlspace

Charming on the outside and amenity-filled on the inside, this country cottage is sure to please. Front and rear covered porches offer outdoor living space. Inside, the dining room is defined by decorative columns and enhanced by a tray ceiling. The island kitchen flows easily with the keeping room and breakfast area while boasting ample counter space, a butler's pantry, and a convenient serving bar. A fireplace in the family room warms the space. The rear porch is accessed through French doors off the breakfast area. The adjoining family room, adorned with a coffered ceiling, features a second fireplace and built-in cabinets. A short hallway leads to the expansive master suite, enhanced by a tray ceiling, a sitting area, a huge walk-in closet, dual-sink vanities, a separate shower and tub, and a private toilet. The second floor houses three additional bedrooms sharing two full baths.

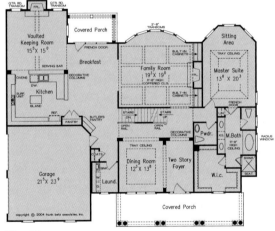

First Floor

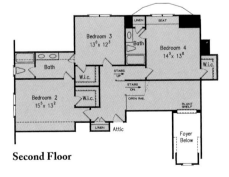

Second Floor

© William E. Poole Designs, Inc.

This handsome brick Colonial would be majestic in any neighborhood—today as well as yesterday and tomorrow. The pedimented entry leads to an open foyer flanked by rooms for formal entertaining. But guests and family members may likely gravitate toward the family room, drawn by the fireplace and its surrounding entertainment center or by the views provided through the massive Palladian window topped with a spectacular fanlight. This room shares its assets with the open island kitchen and adjoining breakfast bay. The master suite is secluded in a corner of the first floor. The second level provides three family bedrooms and two full baths, with an optional fifth bedroom and rec room, which is reached by a separate stair near the garage.

Plan: HPK3200328

First Floor: 2,209 sq. ft.	Bathrooms: 3 ½
Second Floor: 1,136 sq. ft.	Width: 60' - 2"
Total: 3,345 sq. ft.	Depth: 78' - 2"
Bonus Space: 462 sq. ft.	Foundation: Crawlspace,
Bedrooms: 5	Unfinished Basement

Second Floor

First Floor

© The Sater Design Collection, Inc.

Plan: HPK3200329

Square Footage: 3,351	Width: 84' - 0"
Bedrooms: 3	Depth: 92' - 0"
Bathrooms: 2 ½ + ½	Foundation: Slab

Magnificent brick and a Colonial-inspired facade make this home from one of our top designers a new favorite. Inside, the foyer opens to the living room/dining room combination, which allows flexibility in interior arrangement. The country kitchen serves the dining areas with ease and provides plenty of workspace for gourmet meal preparation. The leisure room entertains with a built-in media center and access to the rear veranda. Two family bedrooms share a full bath and extra hall storage. On the far left, the master suite is a dream, with a bayed window, oversized walk-in closets, and a grand spa bath with a whirlpool tub.

© William E. Poole Designs, Inc.

Plan: HPK3200330

First Floor: 2,357 sq. ft.	Bathrooms: 3 ½
Second Floor: 995 sq. ft.	Width: 79' - 0"
Total: 3,352 sq. ft.	Depth: 58' - 2"
Bonus Space: 472 sq. ft.	Foundation: Crawlspace
Bedrooms: 4	

Parasols, high-necked lace collars, white gloves, and gold-tipped canes adorned lovely ladies from the past as they sipped their tea and visited the country gardens. This design, like many antebellum homes that capture the romance of the Old South, graciously reflects the Greek Revival style of architecture. Three bedrooms in addition to the master suite welcome housefuls of guests, and a collection of gathering rooms with warming hearths assure a pleasant stay. With amenities that please visitors and homeowners alike, this design is southern at its best.

Second Floor

First Floor

Family Homes

Plan: HPK3200331

First Floor: 2,258 sq. ft.
Second Floor: 1,100 sq. ft.
Total: 3,358 sq. ft.
Bedrooms: 5
Bathrooms: 3 ½

Width: 78' - 0"
Depth: 52' - 0"
Foundation: Unfinished Basement

Impressive columns rising two stories high end in a simple pediment and offer a grand entrance to this plan. The first floor features a classic center-hall lay-out, with a hearth-warmed great room, a formal din-ing room, and a study. The master suite is also on this level and contains two walk-in closets and a bath with corner whirlpool and separate shower. Upstairs are four additional bedrooms—two with walk-in closets. These family bedrooms share two compartmented baths.

First Floor

Second Floor

© 1999 Donald A. Gardner, Inc.

Plan: HPK3200332

First Floor: 2,672 sq. ft.	Bedrooms: 4
Second Floor: 687 sq. ft.	Bathrooms: 3
Total: 3,359 sq. ft.	Width: 72' - 6"
Bonus Space: 522 sq. ft.	Depth: 64' - 5"

A brick exterior mixed with cedar shakes creates an intriguing facade for this four-bedroom custom home with a dramatic hipped roof and dual chimneys. This home features formal living and dining rooms as well as a more casual family room and breakfast area. The dining room is defined by well-placed interior columns. A second-floor balcony overlooks the vaulted living room, while the family room is expanded by a 13-foot ceiling. Two staircases make access to the second floor convenient from anywhere in the home. A bedroom/study and the master suite are located on the first floor, while the second floor features two more bedrooms and a bonus room.

First Floor

Second Floor

Family Homes

© William E. Poole Designs, Inc.

Plan: HPK3200333

First Floor: 2,099 sq. ft.
Second Floor: 1,260 sq. ft.
Total: 3,359 sq. ft.
Bonus Space: 494 sq. ft.
Bedrooms: 4

Bathrooms: 3 ½
Width: 68' - 4"
Depth: 54' - 0"
Foundation: Crawlspace

This Colonial home gets a Victorian treatment with an expansive covered porch complete with a gazebo-like terminus. Inside, the impressive foyer is flanked by the living room and the formal dining room. The spacious island kitchen is ideally situated between the dining room and the sunny breakfast area. Completing the living area, the family room includes a fireplace, built-ins, and a generous view. The lavish master suite resides on the far right with a private bath and a huge walk-in closet. A second master suite is found on the upper level, along with two additional bedrooms that share a full bath.

First Floor

Second Floor

First Floor

Plan: HPK3200334

First Floor: 2,479 sq. ft.
Second Floor: 884 sq. ft.
Total: 3,363 sq. ft.
Bedrooms: 4
Bathrooms: 3 ½

Width: 63' - 0"
Depth: 62' - 0"
Foundation: Unfinished Basement

A Colonial beauty adorned with European-inspired appointments encases a household of contemporary style. Columns loosely define the formal dining room and grand room from the foyer. Toward the back of the home, an open layout of a kitchen, morning room, and keeping room invites casual gatherings and provides access to a rear veranda. The master suite and a semi-private study are on the left side of the plan. Here, His and Hers walk-in closets and a pleasing master bath grant homeowners with luxury and comfort. Upstairs, three bedrooms, each with its own bath access and walk-in closet, accommodate family and guests alike.

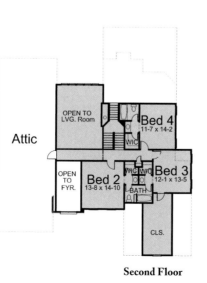

Second Floor

Family Homes

© William E. Poole Designs, Inc.

Plan: HPK3200335

First Floor: 2,168 sq. ft.
Second Floor: 1,203 sq. ft.
Total: 3,371 sq. ft.
Bonus Space: 452 sq. ft.
Bedrooms: 4

Bathrooms: 4 ½
Width: 71' - 2"
Depth: 63' - 4"
Foundation: Crawlspace,
Unfinished Basement

This stately two-story beauty offers the utmost in style and livability. The grand columned entryway is topped by a railed roof, making it the centerpiece of the facade. Formal space resides at the front of the plan, with a living room and dining room flanking the foyer. Secluded behind the staircase is the elegant master suite, with a huge walk-in closet and swanky private bath. The hearth-warmed family room flows into the island kitchen and breakfast nook, making this space the comfortable hub of home life. A laundry room and half-bath are convenient to this area. Upstairs, three bedrooms all have access to separate baths and share space with a future recreation room.

First Floor

Second Floor

Order blueprints anytime at
eplans.com or 1-800-521-6797

© William E. Poole Designs, Inc

First Floor

Second Floor

Plan: HPK3200336

First Floor: 2,193 sq. ft.
Second Floor: 1,179 sq. ft.
Total: 3,372 sq. ft.
Bonus Space: 558 sq. ft.
Bedrooms: 4

Bathrooms: 3 ½ + ½
Width: 66' - 5"
Depth: 75' - 5"
Foundation: Crawlspace

Three fireplaces warm and soothe in this comfortable Colonial cottage. Formal living space is placed at the front of the home, and casual living areas refresh the rest of the plan. A built-in desk and entertainment center enhance the family atmosphere. The master suite is an intimate hideaway with a fireplace, whirlpool tub, and separate shower big enough for two. Five dormer windows brighten the upper level, which includes three bedrooms and future space.

Family Homes

Plan: HPK3200337

First Floor: 1,625 sq. ft.	Width: 63' - 10"
Second Floor: 1,750 sq. ft.	Depth: 48' - 6"
Total: 3,375 sq. ft.	Foundation: Walkout
Bedrooms: 4	Basement
Bathrooms: 3 ½	

This American country home, with its clapboard siding, covered balcony, and shuttered windows, echoes images of traditional small-town living. The two-story great room includes a fireplace, bookcases, and a window wall. Adjacent to the great room are the spacious kitchen and bayed breakfast area. A back staircase is included for easy access to upstairs bedrooms. The second floor provides three bedrooms with various bath combinations. A balcony provides a breathtaking view of the great room and foyer below. The master suite features a tray ceiling and sitting area warmed by sunlight from an angled window combination. The enormous master bath area includes a tray ceiling and His and Hers vanities and closets.

First Floor

Second Floor

Order blueprints anytime at
eplans.com or 1-800-521-6797

Family Homes

© William E. Poole Designs, Inc.

This unique design uses a wall of windows at the rear of the home to showcase the deck area and attempt to expand the living space to the outdoors. Built-in bookcases in the family and living rooms are an added bonus. Three fireplaces on the first floor make a grand impression and provide extra warmth. The lavish master suite boasts large, side-by-side His and Hers wardrobes. Upstairs, Bedrooms 3 and 4 share a full-bath with a dual-sink vanity. A third family bedroom—a possible guest suite—has a private, full bath. A laundry chute is conveniently located on this level.

Plan: HPK3200338

First Floor: 2,320 sq. ft.	Bathrooms: 4 ½
Second Floor: 1,057 sq. ft.	Width: 81' - 4"
Total: 3,377 sq. ft.	Depth: 58' - 2"
Bonus Space: 608 sq. ft.	Foundation: Crawlspace
Bedrooms: 4	

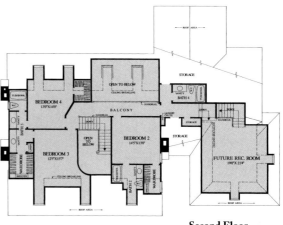

Second Floor

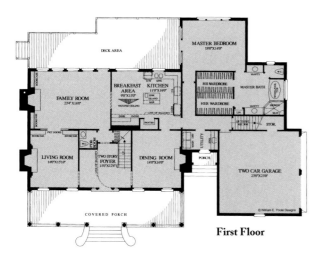

First Floor

Family Homes

Plan: HPK3200339

First Floor: 2,633 sq. ft.
Second Floor: 752 sq. ft.
Total: 3,385 sq. ft.
Bedrooms: 4
Bathrooms: 4

Width: 75' - 2"
Depth: 89' - 6"
Foundation: Crawlspace,
Slab, Unfinished
Basement

A delightful mix of styles combine to give this home plenty of curb appeal. From the foyer, a study, formal dining room, and spacious great room are accessible. The gourmet of the family will enjoy the kitchen, with its work surface/snack-bar island and tons of counter and cabinet space. Two bedrooms are located on the right side of the home, each offering a walk-in closet and a private bath. The deluxe master bedroom suite is lavish in its amenities, which include a large walk-in closet, a fireplace, and a sumptuous bath. Note the huge game room and extra bedroom over the garage—perfect for an in-law suite.

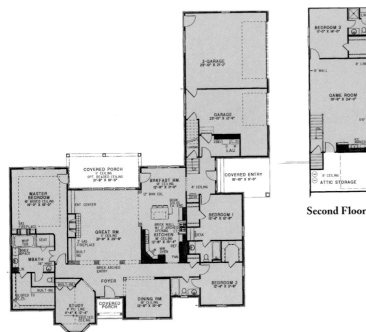

Second Floor

First Floor

Plan: HPK3200340

First Floor: 1,621 sq. ft.	Width: 52' - 0"
Second Floor: 1,766 sq. ft.	Depth: 50' - 6"
Total: 3,387 sq. ft.	Foundation: Walkout
Bedrooms: 4	Basement
Bathrooms: 3 ½	

All-American charm springs from the true Colonial style of this distinguished home. Double French doors partition the casual region of the home, which features the comfortable family room and its lovely fireplace. A guest room is located behind the kitchen area, making it a perfect maid's or nurse's room. The master suite has a private study, a fireplace, and an amenity-laden bath with an extended walk-in closet. Two additional bedrooms share a private, compartmented bath.

Second Floor

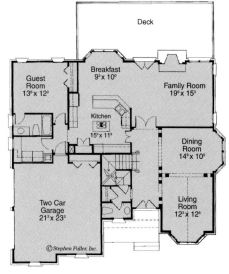

First Floor

Family Homes

Plan: HPK3200341

First Floor: 2,144 sq. ft.
Second Floor: 1,253 sq. ft.
Total: 3,397 sq. ft.
Bedrooms: 3

Bathrooms: 3 ½
Width: 64' - 11"
Depth: 76' - 7"

This two-story beauty is rich in luxurious style. A dramatic entrance welcomes you to the foyer, where a stunning curved staircase leads to the second floor. A turret-style dining room floods with light from the bay windows. Across the gallery, the living room features a through-fireplace to the family room. The island kitchen opens to the breakfast room, which accesses the rear porch and the family room equipped with built-ins. The first-floor master bedroom offers a bath with a whirlpool tub, two walk-in closets, and a dressing room. Two additional bedrooms, a study, and a game room with sundeck access all reside on the second floor.

First Floor

Second Floor

Plan: HPK3200342

First Floor: 1,670 sq. ft.	Width: 64' - 0"
Second Floor: 1,741 sq. ft.	Depth: 78' - 2"
Total: 3,411 sq. ft.	Foundation: Unfinished
Bedrooms: 4	Basement
Bathrooms: 3 ½	

© Stephen Fuller, Inc.

Two Car Garage
21⁶ x 23⁶

Porte Cochère

Porch

Kitchen
14³ x 14³

Breakfast
12³ x 12¹

Dining Room
14⁶ x 11⁶

Great Room
14⁶ x 20⁹

Living Room
14⁶ x 13⁶

Foyer

Porch

First Floor

Guest Bedroom
21³ x 14³

Bedroom #2
14⁶ x 12³

WIC

Master Bathroom

Bedroom #3
12³ x 13⁶

Master Suite
14⁴ x 20⁰

Open to Below

Second Floor

Symmetry is everything in the Federal - Adams style, and this home is a classic Federal - Adams in both plan and exterior. The facade as a whole balances a one-story extended porch under a two-story hipped roof box. Inside, a traditional foyer with a central staircase is flanked by the living/dining rooms on one side and the great room on the other. Rear stairs allow private access to a secluded guest suite over the garage.

Family Homes

© 1995 William E Poole Designs, Inc.

Plan: HPK3200343

First Floor: 2,191 sq. ft.
Second Floor: 1,220 sq. ft.
Total: 3,411 sq. ft.
Bonus Space: 280 sq. ft.
Bedrooms: 4

Bathrooms: 3 ½
Width: 75' - 8"
Depth: 54' - 4"
Foundation: Crawlspace,
Unfinished Basement

This Colonial farmhouse will be the showpiece of your neighborhood. Come in from the wide front porch through French doors topped by a sunburst window. Continue past the formal dining and living rooms to a columned gallery and a large family room with a focal fireplace. The kitchen astounds with a unique layout, an island, and abundant counter and cabinet space. The master bath balances luxury with efficiency. Three upstairs bedrooms feature such amenities as dormer windows and walk-in closets. Bonus space is ready for expansion as your needs change.

First Floor

Second Floor

This two-story design faithfully recalls the 18th-Century homestead of Secretary of Foreign Affairs John Jay. First-floor livability includes a grand living room with a fireplace and a music alcove. The nearby library also sports a fireplace and convenient built-ins. A large country kitchen delights with another fireplace and a snack bar. A large clutter room has an attached half-bath and allows plenty of space for hobbies or a workshop. Three upstairs bedrooms include a large master suite with a walk-in closet, vanity seating, and double sinks. Each family bedroom contains a double closet.

Plan: HPK3200344

First Floor: 2,026 sq. ft.	Width: 84' - 0"
Second Floor: 1,386 sq. ft.	Depth: 65' - 8"
Total: 3,412 sq. ft.	Foundation: Unfinished
Bedrooms: 3	Basement
Bathrooms: 2 ½ + ½	

Second Floor

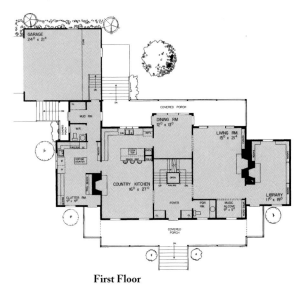

First Floor

Family Homes

Plan: HPK3200345

First Floor: 2,384 sq. ft.
Second Floor: 1,050 sq. ft.
Total: 3,434 sq. ft.
Bonus Space: 228 sq. ft.
Bedrooms: 4
Bathrooms: 3 ½

Width: 65' - 8"
Depth: 57' - 0"
Foundation: Crawlspace,
Unfinished Walkout
Basement

The covered front porch of this stucco home opens to a two-story foyer and one of two staircases. Arched openings lead into both the formal dining room and the vaulted living room. The efficient kitchen features a walk-in pantry, built-in desk, work island, and separate snack bar. Nearby, the large breakfast area opens to the family room. Lavish in its amenities, the master suite offers a separate vaulted sitting room with a fireplace, among other luxuries. Three bedrooms, along with optional bonus space and attic storage, are found on the second floor.

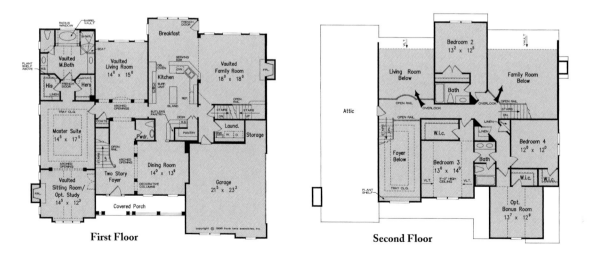

First Floor

Second Floor

First Floor

Second Floor

Plan: HPK3200346

First Floor: 2,199 sq. ft.	Bathrooms: 4
Second Floor: 1,235 sq. ft.	Width: 62' - 6"
Total: 3,434 sq. ft.	Depth: 54' - 3"
Bonus Space: 150 sq. ft.	Foundation: Walkout
Bedrooms: 4	Basement

The covered front porch of this home warmly welcomes family and visitors. To the right of the foyer is a versatile option room. On the other side is the formal dining room. A comfortable great room boasts French doors to a rear deck and easy access to a large breakfast area and sunroom. The adjacent kitchen includes a cooking island/breakfast bar. Secluded on the main level for privacy, the master suite features a lavish bath loaded with amenities. Just off the bedroom is a private deck. Three additional bedrooms and two baths occupy the second level.

Family Homes

Plan: HPK3200347

First Floor: 2,148 sq. ft.
Second Floor: 1,300 sq. ft.
Total: 3,448 sq. ft.
Bonus Space: 444 sq. ft.
Bedrooms: 4

Bathrooms: 4
Width: 85' - 5"
Depth: 73' - 0"
Foundation: Crawlspace

Impressive stone-faced columns frame the entry and give way to an impressive two-story foyer encircled by a curving stairway. Guests may gather around the fireplace in the columned living room, then move on to the formal dining room for a festive meal. A large island kitchen bridges the formal and family areas of the home, and a sunny breakfast nook provides a place to enjoy the morning together. The first floor is completed by a den or guest room with adjoining bath, a convenient utility room, and a back stair to the three family bedrooms and large bonus room above the three-car garage. Also upstairs is an elegant master suite, with a huge walk-in closet, dual vanities, and a soaking tub set in a windowed alcove. Stately ceiling treatments and handsome built-ins heighten the drama of this contemporary home.

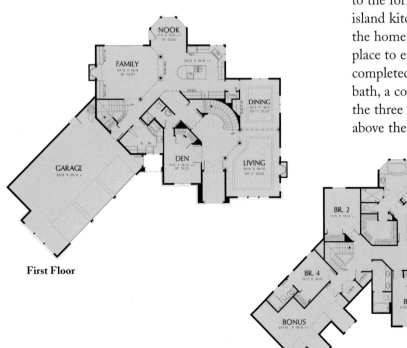

First Floor

Second Floor

Family Homes

This unusual design features curved galleries leading to matching wings. In the main house, the living and dining rooms provide a large open area, with access to the rear porch for additional entertaining possibilities. A keeping room features a pass-through to the kitchen and a fireplace with a built-in wood box. Four bedrooms, including a master suite with a fireplace, are found upstairs. One wing contains separate guest quarters with a full bath, a lounge area, and an upstairs studio—or make it a loft. The other wing features a second-floor room for storage or hobbies above the garage.

Plan: HPK3200348

First Floor: 1,992 sq. ft.
Second Floor: 1,458 sq. ft.
Total: 3,450 sq. ft.
Bonus Space: 380 sq. ft.
Bedrooms: 5

Bathrooms: 3 ½
Width: 108' - 0"
Depth: 64' - 0"
Foundation: Unfinished Basement

Optional Layout

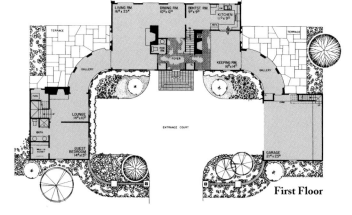

First Floor

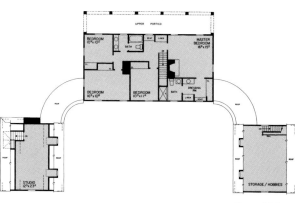

Second Floor

The Big Book of Traditional House Plans   **275**

Family Homes

© Design Traditions

Plan: HPK3200349

First Floor: 1,567 sq. ft.
Second Floor: 1,895 sq. ft.
Total: 3,462 sq. ft.
Bedrooms: 4
Bathrooms: 3 ½

Width: 63' - 0"
Depth: 53' - 6"
Foundation: Walkout Basement

Although the facade may look like a quaint country cottage, this home's fine proportions contain formal living areas, including a dining room and a living room. At the back of the first floor you'll find a spacious kitchen and breakfast nook. A great room with a fireplace and bumped-out window makes everyday living very comfortable. A rear porch allows for outdoor dining and relaxation. Upstairs, four bedrooms include a master suite with lots of notable features. A boxed ceiling, lavish bath, large walk-in closet, and secluded sitting room (which would also make a nice study or exercise room) assure great livability.

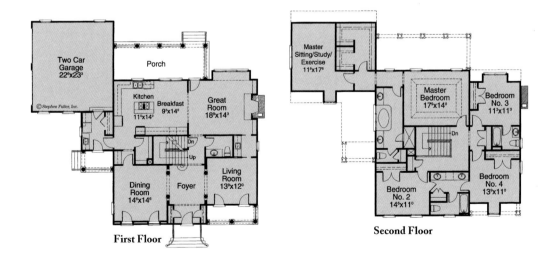

First Floor

Second Floor

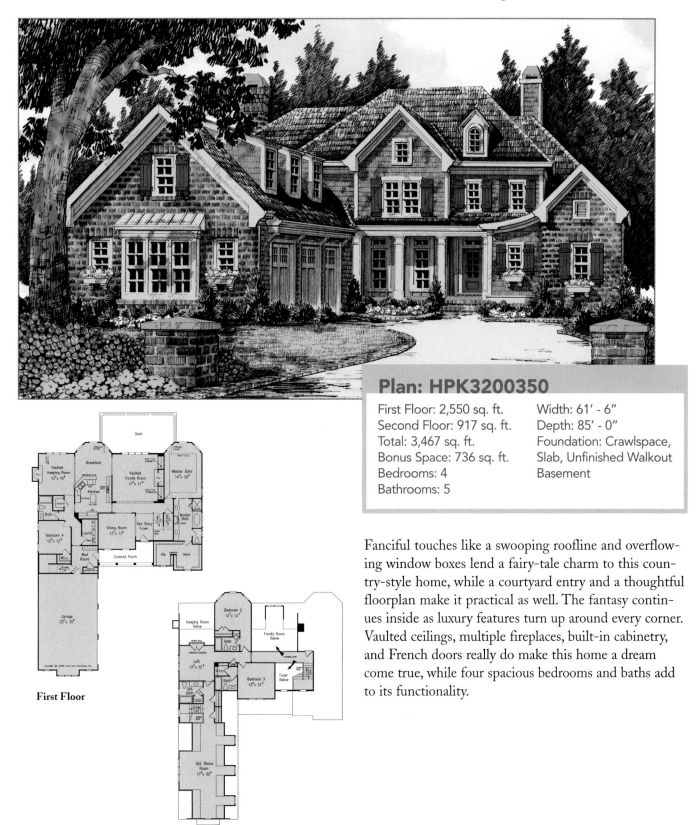

First Floor

Second Floor

Plan: HPK3200350

First Floor: 2,550 sq. ft.
Second Floor: 917 sq. ft.
Total: 3,467 sq. ft.
Bonus Space: 736 sq. ft.
Bedrooms: 4
Bathrooms: 5

Width: 61' - 6"
Depth: 85' - 0"
Foundation: Crawlspace,
Slab, Unfinished Walkout
Basement

Fanciful touches like a swooping roofline and overflowing window boxes lend a fairy-tale charm to this country-style home, while a courtyard entry and a thoughtful floorplan make it practical as well. The fantasy continues inside as luxury features turn up around every corner. Vaulted ceilings, multiple fireplaces, built-in cabinetry, and French doors really do make this home a dream come true, while four spacious bedrooms and baths add to its functionality.

Family Homes

Plan: HPK3200351

First Floor: 1,819 sq. ft.
Second Floor: 1,664 sq. ft.
Total: 3,483 sq. ft.
Bedrooms: 4

Bathrooms: 3 ½
Width: 71' - 0"
Depth: 52' - 0"
Foundation: Crawlspace

This stucco and stone home features an interesting mix of European and French Country accents with northwest contemporary style. Inside, an elegant 14-foot, two-story foyer welcomes you into this exciting home. The main floor offers a minimum ceiling height of 9 feet. The gourmet will be delighted by the island countertop kitchen. Convenient laundry facilities are located on the upper floor. A teen suite serves two secondary bedrooms. The rear staircase leads to a bonus room.

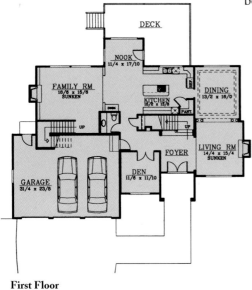

First Floor

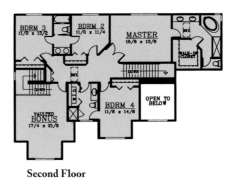

Second Floor

© 1995 William E Poole Designs, Inc.

Five front-facing dormers are part of the allure, but the true appeal can be found inside where three fireplaces reside. The first sits in the corner of the first-floor master suite. The second fireplace is in the living room/ library adjacent to the master bedroom. The third fireplace is along the right wall of the family room, next to a built-in entertainment center. To the right of the family room, the island kitchen boasts a snack bar, built-in desk, a walk-in pantry, and abundant counter space. The mud-room offers a space to doff coats and soiled shoes. A separate utility room houses the washer/dryer, drip/dry area, and sink. The second floor houses three additional bedrooms, three full baths, and space for a future rec room.

Plan: HPK3200352

First Floor: 2,376 sq. ft.	Bathrooms: 4 ½
Second Floor: 1,117 sq. ft.	Width: 72' - 8"
Total: 3,493 sq. ft.	Depth: 67' - 6"
Bonus Space: 597 sq. ft.	Foundation: Unfinished
Bedrooms: 4	Basement

First Floor

Second Floor

Family Homes

Plan: HPK3200353

First Floor: 2,469 sq. ft.
Second Floor: 1,025 sq. ft.
Total: 3,494 sq. ft.
Bonus Space: 320 sq. ft.
Bedrooms: 4
Bathrooms: 3 ½

Width: 67' - 8"
Depth: 74' - 2"
Foundation: Crawlspace,
Slab, Unfinished
Basement

A lovely double arch gives this European-style home a commanding presence. Once inside, a two-story foyer provides an open view directly through the formal living room to the rear grounds beyond. The spacious kitchen with a work island and the bayed breakfast area share space with the family room. The private master suite features dual sinks, twin walk-in closets, a corner garden tub, and a separate shower. A large game room completes this wonderful family home.

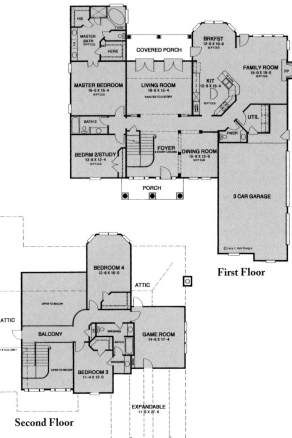

First Floor

Second Floor

Although charming, the front porch of this country cottage provides more than just a pretty facade. Rain or shine, the protective cover will inspire you to enjoy the outdoors. Inside, space for formal entertaining is provided by the living room/study and dining room that flank the foyer. A guest bedroom and an adjacent bath are conveniently located to the rear of the living room/study. An island cooktop enhances the efficient, U-shaped kitchen, which easily serves the breakfast room, the dining room, and the great room with its centered fireplace. The second floor contains three family bedrooms, two full baths, and a relaxing master suite.

Plan: HPK3200354

First Floor: 1,809 sq. ft.
Second Floor: 1,690 sq. ft.
Total: 3,499 sq. ft.
Bedrooms: 5
Bathrooms: 4

Width: 58' - 3"
Depth: 58' - 3"
Foundation: Walkout Basement

Second Floor

First Floor

Family Homes

Plan: HPK3200355

First Floor: 1,795 sq. ft.
Second Floor: 1,708 sq. ft.
Total: 3,503 sq. ft.
Bedrooms: 4
Bathrooms: 3 ½

Width: 72' - 6"
Depth: 53' - 8"
Foundation: Unfinished
Basement, Block

The first floor of this contemporary Colonial home contains all of the spaces and needs of a busy, active family. A bayed parlor and tray-ceilinged dining room accommodate formal occasions; the open great room, morning room, and kitchen are more casual. A powder room and laundry are conveniently located near the kitchen. The second floor houses the four bedrooms, including the master suite, which feature a large bath, dormered sitting area, and His and Hers walk-in closets.

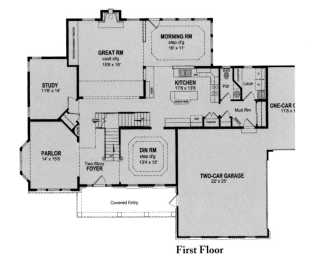

First Floor

Second Floor

Plan: HPK3200356

First Floor: 2,658 sq. ft.
Second Floor: 854 sq. ft.
Total: 3,512 sq. ft.
Bonus Space: 150 sq. ft.
Bedrooms: 4
Bathrooms: 3 ½

Width: 86' - 0"
Depth: 58' - 1"
Foundation: Crawlspace,
Slab, Unfinished
Basement

First Floor

Second Floor

This grand country estate presents an impressive exterior of brick and fieldstone with a hooded bay window as the focal point. This two-story design eatures a magnificent curved staircase from the foyer to the second level. A secluded study and formal dining room are at the front of the house. The master bedroom suite features a unique curved vanity and oversized twin walk-in closets. The main living areas are connected by a tiled gallery. One family bedroom suite is on the first level; two additional bedrooms and full bath share the second level with a playroom and a large bonus room with access to attic storage.

Family Homes

Rear Exterior

Plan: HPK3200357

First Floor: 2,315 sq. ft.
Second Floor: 1,200 sq. ft.
Total: 3,515 sq. ft.
Bedrooms: 4
Bathrooms: 3 ½

Width: 77' - 4"
Depth: 46' - 8"
Foundation: Walkout
Basement

This grand home displays the finest in farmhouse design. Dormer windows and a traditional brick and siding exterior create a welcoming facade. Inside, the entry foyer opens to a formal zone consisting of a living room to the left and a dining room to the right. The kitchen offers a pass-through to the breakfast area; the great room is just a step away. Here, a fireplace graces the far end of the room while a wall of glass allows light to penetrate the interior of the room. Double doors grant passage to the backyard. Beyond the first-floor gallery, the master bedroom boasts a tray ceiling, bay window, and lavish bath. Upstairs, three family bedrooms all have walk-in closets.

First Floor

Second Floor

Plan: HPK3200358

First Floor: 2,200 sq. ft.
Second Floor: 1,338 sq. ft.
Total: 3,538 sq. ft.
Bedrooms: 4

Bathrooms: 3 ½
Width: 83' - 5"
Depth: 68' - 11"

This New American manor possesses the amenities a modern family wants and the features that impress—inside and out. From the entry, be immediately welcomed by a winding staircase to the second floor with three bedrooms, two baths, and a game room. An octagonal dining room is in the turret at the front of the home, and the octagonal great room with fireplace and built-ins is toward the back. The island kitchen is perfectly positioned to serve all public rooms. A study lies in another turret on the side of the plan, in front of the master suite. A palladian window illuminates the master bedroom; His and Hers walk-in closets branch off from the master bath.

Optional Layout

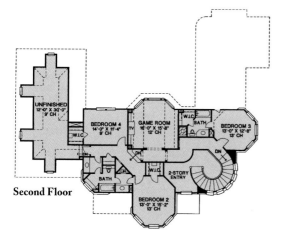

Second Floor

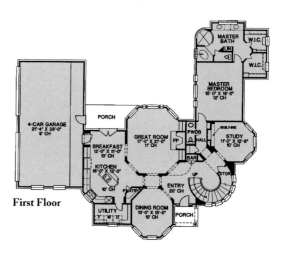

First Floor

Family Homes

© Stephen Fuller, Inc.

Plan: HPK3200359

First Floor: 2,034 sq. ft.
Second Floor: 1,514 sq. ft.
Total: 3,548 sq. ft.
Bonus Space: 460 sq. ft.
Bedrooms: 4

Bathrooms: 4
Width: 72' - 9"
Depth: 54' - 0"
Foundation: Unfinished
Walkout Basement

This traditional home exudes charm with cedar shake, stacked stone, and a petite portico. The dining room features a cozy window seat and coffered ceilings, while the great room has access to the rear porch and a large fireplace. The breakfast room has an abundance of windows to illuminate warm meals prepared in the adjacent kitchen. A guest room and study with fireplace are at the left side of the plan for privacy. Dual staircases lead upstairs to a spacious master suite and two additional bedrooms with private baths. The bonus room would be perfect as a Media Room or a children's playroom.

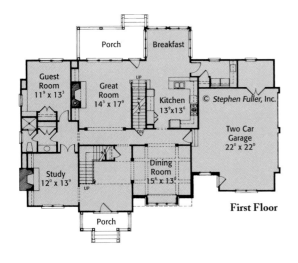

First Floor

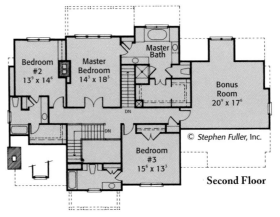

Second Floor

© 2001 Donald A. Gardner, Inc.

An abundance of windows and an attractive brick facade enhance the exterior of this traditional two-story home. Inside, a study and formal dining room flank the two-story foyer. Fireplaces warm both the great room and first-floor master suite. The suite also provides a separate sitting room, two walk-in closets, and a private bath. The island kitchen extends into the breakfast room. The second floor features three additional family bedrooms, two baths, and a bonus room fit for a home office.

Plan: HPK3200360

First Floor: 2,511 sq. ft.	Bedrooms: 4
Second Floor: 1,062 sq. ft.	Bathrooms: 3 ½
Total: 3,573 sq. ft.	Width: 84' - 11"
Bonus Space: 465 sq. ft.	Depth: 55' - 11"

Second Floor

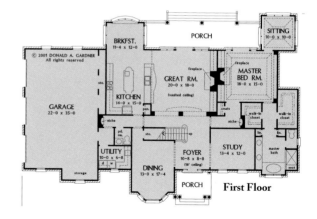

First Floor

Family Homes

Plan: HPK3200361

First Floor: 2,461 sq. ft.
Second Floor: 1,114 sq. ft.
Total: 3,575 sq. ft.
Bedrooms: 4
Bathrooms: 3 ½

Width: 84' - 4"
Depth: 63' - 0"
Foundation: Walkout
Basement

A myriad of glass and ornamental stucco detailing complements the asymmetrical facade of this two-story home. Inside, the striking, two-story foyer provides a dramatic entrance. To the right is the formal dining room. An efficient L-shaped kitchen and bayed breakfast nook are conveniently located near the dining area. The living room, with its welcoming fireplace, opens through double doors to the rear terrace. The private master suite provides access to the rear terrace and adjacent study. The master bath is sure to please with its relaxing garden tub, separate shower, grand His and Hers walk-in closets, and a compartmented toilet. The second floor contains three large bedrooms, one with a private bath, while the others share a bath.

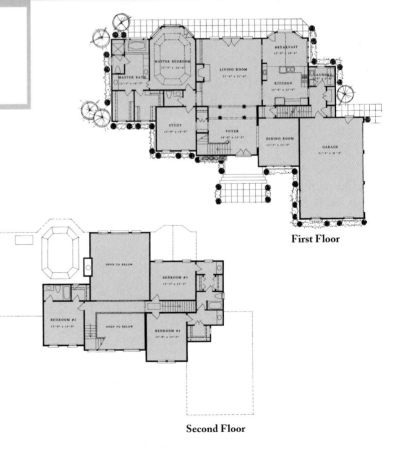

First Floor

Second Floor

This breathtaking stone-and-shingle European cottage will turn the home of your dreams into a reality. Enter a formal foyer with an elegant box-bay dining room on the left and vast, vaulted family room ahead. A fireplace here gives the room a definite focus; tall windows bring in floods of natural light. An expansive kitchen makes it easy for multiple cooks to share space and effortlessly serve the bayed breakfast nook. A vaulted keeping room at the rear is a cozy hideaway. The master suite shines with a bayed sitting area and majestic vaulted bath with a corner garden tub.

Plan: HPK3200362

First Floor: 2,225 sq. ft.
Second Floor: 1,360 sq. ft.
Total: 3,585 sq. ft.
Bonus Space: 277 sq. ft.
Bedrooms: 4
Bathrooms: 3 ½

Width: 68' - 10"
Depth: 60' - 0"
Foundation: Crawlspace, Unfinished Walkout Basement

First Floor

Second Floor

Family Homes

Plan: HPK3200363

First Floor: 2,064 sq. ft.
Second Floor: 1,521 sq. ft.
Total: 3,585 sq. ft.
Bonus Space: 427 sq. ft.
Bedrooms: 4

Bathrooms: 3
Width: 84' - 8"
Depth: 65' - 0"
Foundation: Crawlspace

The best of southern tradition combines with an easy-going floor plan to make this home a sure neighborhood favorite. The elegant portico at the front is a unique touch. Formal rooms—a library, living room, and dining room—surround the two-story foyer, which leads past the staircase to the hearth-warmed family room. In the very back, the kitchen is amplified by a gorgeous vaulted sunroom featuring two walls of windows to let in light. The second floor is home to a deluxe master suite as well as two family bedrooms that share a bath. A utility room is conveniently located upstairs as well. Future space is available for expansion over the garage.

First Floor

Second Floor

Plan: HPK3200364

First Floor: 1,599 sq. ft.
Second Floor: 1,987 sq. ft.
Total: 3,586 sq. ft.
Bedrooms: 4
Bathrooms: 4 ½
Width: 65' - 0"

Depth: 45' - 0"
Foundation: Crawlspace,
Unfinished Walkout
Basement

First Floor

Second Floor

Stone and shingles give this home a decidedly country facade. The interior, however, offers every modern convenience. Double doors lead into the house as well as the study. A wide pass-through opens the dining room to the foyer, and a smaller pass-through meanders to the kitchen for easy serving access. The breakfast room is open to the kitchen and has a doorway to the rear deck. Another pass-through leads to the coffered-ceilinged family room with fireplace and framing windows. An angled staircase ventures to the packed second floor. That houses all four bedrooms—including the master— and the laundry room. The master suite features a tray ceiling in the spacious bedroom, a sitting room, a large bath with many amenities, and His and Hers walk-in closets.

Family Homes

© William E. Poole Designs, Inc.

Plan: HPK3200365

Square Footage: 3,600
Bedrooms: 4
Bathrooms: 3 ½
Width: 76' - 2"

Depth: 100' - 10"
Foundation: Crawlspace,
Unfinished Basement

Graceful columns combine with stunning symmetry on this fine four-bedroom home. Inside, the foyer opens to the formal living room on the left and then leads back to the spacious family room. Here, a fireplace waits to warm cool fall evenings and built-ins accommodate your book collection. The efficient island kitchen offers plenty of counter and cabinet space, easily serving both the formal dining room and the sunny breakfast area. A separate bedroom resides back by the garage and features a walk-in closet. Two more family bedrooms are at the front right side of the home and share a full bath. The lavish master suite is complete with a huge walk-in closet, a bayed sitting area, and a sumptuous bath.

© William E. Poole Designs

Plan: HPK3200366

First Floor: 1,850 sq. ft.
Second Floor: 1,760 sq. ft.
Total: 3,610 sq. ft.
Bedrooms: 4
Bathrooms: 4

Width: 56' - 0"
Depth: 55' - 0"
Foundation: Walkout Basement

This American country-style home, with wood siding and shuttered windows, echoes images of the warmth and strength of traditional southern living. The two-story foyer opens to a dining room and formal parlor. Pass the open-rail stairs to the large family room with its fireplace and hearth, flanking bookcases, and squared column supports. The spacious kitchen has a breakfast area that opens to the outside. There is also an "option room" which may serve as the guest quarters with a private bath, a private study, or a children's den. Upstairs, the master suite has its own sitting area and an unusual vaulted ceiling. Two other bedrooms share a bath; a fourth has a private bath as well as access to the second-floor porch.

First Floor

Second Floor

Family Homes

Plan: HPK3200367

First Floor: 2,384 sq. ft.
Second Floor: 1,234 sq. ft.
Total: 3,618 sq. ft.
Bonus Space: 344 sq. ft.
Bedrooms: 5
Bathrooms: 4 ½

Width: 64' - 6"
Depth: 57' - 10"
Foundation: Crawlspace, Slab, Unfinished Walkout Basement

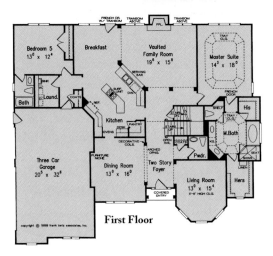

First Floor

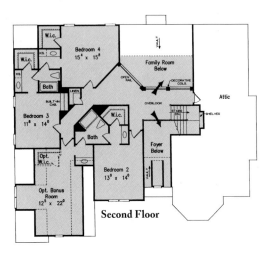

Second Floor

Stucco and stone, French shutters, a turret-style bay, and lovely arches create a magical, timeless style. A formal arch romanticizes the front entry, which opens to a two-story foyer. A bayed living room resides to the right, and a formal dining room is set to the left. Straight ahead, the vaulted two-story family room is warmed by an enchanting fireplace. The island kitchen is set between the breakfast and dining rooms. The master suite is enhanced by a tray ceiling and offers a lavish master bath with a whirlpool tub. Upstairs, Bedroom 2 offers another private bath and a walk-in closet. Bedrooms 3 and 4 each provide their own walk-in closets and share a full bath. The bonus room is perfect for a future home office or playroom.

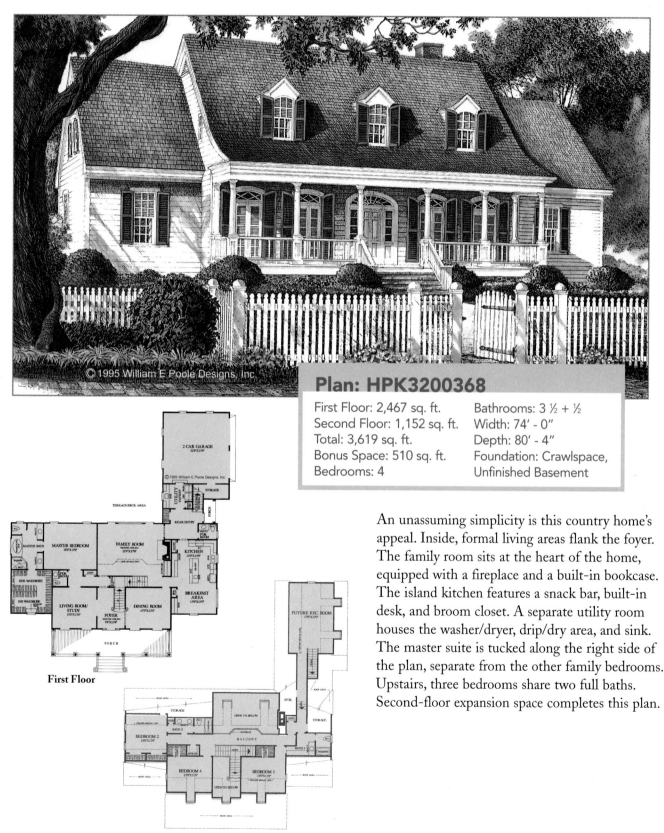

First Floor

Second Floor

© 1995 William E Poole Designs, Inc.

Plan: HPK3200368

First Floor: 2,467 sq. ft.
Second Floor: 1,152 sq. ft.
Total: 3,619 sq. ft.
Bonus Space: 510 sq. ft.
Bedrooms: 4

Bathrooms: 3 ½ + ½
Width: 74' - 0"
Depth: 80' - 4"
Foundation: Crawlspace,
Unfinished Basement

An unassuming simplicity is this country home's appeal. Inside, formal living areas flank the foyer. The family room sits at the heart of the home, equipped with a fireplace and a built-in bookcase. The island kitchen features a snack bar, built-in desk, and broom closet. A separate utility room houses the washer/dryer, drip/dry area, and sink. The master suite is tucked along the right side of the plan, separate from the other family bedrooms. Upstairs, three bedrooms share two full baths. Second-floor expansion space completes this plan.

Family Homes

Plan: HPK3200369

First Floor: 2,778 sq. ft.
Second Floor: 841 sq. ft.
Total: 3,619 sq. ft.
Bedrooms: 4
Bathrooms: 3 ½ + ½

Width: 100' - 9"
Depth: 67' - 5"
Foundation: Unfinished
Basement

For a change of pace, this California transitional design offers the finest in modern livability. The large living room and library will make impressive entertaining spaces while the family room, with its oversized fireplace, provides a comfortable atmosphere for casual living. The three-car garage opens to a utility area off the kitchen and breakfast room. Located on the first floor for privacy, the master bedroom boasts a curved wall of glass and a pampering bath with a whirlpool tub, separate vanities, and a walk-in closet. Upstairs, three bedrooms include one with a balcony and one with a private bath.

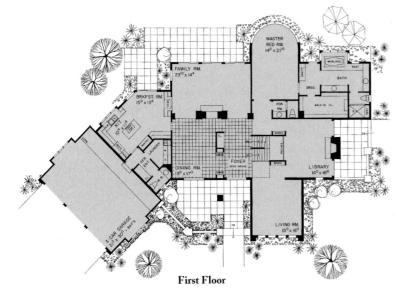

First Floor

Second Floor

Family Homes

Plan: HPK3200370

First Floor: 1,923 sq. ft.
Second Floor: 1,710 sq. ft.
Total: 3,633 sq. ft.
Bedrooms: 4

Bathrooms: 2 ½
Width: 66' - 0"
Depth: 60' - 0"
Foundation: Crawlspace

This uniquely designed home is dazzled in Mediterranean influences and eye-catching luxury. A grand arching entrance welcomes you inside to a spacious foyer that introduces a curved staircase and flanking living and dining rooms on either side. Casual areas of the home are clustered to the rear left of the plan and include a kitchen, nook, and family room warmed by a fireplace. The professional study is a quiet retreat. The three-car garage offers spacious storage. Upstairs, the master bedroom has a private bath and roomy walk-in closet. Three additional bedrooms share a hall bath and open playroom.

First Floor

Second Floor

Family Homes

Plan: HPK3200371

First Floor: 2,521 sq. ft.
Second Floor: 1,116 sq. ft.
Total: 3,637 sq. ft.
Bonus Space: 650 sq. ft.
Bedrooms: 4
Bathrooms: 4 ½

Width: 70' - 0"
Depth: 82' - 0"
Foundation: Crawlspace,
Unfinished Walkout
Basement

The exterior appeal of this country cottage is just the beginning. Once inside, the open floor plan joins the living areas seamlessly. The foyer connects with the coffered-ceilinged family room adding warmth to the space with a fireplace. A second fireplace in the keeping room warms the adjoining kitchen and breakfast area. The master suite, enhanced by a tray ceiling, boasts a private sitting room, His and Hers closets, a roomy bath with dual-sink vanities, a separate shower and tub, and a private toilet. Upstairs houses three additional bedrooms, each with a full bath. Bonus space completes the second floor.

First Floor

Second Floor

© William E. Poole Designs, Inc.

A country cottage with curb appeal, this design will surely please family members and visitors alike. The master suite, nestled in the far left corner of the first floor, is a quiet retreat for the homeowners. The great room is centrally located with a fireplace on the left wall and built-in bookcases. The U-shaped kitchen features a corner snack bar that serves the adjoining sunroom/breakfast area. A rear screen porch is accessed from here. A first-floor bedroom with full bath could serve as a guest suite or study. Upstairs houses two additional family bedrooms sharing a full bath, two storage areas, and a rec room.

Plan: HPK3200372

First Floor: 2,620 sq. ft.	Bathrooms: 3
Second Floor: 1,019 sq. ft.	Width: 77' - 6"
Total: 3,639 sq. ft.	Depth: 59' - 10"
Bedrooms: 4	Foundation: Crawlspace

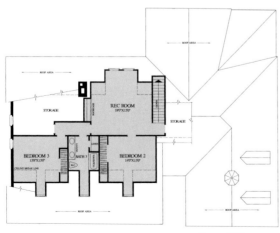

Second Floor

First Floor

Family Homes

Plan: HPK3200373

First Floor: 1,882 sq. ft.
Second Floor: 1,763 sq. ft.
Total: 3,645 sq. ft.
Bedrooms: 4
Bathrooms: 3 ½

Width: 94' - 2"
Depth: 57' - 0"
Foundation: Unfinished Basement

Traditional styling takes on added dimension in this stately two-story home. An angled wing encloses the sunken living room and a spacious study. Both rooms access a large terrace—perfect for formal entertaining. The dining room, with its window bay, introduces the other half of the house. Here, the resident gourmet will take great delight in the kitchen with ample counter space and island cook-top. The breakfast room remains open to the kitchen and, through a pair of columns, the family room. The second floor offers excellent sleeping quarters with four bedrooms. The master suite spoils its occupants with a sloped ceiling, balcony, and fireplace. A huge walk-in closet and a divine bath finish off the room. Three additional bedrooms include one with a private bath.

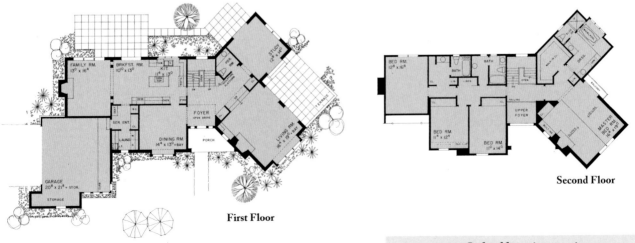

First Floor

Second Floor

© William E. Poole Designs, Inc.

Plan: HPK3200374

First Floor: 2,273 sq. ft.	Bathrooms: 4 ½
Second Floor: 1,391 sq. ft.	Width: 77' - 2"
Total: 3,664 sq. ft.	Depth: 48' - 0"
Bonus Space: 547 sq. ft.	Foundation: Crawlspace
Bedrooms: 4	

An easy and charming interpretation of the late Georgian style, this plan is carefully adapted to meet the practical requirements of a modern lifestyle. Cased openings, high ceilings, and well-placed windows keep the expansive, comfortable interiors well-lit and open. The spacious family room, which features a fireplace flanked by built-in shelves, opens to the rear terrace. The lavish master suite offers privacy on the first level; the other three bedrooms—each with private baths—are comfortably situated on the second floor. Additional space is available upstairs to develop a recreation room.

Second Floor

First Floor

Family Homes

© Stephen Fuller, Inc.

Plan: HPK3200375

First Floor: 2,380 sq. ft.
Second Floor: 1,295 sq. ft.
Total: 3,675 sq. ft.
Bedrooms: 4
Bathrooms: 3 ½

Width: 77' - 4"
Depth: 58' - 4"
Foundation: Walkout Basement

Finely crafted porches—front, side, and rear—make this home a classic in traditional southern living. Past the large French doors, the impressive foyer is flanked by the formal living and dining rooms. Beyond the stair is a vaulted great room with an expanse of windows, a fireplace, and built-in bookcases. From here, the breakfast room and kitchen are easily accessible and open to a private side porch. The master suite provides a large bath, two spacious closets, and a fireplace. The second floor contains three bedrooms with private bath access and a playroom.

Rear Exterior

First Floor

Second Floor

Plan: HPK3200376

First Floor: 2,009 sq. ft.
Second Floor: 1,667 sq. ft.
Total: 3,676 sq. ft.
Bedrooms: 4
Bathrooms: 3 ½

Width: 81' - 0"
Depth: 55' - 0"
Foundation: Unfinished Basement

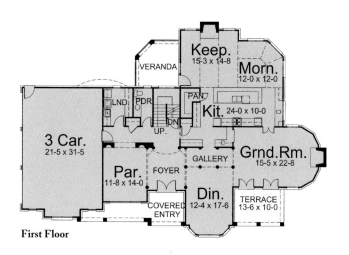

First Floor

Second Floor

Your friends and neighbors will be impressed by this grand home. It's not only the brick facade with many mutipaned windows and a covered entry supported by compelling pillars, but the superb interior layout. To the rear, an extravagant kitchen that will make any family cook's mouth water opens to a cozy keeping room. This room is flanked to the left by a veranda and to the right by a tray-ceiling breakfast niche designed to draw in morning sunshine. Between the grand room and dining area, a gallery for your favorite paintings or photographs truly personalizes your home. All the sleeping quarters are on the second level; a ravishing master suite, a bedroom with a private bath, and two bedrooms that share a large dual vanity bath.

Family Homes

Plan: HPK3200377

First Floor: 2,362 sq. ft.
Second Floor: 1,319 sq. ft.
Total: 3,681 sq. ft.
Bedrooms: 4

Bathrooms: 3 ½
Width: 77' - 11"
Depth: 64' - 11"

Unique angles and bold lines on this distinctive home create an attention-getting facade, as tall arched windows soften the design. A two-story arched entry opens to the formal foyer; to the left, the study is a quiet retreat. Continue to the living room, where a see-through fireplace shares its warmth with the angled family room. Natural light enters through a bay window and shines on the well-planned gourmet kitchen. The master suite is thoughtfully located for privacy and has a bayed sitting area and whirlpool bath. Upstairs, three splendid bedrooms share a vaulted game room. Future space will complete the plan when you desire.

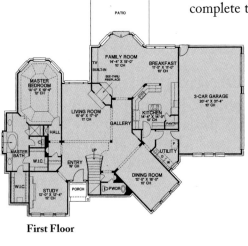

First Floor

Second Floor

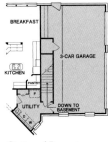

Optional Layout

Plan: HPK3200378

First Floor: 2,657 sq. ft.	Bathrooms: 3 ½
Second Floor: 1,026 sq. ft.	Width: 75' - 8"
Total: 3,683 sq. ft.	Depth: 74' - 2"
Bonus Space: 308 sq. ft.	Foundation: Crawlspace,
Bedrooms: 4	Slab, Unfinished Basement

This breathtaking traditional manor looks great from the curb, but it is the interior that will steal your heart. The entry is lit by twin two-story Palladian windows for subtle drama. On the right, the dining room is defined by columns. The living room makes an elegant impression with a vaulted ceiling and French doors to the rear porch. The kitchen is nearby and sports a "boomerang" counter and a central island. A breakfast bay creates a cheerful place for casual meals. The family room is warmed by a fireplace and brightened by a rear wall of windows. The master suite is in the left wing, decadent with a bayed sitting area, porch access, and an indulgent spa bath. A nearby bedroom makes a great guest suite or home office. Upstairs, two lovely bedrooms share a full bath and a game room.

First Floor

Second Floor

Family Homes

© 2000 Donald A. Gardner, Inc.

Plan: HPK3200379

First Floor: 2,908 sq. ft.
Second Floor: 790 sq. ft.
Total: 3,698 sq. ft.
Bonus Space: 521 sq. ft.

Bedrooms: 4
Bathrooms: 4 ½
Width: 86' - 11"
Depth: 59' - 5"

A stately hipped roof crowns this impressive executive home's brick exterior, which includes arch-topped windows, keystones, and a covered entry with a balustrade. The spacious floor plan boasts formal and casual living areas. A two-story ceiling in the foyer and family room highlights an exciting curved balcony on the second floor. The generously proportioned kitchen includes a center island sink and plenty of work space. Distinctive shelving is built into either end of the home's center hall. The master suite and a guest suite, each with tray ceilings and private baths, are located on the first floor. Two vaulted bedrooms, two full baths, and a bonus room can be found upstairs.

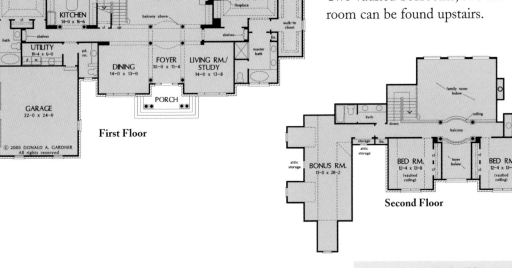

First Floor

Second Floor

Plan: HPK3200380

First Floor: 2,772 sq. ft.
Second Floor: 933 sq. ft.
Total: 3,705 sq. ft.
Bedrooms: 4
Bathrooms: 4 ½

Width: 74' - 8"
Depth: 61' - 10"
Foundation: Crawlspace, Slab

A truly grand entry—absolutely stunning on a corner lot—sets the eclectic yet elegant tone of this four-bedroom home. The foyer opens to a dramatic circular stair, then on to the two-story great room that's framed by a second-story balcony. An elegant dining room is set to the side, distinguished by a span of arches. The gourmet kitchen features wrapping counters, a cooktop island, and a breakfast room. A front study and a secondary bedroom are nice accompaniments to the expansive master suite. A through-fireplace, a spa-style bath, and a huge walk-in closet highlight this area. Upstairs, a loft opens to two balconies overlooking the porch and leads to two family bedrooms and a game room.

Second Floor

First Floor

Family Homes

Plan: HPK3200381

First Floor: 1,947 sq. ft.
Second Floor: 1,773 sq. ft.
Total: 3,720 sq. ft.
Bedrooms: 4
Bathrooms: 4 ½

Width: 73' - 0"
Depth: 46' - 0"
Foundation: Unfinished Basement

The large and efficient kitchen is at the very heart of this warm and tasteful home. Because the kitchen is connected to both a morning room and a keeping room, with access to a porch and veranda, it is ideal for everyday family life and casual entertaining. For more formal occasions, the columned dining room stately grand room with a front porch are easily accessible. A spacious home office is near the three-car garage and laundry room. The master suite with a private sitting room and three other bedrooms—each with its own bath and walk-in closets—can be found on the second floor.

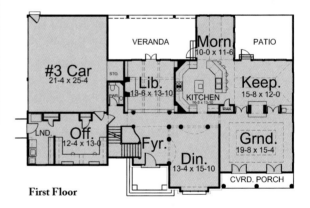

First Floor

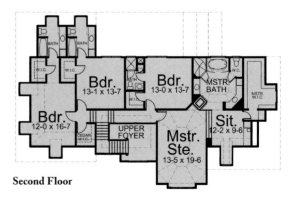

Second Floor

Plan: HPK3200382

First Floor: 2,369 sq. ft.
Second Floor: 1,363 sq. ft.
Total: 3,732 sq. ft.
Bedrooms: 4
Bathrooms: 3 ½

Width: 71' - 10"
Depth: 75' - 6"
Foundation: Crawlspace, Slab

Formal and informal needs are met in this attractive four-bedroom home. For fine dinner parties, the formal dining room flows into the formal living room, separated by graceful columns, for after-dinner conversation. Casual gatherings will thrive in the spacious family room, where a warming fireplace will add just the right glow to festivities. The nearby kitchen will make serving a breeze. For more intimate meetings, the study is available. Located on the main floor for privacy, the master suite is designed to pamper, with His and Hers walk-in closets, a whirlpool tub, and separate shower. Upstairs, three secondary bedrooms share two full baths, a walk-in linen closet, and access to a large game room.

Second Floor

First Floor

Family Homes

© William E. Poole Designs, Inc.

Plan: HPK3200383

First Floor: 2,746 sq. ft.
Second Floor: 992 sq. ft.
Total: 3,738 sq. ft.
Bonus Space: 453 sq. ft.
Bedrooms: 4

Bathrooms: 3 ½
Width: 80' - 0"
Depth: 58' - 6"
Foundation: Crawlspace

The columned entry of this Colonial home speaks for itself, but the inside actually seals the deal. The cook-top-island kitchen flows easily into the breakfast area and great room. The vaulted sunroom accesses a rear covered porch perfect for outdoor entertaining. The master suite includes a private entrance to the rear porch, central His and Hers wardrobes, and a spacious bath. Upstairs, three family bedrooms share two full baths. Expansion space makes a future rec room an option. Extra storage space in the garage is an added convenience.

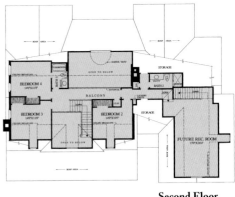

Second Floor

First Floor

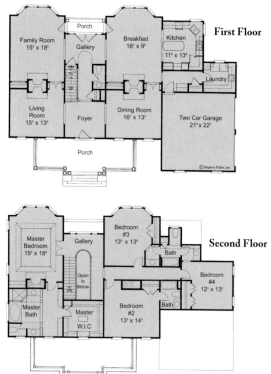

Rear Exterior

Plan: HPK3200384

First Floor: 1,880 sq. ft.	Width: 66' - 4"
Second Floor: 1,860 sq. ft.	Depth: 44' - 0"
Total: 3,740 sq. ft.	Foundation: Walkout
Bedrooms: 4	Basement
Bathrooms: 3 ½	

This traditional home offers a pleasing exterior and an interior filled with old-fashioned country splendor. Upon entering, family and friends will notice the gallery just beyond the foyer. To the left, a formal living room shares a fireplace with the family room; the family room offers a winsome bayed window and a door that opens to the back porch. To the right, the dining room and keeping room open to the breakfast room brightened by a bayed window and share another fireplace. The kitchen, adjacent to the keeping room, features a pantry, island work area and plenty of counter space; also adjoining the kitchen is a laundry/mudroom. Upstairs, a lavish master suite provides yet another warming fireplace, a private bath with garden tub, and an expansive walk-in closet. Three family bedrooms, one with a private bath, complete the second level.

First Floor

Porch · Family Room 15' x 18' · Gallery · Breakfast 16' x 9' · Kitchen 11' x 13' · Living Room 15' x 13' · Foyer · Dining Room 16' x 13' · Two Car Garage 21' x 22' · Laundry · Porch

Second Floor

Master Bedroom 15' x 18' · Gallery · Bedroom #3 13' x 13' · Bath · Open to Below · Bedroom #4 12' x 13' · Master Bath · Master W.I.C · Bedroom #2 13' x 14' · Bath

Family Homes

Plan: HPK3200385

First Floor: 1,870 sq. ft.
Second Floor: 1,881 sq. ft.
Total: 3,751 sq. ft.
Bedrooms: 5
Bathrooms: 4 ½

Width: 60' - 0"
Depth: 55' - 0"
Foundation: Crawlspace,
Unfinished Walkout
Basement

A grand entrance is just one of the highlights of this fine brick home. Inside, the two-story foyer leads through French doors to a quiet study—or make it a private guest suite. The formal living room on the right flows through an arched opening to the dining room, making entertaining a breeze. The spacious kitchen provides a large island with a serving bar as well as an adjacent breakfast area. Featuring a fireplace flanked by built-ins and a two-stories-tall ceiling, the family room is sure to be a favorite gathering spot. Upstairs, Bedrooms 2 and 3 share a full bath, while Bedroom 4 offers a private bath and a large walk-in closet. The master suite is sure to please with its His and Hers walk-in closet, pampering bath, and tray ceiling treatment.

First Floor

Second Floor

© William E. Poole Designs, Inc.

Plan: HPK3200386

First Floor: 2,327 sq. ft.	Bathrooms: 3 ½
Second Floor: 1,431 sq. ft.	Width: 78' - 10"
Total: 3,758 sq. ft.	Depth: 58' - 2"
Bonus Space: 473 sq. ft.	Foundation: Crawlspace,
Bedrooms: 5	Unfinished Basement

This Early American classic was built with attention to the needs of an active family. The formal entrance allows guests to come and go in splendor, and family members can kick off their shoes in the mudroom. The step-saving kitchen is accented by an island for dinner preparations or school projects, and a pantry with tons of space. In the master suite, homeowners can relax in the whirlpool tub and revel in the ample walk-in closet. Second-floor family bedrooms provide privacy, walk-in closets, and two shared baths, both with dual vanities.

Second Floor

First Floor

Family Homes

Plan: HPK3200387

First Floor: 2,350 sq. ft.
Second Floor: 1,425 sq. ft.
Total: 3,775 sq. ft.
Bonus Space: 219 sq. ft.
Bedrooms: 4
Bathrooms: 4 ½

Width: 79' - 0"
Depth: 69' - 6"
Foundation: Crawlspace,
Unfinished Walkout
Basement

First Floor

Second Floor

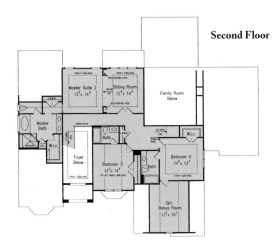

This country cottage has more than a little European flair to create great curb appeal. Take your pick from either of the master suites in this gorgeous home; there's one on the first floor and another on the second, both complete with adjacent sitting rooms and fully pampering baths. Two more bedrooms with private baths are also located upstairs. Living spaces have been wisely placed on the main level. Here you'll find built-in shelves in the living room and cabinets in the family room. Decorative columns mark the entrance to the formal dining area, easily served by the nearby island kitchen. A vaulted porch and laundry room add finishing touches to the plan.

Family Homes

A covered, columned porch and symmetrically placed windows welcome you to this elegant brick home. The formal living room offers built-in bookshelves and one of two fireplaces; the other is in the spacious family room. A gallery running between these rooms leads to the sumptuous master suite, which includes a sitting area, a private covered patio, and a bath with two walk-in closets, dual vanities, a large shower, and a garden tub. The step-saving kitchen features a work island and a snack bar. The breakfast and family rooms offer doors to the large covered veranda. Upstairs you'll find three bedrooms and attic storage space. The three-car garage even has room for a golf cart.

Plan: HPK3200388

First Floor: 2,814 sq. ft.
Second Floor: 979 sq. ft.
Total: 3,793 sq. ft.
Bedrooms: 4
Bathrooms: 3 ½

Width: 98' - 0"
Depth: 45' - 10"
Foundation: Slab,
Unfinished Basement

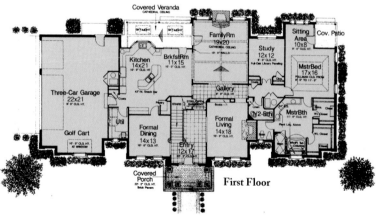

First Floor

Second Floor

Family Homes

© William E. Poole Designs, Inc.

Plan: HPK3200389

First Floor: 2,492 sq. ft.
Second Floor: 1,313 sq. ft.
Total: 3,805 sq. ft.
Bonus Space: 687 sq. ft.
Bedrooms: 4

Bathrooms: 3 ½ + ½
Width: 85' - 10"
Depth: 54' - 6"
Foundation: Crawlspace,
Unfinished Basement

Although the exterior of this Georgian home is entirely classical, the interior boasts an up-to-date floor plan that's a perfect fit for today's lifestyles. The large central family room, conveniently near the kitchen and breakfast area, includes a fireplace and access to the rear terrace; fireplaces also grace the formal dining room and library. The master suite, also with terrace access, features a spacious walk-in closet and a bath with a whirlpool tub. Upstairs, a second master suite—great for guests—joins two family bedrooms. Nearby, a large open area can serve as a recreation room.

First Floor

Second Floor

Plan: HPK3200390

First Floor: 1,656 sq. ft.
Second Floor: 1,440 sq. ft.
Third Floor: 715 sq. ft.
Total: 3,811 sq. ft.
Bedrooms: 4

Bathrooms: 3 ½
Width: 72' - 0"
Depth: 36' - 0"
Foundation: Unfinished Basement

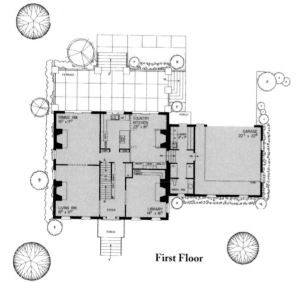

First Floor

Second Floor

Third Floor

This home recalls the home built by George Read II in New Castle, Delaware, around 1791. Its Georgian roots are evident in its symmetry and the Palladian window, keystone lintels, and parapeted chimneys. Notice, however, the round-head dormer windows, roof balustrades, and arched front-door transom, which reflect the Federal styling that was popular at the end of the 18th Century. Three massive chimneys support six fireplaces, including one in each first-floor room and two in the master suite. The country kitchen also boasts an island cooktop, a built-in desk, a pantry, and sliding glass doors to the terrace. The second floor contains two family bedrooms, in addition to the luxurious master suite, while the top floor adds a fourth bedroom and a hobby/studio area. The garage includes an L-shaped curb for a work table and storage.

Family Homes

Plan: HPK3200391

First Floor: 2,269 sq. ft.
Second Floor: 1,551 sq. ft.
Total: 3,820 sq. ft.
Bedrooms: 4
Bathrooms: 3 ½

Width: 79' - 0"
Depth: 73' - 4"
Foundation: Crawlspace,
Unfinished Walkout
Basement

Multiple gables with trusses and a brick exterior reveal European cottage influences in the design. The layout is thoroughly modern and American: a large family room with coffered ceiling, spacious flow-through kitchen and nook, vaulted keeping room with fireplace, and a luxurious master suite. Upstairs, three more bedrooms share two baths, surrounding a large common area to be used as a den, media room, or recreation room. Separate garages offer a chance to customize one into a utility or storage area.

First Floor

Second Floor

Plan: HPK3200392

First Floor: 1,634 sq. ft.	Bathrooms: 3 ½
Second Floor: 2,207 sq. ft.	Width: 64' - 0"
Total: 3,841 sq. ft.	Depth: 50' - 0"
Bedrooms: 4	Foundation: Crawlspace

The stone-and-siding exterior lends a stately appeal to this 3,800-square-foot, four-bedroom home. The first floor is dedicated to amenity-filled common living spaces that flow easily for an efficient layout. The great room sits at the heart of the home with a central fireplace, built-in bookshelves, and a built-in media center. The expansive, gourmet kitchen conveniently serves the adjacent dining room. Upstairs, the master suite is a homeowner's dream, complete with an enormous walk-in closet, a private fireplace, and a spa tub. Three additional family bedrooms are housed on this level: Bedroom 4 boasts a full bath and Bedrooms 2 and 3 are separated by a Jack-and-Jill bath. The media room is equipped with a snack bar, perfect for entertaining. A second-floor laundry room is an added bonus.

Second Floor

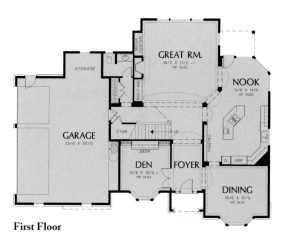

First Floor

Family Homes

Plan: HPK3200393

First Floor: 2,496 sq. ft.	Bathrooms: 3 ½
Second Floor: 1,348 sq. ft.	Width: 64' - 0"
Total: 3,844 sq. ft.	Depth: 60' - 0"
Bedrooms: 4	

This grand estate employs European elements and fairy-tale charm to create a home that will be the hallmark of any neighborhood. Inside, an impressive foyer stretches two-stories high; on the left, a study set in a turret is warmed by a fireplace. The dining room, lit by a box-bay window, is on the right, equipped with a butler's pantry. A formal living room receives guests, and the hearth-warmed family room welcomes casual relaxation. The master suite is the real star of this design, with a carousel-bay sitting room, romantic fireplace, porch access, and resplendent bath. Upstairs, three bedrooms share three full baths and a versatile game room.

First Floor

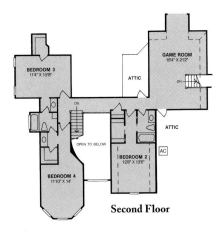

Second Floor

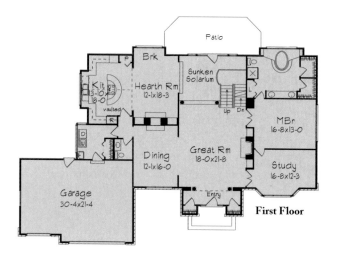

First Floor

Plan: HPK3200394

First Floor: 2,306 sq. ft.	Width: 80' - 8"
Second Floor: 1,544 sq. ft.	Depth: 51' - 8"
Total: 3,850 sq. ft.	Foundation: Unfinished
Bedrooms: 5	Basement
Bathrooms: 3 ½	

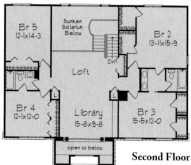

Second Floor

The detailed keystone arch highlights the grand entryway of this home. The vast windows flood the home with natural light throughout. The entry leads into a splendid great room with a sunken solarium. The solarium features U-shaped stairs and a balcony with an arched window. The secluded master suite includes a luxurious bath and a large study with a bay window. A loft, the library, and four family bedrooms occupy the second floor.

Family Homes

Plan: HPK3200395

First Floor: 2,060 sq. ft.
Second Floor: 1,817 sq. ft.
Total: 3,877 sq. ft.
Bedrooms: 5
Bathrooms: 4 ½

Width: 54' - 0"
Depth: 78' - 4"
Foundation: Crawlspace, Slab, Unfinished Walkout Basement

Mesmerizing details make this luxurious home a distinct sensation. Stucco and stone, opulent arches, and French shutters romanticize the exterior. Inside, a radiant staircase cascades into the two-story foyer. The eye-catching stone turret encloses the dining room. The formal living room is illuminated by two enormous arched windows. A wall of windows in the family room offers a breathtaking view of the backyard. The island kitchen adjoins the breakfast area and a walk-in pantry. A three-car garage completes the ground level. Upstairs, the master wing is almost doubled by its private sitting area. Double doors open into the master bath with a corner whirlpool tub. Enormous His and Hers walk-in closets are efficiently designed.

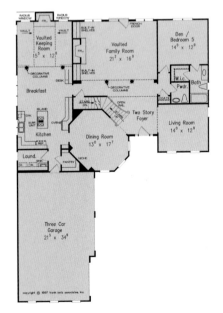

First Floor

Second Floor

This beautiful Folk Victorian home is in a class of its own. Living areas include a formal Victorian parlor, a private study, and large gathering room. The formal dining room has a more casual counterpart in the bay-windowed breakfast room. Both are near the well-appointed kitchen. Five bedrooms readily serve family and guest needs handily; three are on the second floor and two more are on the third floor. The master suite includes a bath with whirlpool tub, separate shower, and two sinks. For outdoor entertaining there is a covered rear porch leading to a terrace. The two-car garage is arranged to the rear of the home and attaches to the main house at a service entrance near the laundry and mudroom.

Plan: HPK3200396

First Floor: 1,683 sq. ft.	Bathrooms: 3 ½
Second Floor: 1,388 sq. ft.	Width: 64' - 0"
Third Floor: 808 sq. ft.	Depth: 67' - 0"
Total: 3,879 sq. ft.	Foundation: Unfinished
Bedrooms: 5	Basement

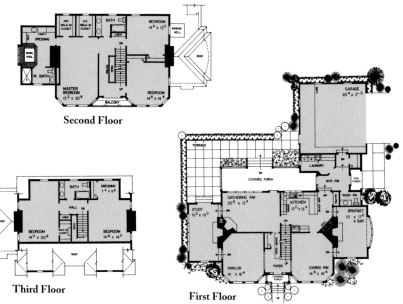

Second Floor

Third Floor

First Floor

Family Homes

Plan: HPK3200397

First Floor: 2,319 sq. ft.
Second Floor: 1,570 sq. ft.
Total: 3,889 sq. ft.
Bedrooms: 4

Bathrooms: 3 ½
Width: 72' - 0"
Depth: 58' - 0"
Foundation: Crawlspace

Fine brick detailing, multiple arches and gables, and a grand entry give this four-bedroom home plenty of charm. The graceful, window-filled entry leads to a foyer flanked by a formal dining room and a study perfect for a home office. The great room, directly ahead, offers a fireplace and access to outside. A butler's pantry is located between the kitchen and dining room. The master suite is on the first floor. On the second floor, three family bedrooms, each with a walk-in closet, share two baths and a game room.

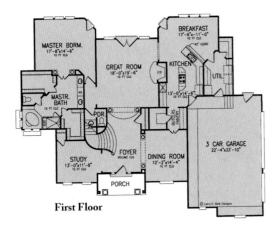

First Floor

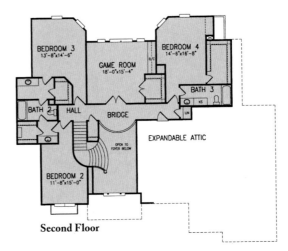

Second Floor

Plan: HPK3200398

First Floor: 2,670 sq. ft.
Second Floor: 1,225 sq. ft.
Total: 3,895 sq. ft.
Bonus Space: 271 sq. ft.
Bedrooms: 4

Bathrooms: 3 ½ + ½
Width: 70' - 6"
Depth: 66' - 6"
Foundation: Unfinished Basement

European extravagance, dazzled with chateau style, makes this manor home the epitome of luxury. A dramatic display of windows and a glorious arched entrance beautify the exterior. Inside, a dramatic staircase cascades into the foyer, which is flanked by the formal dining room and parlor. Straight ahead, the lofty grand room is illuminated by a curved wall of windows. An enormous hearth warms the room and is flanked by built-in shelves. The cozy keeping room, warmed by a second fireplace, is open to both the bayed breakfast room and the island kitchen. The left wing is almost entirely devoted to the master suite, which provides a bath with a whirlpool tub and a large walk-in closet. Upstairs, all three family bedrooms feature their own private baths. An optional fifth bedroom provides future additional space.

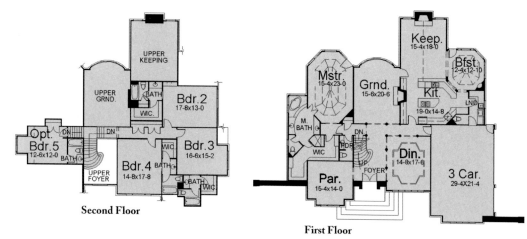

Second Floor

First Floor

Family Homes

Plan: HPK3200399

First Floor: 2,346 sq. ft.	Bathrooms: 2 ½
Second Floor: 1,554 sq. ft.	Width: 97' - 4"
Total: 3,900 sq. ft.	Depth: 58' - 6"
Bonus Space: 455 sq. ft.	Foundation: Crawlspace
Bedrooms: 3	

A complex roofline astrides a brick facade, with bay and dormer windows dappling this sweeping exterior. Inside, you'll be in awe of the corner master suite on the main level, which provides plenty of views through the windows and private outdoor access, not to mention its own spectacular bath. The great room has more of those views in store, plus a pair of stunning French doors. A sunroom allows access to a small patio and to the garage.

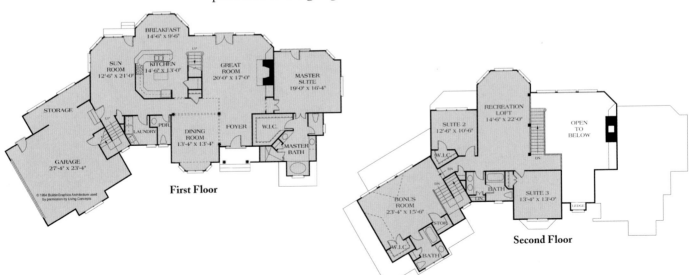

First Floor

Second Floor

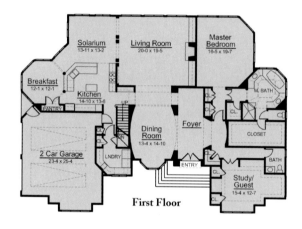

First Floor

Second Floor

Plan: HPK3200400

First Floor: 2,836 sq. ft.
Second Floor: 1,064 sq. ft.
Total: 3,900 sq. ft.
Bedrooms: 5
Bathrooms: 4 ½

Width: 78' - 0"
Depth: 55' - 0"
Foundation: Unfinished Basement

View your garden or a lakeside from a multitude of vantage points in this European-style home. The solarium is a sunlit space shared by the living room and kitchen. A wall of windows extends through these spaces and around the corner to the breakfast bay. A turret-style bay at the front of the plan houses the formal dining room. Even the master suite takes advantage of views of the rear and side property. Such ocular luxuries, however, are not reserved for the main level alone; each of the three upstairs bedrooms has its own unique perspective as well as a private bath.

Family Homes

© William E. Poole Designs, Inc.

Plan: HPK3200401

First Floor: 2,648 sq. ft.
Second Floor: 1,253 sq. ft.
Total: 3,901 sq. ft.
Bonus Space: 540 sq. ft.
Bedrooms: 4

Bathrooms: 3 ½
Width: 82' - 0"
Depth: 60' - 4"
Foundation: Crawlspace

This delightful home packs quite a punch. The grand staircase in the elegant foyer makes a dazzling first impression. To the left is the living room and on the right is the library, which opens to the sunroom overlooking the deck. The angled island kitchen is situated conveniently between the breakfast area and the dining room. The master suite finds privacy on the far right. Here, the private bath pampers with spaciousness and twin wardrobes. Three additional bedrooms are found on the second floor, along with two full baths. Future space provides an additional bedroom, bath, and rec room.

First Floor

Second Floor

Rear Exterior

Plan: HPK3200402

First Floor: 2,813 sq. ft.
Second Floor: 1,091 sq. ft.
Total: 3,904 sq. ft.
Bedrooms: 4

Bathrooms: 3 ½
Width: 85' - 5"
Depth: 74' - 8"

Keystone lintels and an arched transom over the entry spell classic design for this four-bedroom home. The tiled foyer offers entry to any room you choose, whether it's the secluded den with built-in bookshelves, the formal dining room, the formal living room with fireplace, or the spacious rear family room and kitchen area with a sunny breakfast nook. The first-floor master suite features a sitting room with bookshelves, two walk-in closets, and a private bath with a corner whirlpool tub. Upstairs, two family bedrooms share a bath and have separate vanities. A third family bedroom features its own full bath and a built-in, box-bayed window seat.

First Floor

Second Floor

Family Homes

Plan: HPK3200403

First Floor: 2,506 sq. ft.
Second Floor: 1,415 sq. ft.
Total: 3,921 sq. ft.
Bedrooms: 4
Bathrooms: 3 ½

Width: 80' - 5"
Depth: 50' - 4"
Foundation: Slab,
Unfinished Basement

A stately two-story home with a gracious, manorly exterior features a large, arched entryway as its focal point. Excellent brick detailing and quoins help make this exterior one of a kind. The large, two-story family area is adjacent to the living room with a cathedral ceiling and formal fireplace—a convenient arrangement for entertaining large groups or just a cozy evening at home. A wrapping patio area allows for dining outdoors. The large kitchen is centrally located, with a second stairway leading to the second floor. The master suite features a volume ceiling and a sitting area overlooking the rear yard. The huge master bath includes two walk-in closets. The upper balcony overlooks the family area and the entryway.

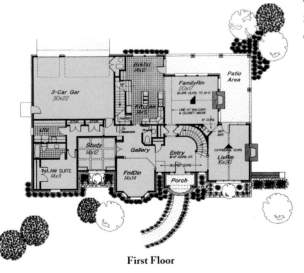

First Floor

Second Floor

© The Sater Design Collection, Inc.

First Floor

Second Floor

Plan: HPK3200404

First Floor: 2,794 sq. ft.	Bathrooms: 3 ½
Second Floor: 1,127 sq. ft.	Width: 85' - 0"
Total: 3,921 sq. ft.	Depth: 76' - 8"
Bedrooms: 4	Foundation: Slab

Elegance is well-displayed on this European manor by its stone-and-stucco facade, multipane windows, grand entrance, and varied rooflines. The grand foyer introduces the formal dining room on the left and a spacious formal living room directly ahead. The study and living room share a through-fireplace, and both have access to the backyard. The kitchen features a walk-in pantry, a cooktop island, a pass-through to the rear veranda, and an adjacent octagonal breakfast nook. Nearby, the leisure room is complete with a coffered ceiling, built-ins, and another fireplace. The master suite resides on the right side of the home and provides two walk-in closets and a lavish bath.

Family Homes

Plan: HPK3200405

First Floor: 2,513 sq. ft.
Second Floor: 1,421 sq. ft.
Total: 3,934 sq. ft.
Bonus Space: 596 sq. ft.
Bedrooms: 4

Bathrooms: 4 ½
Width: 72' - 0"
Depth: 93' - 0"
Foundation: Crawlspace

This luxury countryside cottage is at home in New England-style neighborhoods—perfect for the ideal American home. The foyer is flanked by a dining room and study. The great room is central, while the kitchen and breakfast nook are located to the left of the plan. A luxurious bath and walk-in closet are featured in the master suite. Three additional bedrooms and a media room are upstairs. A bonus room is above the garage.

First Floor

Second Floor

Plan: HPK3200406

First Floor: 2,751 sq. ft.	Width: 79' - 0"
Second Floor: 1,185 sq. ft.	Depth: 66' - 4"
Total: 3,936 sq. ft.	Foundation: Slab,
Bedrooms: 4	Unfinished Basement
Bathrooms: 3 ½	

With a grand brick facade, this home also boasts muntin windows, multilevel rooflines, keystone arches, and a dramatic entry. A cathedral-ceilinged living room, complete with a fireplace, and a family dining room flank the 20-foot-high entry. Relax in the family room, mix a drink from the wet bar, and look out through multiple windows to the covered veranda. A luxurious master suite includes a windowed sitting area overlooking the rear view and private patio, a full bath boasting a 10-foot ceiling, and a spacious walk-in closet. On the second level, three bedrooms share two full baths and a study area with a built-in desk.

First Floor

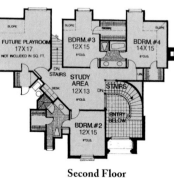

Second Floor

Family Homes

© William E. Poole Designs, Inc.

Plan: HPK3200407

First Floor: 2,653 sq. ft.
Second Floor: 1,286 sq. ft.
Total: 3,939 sq. ft.
Bonus Space: 583 sq. ft.
Bedrooms: 4

Bathrooms: 3 ½
Width: 77' - 8"
Depth: 81' - 6"
Foundation: Crawlspace

One covered front porch, twin chimneys, and a triplet of dormers add up to create the gorgeous facade of this country cottage. Through the impressive entry and into the foyer, look left to find a convenient powder room, straight ahead to see the friendly family room, and to the right to locate the living room (or library). The kitchen/breakfast area is convenient to the dining room and also provides access to the utility room near a double garage. To the far right of the first level sits the master suite and master bath, complete with a lavish tub and an enormous walk-in closet. The second level includes three bedrooms, two full baths, and a future rec room.

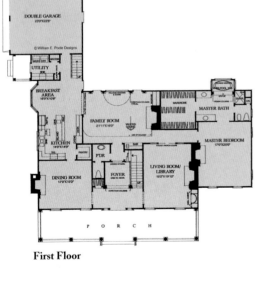

First Floor

Second Floor

© Stephen Fuller, Inc.

A symmetrical facade with twin chimneys makes a grand statement. A covered porch welcomes visitors and provides a pleasant place to spend a mild evening. The entry foyer is flanked by formal living areas—a dining room and a living room—each with a fireplace. A third fireplace is the highlight of the expansive great room to the rear. An L-shaped kitchen offers a work island and a walk-in pantry, and easily serves the nearby breakfast and sunrooms. The master suite provides lavish luxuries.

Plan: HPK3200408

First Floor: 2,565 sq. ft.	Width: 88' - 6"
Second Floor: 1,375 sq. ft.	Depth: 58' - 6"
Total: 3,940 sq. ft.	Foundation: Unfinished
Bedrooms: 4	Walkout Basement
Bathrooms: 3 ½	

First Floor

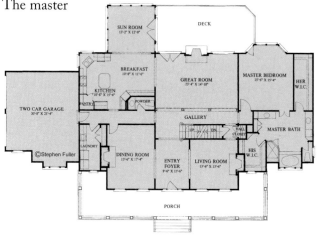

Second Floor

Family Homes

© The Sater Design Collection, Inc.

Plan: HPK3200409

Square Footage: 3,942	Width: 83' - 10"
Bedrooms: 3	Depth: 106' - 0"
Bathrooms: 4	Foundation: Slab

Welcome home to a country manor with Renaissance flair. Full-length, squint-style windows and brick accents bring Old World charm to a modern plan. Designed for flexibility, the open foyer, living room, and dining room have infinite decor options. Down a gallery (with art niches), two bedroom suites include private baths. The bon-vivant island kitchen is introduced with a wet bar and pool bath. In the leisure room, family and friends will revel in expansive views of the rear property. An outdoor kitchen on the lanai invites alfresco dining. Separated for ultimate privacy, the master suite is an exercise in luxurious living. Past the morning kitchen and into the grand bedroom, an octagonal sitting area is bathed in light. The bath is gracefully set in the turret, with a whirlpool tub and views of the master garden.

© William E. Poole Designs, Inc.

First Floor

Second Floor

© William E. Poole Designs

Plan: HPK3200410

First Floor: 2,767 sq. ft.
Second Floor: 1,179 sq. ft.
Total: 3,946 sq. ft.
Bonus Space: 591 sq. ft.
Bedrooms: 4

Bathrooms: 3 ½ + ½
Width: 79' - 11"
Depth: 80' - 6"
Foundation: Crawlspace

The grand entrance is reminiscent of Early American homes, and the exquisite interior does not disappoint. Formal living areas give way to the informal openness of the family room and adjoining breakfast area and island kitchen. Access to the rear terrace from this area makes alfresco meals an option. Upstairs houses three additional family bedrooms—two share a Jack-and-Jill bath—the third boasts a private, full bath. A future rec room completes this level.

Family Homes

Plan: HPK3200411

First Floor: 2,628 sq. ft.	Bathrooms: 4
Second Floor: 1,320 sq. ft.	Width: 92' - 0"
Total: 3,948 sq. ft.	Depth: 63' - 0"
Bedrooms: 5	Foundation: Slab

A centered cupola sets off the clean, simple lines of this cottage. Horizontal siding and history-rich details rethink tradition in a thoroughly modern plan drawn for livability and comfort. At the front of the home, massive columns line the wrapping entry porch. Inside, an unrestrained floor plan permits public and casual spaces to flex, with rooms that facilitate planned events as easily as they do family gatherings. Pocket doors seclude a library or study, which sports a beamed ceiling and grants private access to the solana. A main-level master suite features a tray ceiling, while upper-level secondary bedrooms access separate sun decks.

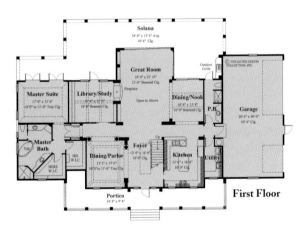

First Floor

Second Floor

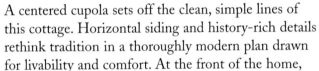

© William E. Poole Designs, Inc.

Plan: HPK3200412

First Floor: 2,416 sq. ft.	Bathrooms: 3 ½
Second Floor: 1,535 sq. ft.	Width: 79' - 2"
Total: 3,951 sq. ft.	Depth: 63' - 6"
Bonus Space: 552 sq. ft.	Foundation: Crawlspace,
Bedrooms: 5	Unfinished Basement

A curved front porch, graceful symmetry in the details, and the sturdiness of brick all combine to enhance this beautiful two-story home. Inside, the two-story foyer introduces the formal rooms—the living room to the right and the dining room to the left—and presents the elegant stairwell. The L-shaped kitchen provides a walk-in pantry, an island with a sink, a butler's pantry, and an adjacent breakfast area. Perfect for casual gatherings, the family room features a fireplace and backyard access. Located on the first floor for privacy, the master suite offers a large walk-in closet and a lavish bath. Upstairs, four bedrooms—each with a walk-in closet—share two full baths and access to the future recreation room over the garage.

First Floor

Second Floor

Family Homes

Plan: HPK3200413

First Floor: 1,541 sq. ft.
Second Floor: 1,408 sq. ft.
Third Floor: 1,016 sq. ft.
Total: 3,965 sq. ft.
Bedrooms: 4

Bathrooms: 3 ½
Width: 44' - 0"
Depth: 43' - 0"
Foundation: Unfinished
Basement

This Federal-style home is beautiful in its simplicity, with lintels above the windows and a row of dormers lining the side-gabled roof. The interior is a traditional center-hall layout, with formal rooms toward the front and more relaxed spaces in the back. A U-shaped kitchen is ideally positioned for serving the dining room, and is also near a circular breakfast room. Three fireplaces warm the rooms on the first floor, while a fourth hearth warms the master bedroom upstairs. A serene retreat, the master suite also includes a large bath with a double vanity and a long walk-in closet. The two remaining bedrooms on this floor share a full hall bath. There is an additional guest suite on the third floor, complete with its own bath and walk-in closet, as well as a spacious studio.

Second Floor

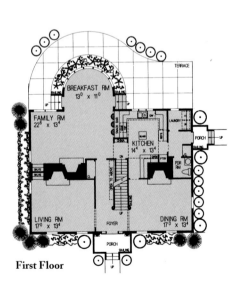

First Floor

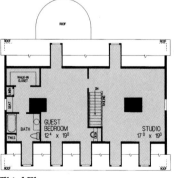

Third Floor

© The Sater Design Collection, Inc.

First Floor

Second Floor

Plan: HPK3200414

First Floor: 2,834 sq. ft.	Bathrooms: 3 ½
Second Floor: 1,143 sq. ft.	Width: 85' - 0"
Total: 3,977 sq. ft.	Depth: 76' - 8"
Bedrooms: 4	Foundation: Slab

Mediterranean accents enhance the facade of this contemporary estate home. Two fanciful turret bays add a sense of grandeur to the exterior. Double doors open inside to a grand two-story foyer. A two-sided fireplace warms the study and the coffered living room. To the right, the master suite includes a private bath, two walk-in closets, and double-door access to the sweeping rear veranda. Casual areas of the home include the gourmet island kitchen, breakfast nook, and leisure room warmed by a fireplace. A spiral staircase leads upstairs, where a second-floor balcony separates two family bedrooms from the luxurious guest suite.

Family Homes

Plan: HPK3200415

First Floor: 2,591 sq. ft.
Second Floor: 1,399 sq. ft.
Total: 3,990 sq. ft.
Bedrooms: 4

Bathrooms: 3 ½
Width: 61' - 4"
Depth: 75' - 0"
Foundation: Slab

A dramatic front stairway announces visitors and welcomes all onto a cozy covered porch. The foyer introduces the living room on the right and the dining area on the left. Straight ahead, the family room boasts a fireplace. The kitchen is set between the breakfast room and a petite outdoor porch—perfect for grilling. Secluded on the first floor for privacy, the master suite includes two luxuriously sized walk-in closets, private access to the rear deck, and a master bath with access to another porch out front. Upstairs, dormers enhance sunlight in two family bedrooms that share a full bath between them. A third bedroom uses the hall bath.

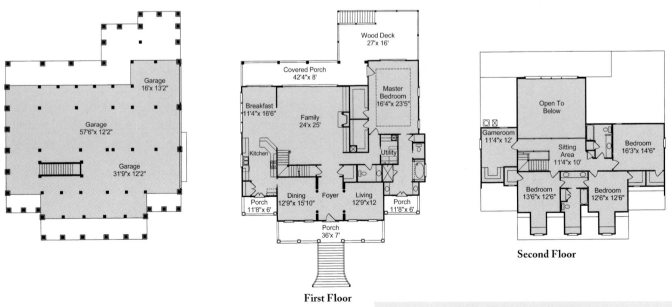

First Floor

Second Floor

Balancing Act

The exterior shows a seamless blend of complementing historical elements.

This home beautifully shows the great range of possibilities that a traditional facade can offer. First of all, the wide front porch, which wraps on the left side of the plan and allows for an alternate entry into the keeping room, is a feature normally found in farmhouses. But the nearly symmetrical facade and center gable are elements of Colonial architecture, as is the prominent chimney at the gable end. Lastly, the porte cochere was a popular Victorian extension. That the resulting exterior feels balanced and recognizable speaks for the skill with which the designer has combined these historical elements.

Interior spaces have been designed for high luxury. The left part of the plan is dominated by the home's kitchen and keeping room, which work together to form a large casual space for family dining and gathering. Still, decorative ceilings and a fireplace keep the area elegant. A host of utility rooms, such as the office and mudroom, handle household work.

At the home's center are the formal dining room, study, and great room. Two more fireplaces, arched openings, ornamental trim, and built-in shelves make this the home's showcase for fine furnishings and art. Two French doors from the great room allow access onto the covered rear deck.

The master suite is located at the right part of the plan and offers a long list of amenities: separate walk-ins and vanities, garden tub, bar, reading nook, private access to the deck, and wide views of the rear property. The result is a very fine and secluded getaway for the homeowners.

The plan's remaining bedrooms reside upstairs, spaced apart for privacy. Each room receives a deep walk-in closet and clear views of the surrounding landscape. Finishing the bonus space as a second suite is a good option for larger families or those with live-in parents.

Luxury Homes

ABOVE and BELOW: Upstairs bedrooms are spacious and come with unique views of the surrounding property.

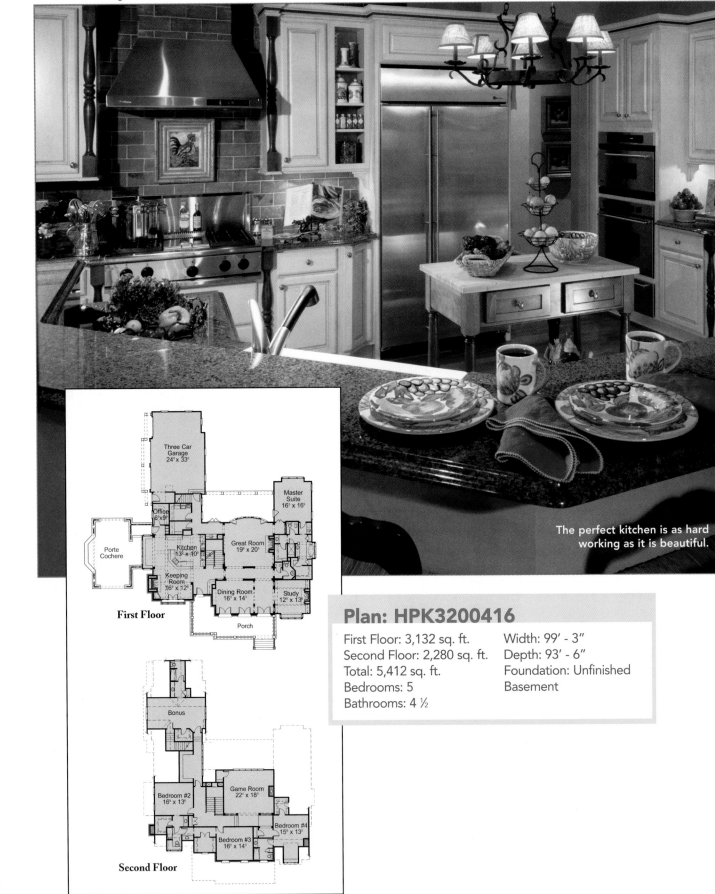

The perfect kitchen is as hard working as it is beautiful.

First Floor

Three Car Garage
24⁰ x 33⁰

Master Suite
16³ x 16⁶

Office
16⁶ x 9⁶

Porte Cochere

Kitchen
13⁶ x 10⁶

Great Room
19⁶ x 20³

Keeping Room
16⁶ x 12⁶

Dining Room
16³ x 14³

Study
12³ x 13⁶

Porch

Second Floor

Bonus

Bedroom #2
16⁸ x 13⁶

Game Room
22⁰ x 18⁰

Bedroom #4
15⁶ x 13⁶

Bedroom #3
16⁰ x 14⁰

Plan: HPK3200416

First Floor: 3,132 sq. ft.
Second Floor: 2,280 sq. ft.
Total: 5,412 sq. ft.
Bedrooms: 5
Bathrooms: 4 ½

Width: 99' - 3"
Depth: 93' - 6"
Foundation: Unfinished Basement

LEFT: Retire to the keeping room for warm, cozy evenings in with family and friends.

BELOW: The versatile bonus space can be finished as an art studio or study room.

Luxury Homes

Plan: HPK3200417

First Floor: 2,126 sq. ft.
Second Floor: 1,882 sq. ft.
Total: 4,008 sq. ft.
Bedrooms: 4
Bathrooms: 2 ½

Width: 92' - 0"
Depth: 64' - 4"
Foundation: Unfinished
Basement

This historical Georgian home has its roots in the 18th Century. The full two-story center section is delightfully complemented by the one-and-a-half-story wings. An elegant gathering room, three steps down from the rest of the house, provides ample space for entertaining on a grand scale. The study and the formal dining room flank the foyer. Each of these rooms has a fireplace as its highlight. The breakfast room, kitchen, powder room, and laundry room are arranged for maximum efficiency. The second floor houses the family bedrooms. Take special note of the spacious master suite.

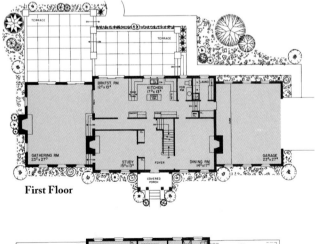

First Floor

Second Floor

First Floor

Second Floor

© The Sater Design Collection, Inc.

Plan: HPK3200418

First Floor: 2,867 sq. ft.	Bathrooms: 4 ½
Second Floor: 1,155 sq. ft.	Width: 71' - 6"
Total: 4,022 sq. ft.	Depth: 82' - 2"
Bonus Space: 371 sq. ft.	Foundation: Slab
Bedrooms: 4	

First Floor

Second Floor

Plan: HPK3200419

First Floor: 3,323 sq. ft.	Bathrooms: 4 ½
Second Floor: 700 sq. ft.	Width: 112' - 0"
Total: 4,023 sq. ft.	Depth: 65' - 0"
Bonus Space: 344 sq. ft.	Foundation: Slab
Bedrooms: 4	

Luxury Homes

First Floor

Second Floor

Plan: HPK3200420

First Floor: 2,608 sq. ft.
Second Floor: 1,432 sq. ft.
Total: 4,040 sq. ft.
Bedrooms: 4
Bathrooms: 3 ½

Width: 89' - 10"
Depth: 63' - 8"
Foundation: Crawlspace, Slab

First Floor

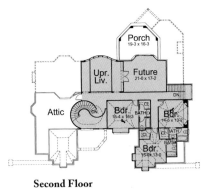

Second Floor

Plan: HPK3200421

First Floor: 2,901 sq. ft.
Second Floor: 1,140 sq. ft.
Total: 4,041 sq. ft.
Bonus Space: 522 sq. ft.
Bedrooms: 4

Bathrooms: 4 ½
Width: 80' - 0"
Depth: 70' - 0"
Foundation: Finished
Walkout Basement

Order blueprints anytime at
eplans.com or 1-800-521-6797

First Floor

Second Floor

Plan: HPK3200422

First Floor: 2,739 sq. ft.
Second Floor: 1,231 sq. ft.
Total: 3,970 sq. ft.
Bedrooms: 5
Bathrooms: 3 ½

Width: 98' - 0"
Depth: 45' - 10"
Foundation: Slab,
Unfinished Basement

photography, may differ from the actual blueprints. For more detailed information, please check the floor plans carefully.

Plan: HPK3200423

First Floor: 2,095 sq. ft.
Second Floor: 1,954 sq. ft.
Total: 4,049 sq. ft.
Bedrooms: 5
Bathrooms: 4 ½

Width: 56' - 0"
Depth: 63' - 0"
Foundation: Crawlspace,
Unfinished Walkout
Basement

First Floor

Second Floor

Luxury Homes

First Floor

Second Floor

Plan: HPK3200424

First Floor: 2,672 sq. ft.
Second Floor: 1,392 sq. ft.
Total: 4,064 sq. ft.
Bedrooms: 4

Bathrooms: 3 ½ + ½
Width: 80' - 0"
Depth: 57' - 0"
Foundation: Crawlspace

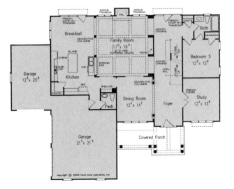

First Floor

Second Floor

Plan: HPK3200425

First Floor: 1,773 sq. ft.
Second Floor: 2,293 sq. ft.
Total: 4,066 sq. ft.
Bedrooms: 5
Bathrooms: 4 ½

Width: 69' - 0"
Depth: 54' - 4"
Foundation: Crawlspace,
Unfinished Walkout
Basement

Plan: HPK3200426

Square Footage: 4,095
Bonus Space: 599 sq. ft.
Bedrooms: 4

Bathrooms: 3 ½
Width: 98' - 0"
Depth: 77' - 6"

First Floor

Second Floor

Plan: HPK3200427

First Floor: 2,995 sq. ft.
Second Floor: 1,102 sq. ft.
Total: 4,097 sq. ft.
Bedrooms: 4

Bathrooms: 3 ½
Width: 120' - 6"
Depth: 58' - 8"
Foundation: Slab

Luxury Homes

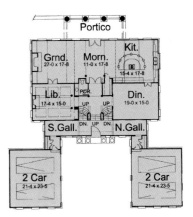

First Floor

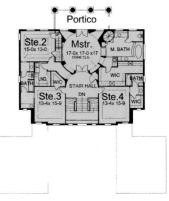

Second Floor

Plan: HPK3200428

First Floor: 2,175 sq. ft.
Second Floor: 1,927 sq. ft.
Total: 4,102 sq. ft.
Bedrooms: 4
Bathrooms: 3 ½

Width: 74' - 0"
Depth: 82' - 0"
Foundation: Finished
Walkout Basement

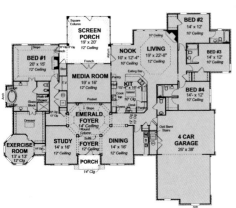

Plan: HPK3200429

Square Footage: 4,121
Bedrooms: 4
Bathrooms: 4 ½

Width: 99' - 10"
Depth: 81' - 0"

First Floor

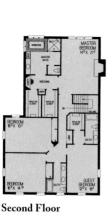

Second Floor

Plan: HPK3200430

First Floor: 2,086 sq. ft.
Second Floor: 2,040 sq. ft.
Total: 4,126 sq. ft.
Bedrooms: 4
Bathrooms: 3 ½

Width: 66' - 0"
Depth: 68' - 4"
Foundation: Unfinished
Basement

Plan: HPK3200431

First Floor: 2,037 sq. ft.
Second Floor: 2,098 sq. ft.
Total: 4,135 sq. ft.
Bedrooms: 5
Bathrooms: 4 ½

Width: 68' - 6"
Depth: 53' - 0"
Foundation: Crawlspace,
Slab, Unfinished Walkout
Basement

First Floor

Second Floor

Luxury Homes

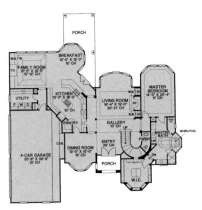

First Floor

Second Floor

Plan: HPK3200432

First Floor: 2,489 sq. ft.	Bedrooms: 4
Second Floor: 1,650 sq. ft.	Bathrooms: 3 ½
Total: 4,139 sq. ft.	Width: 72' - 8"
Bonus Space: 366 sq. ft.	Depth: 77' - 0"

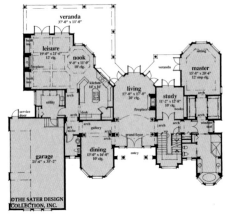

First Floor

©THE SATER DESIGN COLLECTION, INC.

© The Sater Design Collection, Inc.

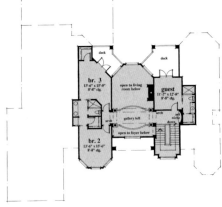

Second Floor

Plan: HPK3200433

First Floor: 3,053 sq. ft.	Width: 87' - 4"
Second Floor: 1,087 sq. ft.	Depth: 80' - 4"
Total: 4,140 sq. ft.	Foundation: Unfinished
Bedrooms: 4	Basement
Bathrooms: 3 ½	

Luxury Homes

First Floor

Second Floor

Plan: HPK3200434

First Floor: 2,572 sq. ft.
Second Floor: 1,578 sq. ft.
Total: 4,150 sq. ft.
Bonus Space: 315 sq. ft.
Bedrooms: 4

Bathrooms: 4 ½
Width: 78' - 2"
Depth: 68' - 0"
Foundation: Crawlspace

First Floor

Second Floor

Plan: HPK3200435

First Floor: 2,665 sq. ft.
Second Floor: 1,496 sq. ft.
Total: 4,161 sq. ft.
Bedrooms: 4
Bathrooms: 3 ½ + ½

Width: 73' - 8"
Depth: 65' - 0"
Foundation: Unfinished
Walkout Basement

Luxury Homes

First Floor

Second Floor

Plan: HPK3200436

First Floor: 3,168 sq. ft.
Second Floor: 998 sq. ft.
Total: 4,166 sq. ft.
Bonus Space: 210 sq. ft.
Bedrooms: 4

Bathrooms: 3 ½
Width: 90' - 0"
Depth: 63' - 5"
Foundation: Crawlspace, Slab, Unfinished Basement

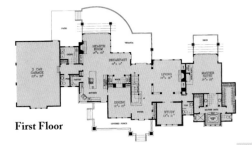

First Floor

Second Floor

Plan: HPK3200437

First Floor: 2,934 sq. ft.
Second Floor: 1,233 sq. ft.
Total: 4,167 sq. ft.
Bedrooms: 4
Bathrooms: 3 ½ + ½

Width: 118' - 7"
Depth: 48' - 11"
Foundation: Unfinished Basement

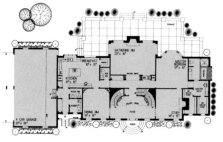

First Floor

Second Floor

Plan: HPK3200438

First Floor: 2,807 sq. ft.
Second Floor: 1,363 sq. ft.
Total: 4,170 sq. ft.
Bedrooms: 5
Bathrooms: 3 ½ + ½

Width: 109' - 4"
Depth: 47' - 0"
Foundation: Unfinished Basement

First Floor

Second Floor

Plan: HPK3200439

First Floor: 2,547 sq. ft.
Second Floor: 1,637 sq. ft.
Total: 4,184 sq. ft.
Bonus Space: 802 sq. ft.
Bedrooms: 4

Bathrooms: 3 ½
Width: 74' - 0"
Depth: 95' - 6"
Foundation: Crawlspace

Luxury Homes

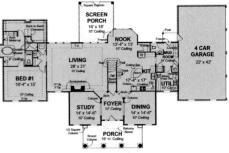

First Floor

Second Floor

Plan: HPK3200440

First Floor: 2,706 sq. ft.
Second Floor: 1,480 sq. ft.
Total: 4,186 sq. ft.
Bedrooms: 4

Bathrooms: 4 ½
Width: 102' - 0"
Depth: 63' - 0"

First Floor

Second Floor

Plan: HPK3200441

First Floor: 2,988 sq. ft.
Second Floor: 1,216 sq. ft.
Total: 4,204 sq. ft.
Bonus Space: 485 sq. ft.
Bedrooms: 4

Bathrooms: 4 ½ + ½
Width: 83' - 0"
Depth: 70' - 4"
Foundation: Crawlspace,
Unfinished Basement

Order blueprints anytime at
eplans.com or 1-800-521-6797

First Floor

Second Floor

Plan: HPK3200442

First Floor: 3,098 sq. ft.
Second Floor: 1,113 sq. ft.
Total: 4,211 sq. ft.
Bonus Space: 567 sq. ft.
Bedrooms: 4

Bathrooms: 3 ½
Width: 112' - 0"
Depth: 69' - 9"
Foundation: Crawlspace

© William E. Poole Designs, Inc.

Plan: HPK3200443

First Floor: 2,891 sq. ft.
Second Floor: 1,336 sq. ft.
Total: 4,227 sq. ft.
Bonus Space: 380 sq. ft.
Bedrooms: 4

Bathrooms: 3 ½ + ½
Width: 90' - 8"
Depth: 56' - 4"
Foundation: Crawlspace,
Unfinished Basement

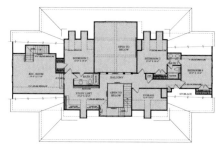

First Floor

Second Floor

Luxury Homes

First Floor

Second Floor

Plan: HPK3200444

First Floor: 2,950 sq. ft.
Second Floor: 1,278 sq. ft.
Total: 4,228 sq. ft.
Bedrooms: 4
Bathrooms: 4 ½

Width: 91' - 8"
Depth: 71' - 10"
Foundation: Crawlspace, Slab, Unfinished Basement

Optional Layout

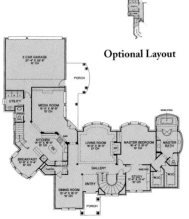

First Floor

Second Floor

Plan: HPK3200445

First Floor: 2,688 sq. ft.
Second Floor: 1,540 sq. ft.
Total: 4,228 sq. ft.
Bedrooms: 4

Bathrooms: 3 ½
Width: 84' - 3"
Depth: 80' - 1"

First Floor

Second Floor

Plan: HPK3200446

First Floor: 2,469 sq. ft.
Second Floor: 1,786 sq. ft.
Total: 4,255 sq. ft.
Bedrooms: 4

Bathrooms: 4
Width: 66' - 8"
Depth: 69' - 3"
Foundation: Crawlspace

First Floor

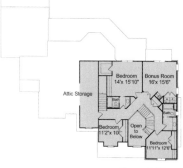

Second Floor

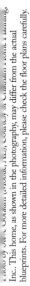

Plan: HPK3200447

First Floor: 2,859 sq. ft.
Second Floor: 1,398 sq. ft.
Total: 4,257 sq. ft.
Bonus Space: 253 sq. ft.
Bedrooms: 4

Bathrooms: 4
Width: 85' - 10"
Depth: 88' - 11"
Foundation: Slab

Luxury Homes

First Floor

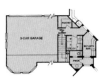

Optional Layout

Second Floor

Plan: HPK3200448

First Floor: 2,551 sq. ft.
Second Floor: 1,709 sq. ft.
Total: 4,260 sq. ft.
Bedrooms: 4

Bathrooms: 3 ½
Width: 98' - 8"
Depth: 67' - 0"

First Floor

Second Floor

Plan: HPK3200449

First Floor: 2,603 sq. ft.
Second Floor: 1,660 sq. ft.
Total: 4,263 sq. ft.
Bonus Space: 669 sq. ft.
Bedrooms: 4

Bathrooms: 4 ½ + ½
Width: 98' - 0"
Depth: 56' - 8"
Foundation: Unfinished
Basement

First Floor

Second Floor

Plan: HPK3200450

First Floor: 2,639 sq. ft.
Second Floor: 1,625 sq. ft.
Total: 4,264 sq. ft.
Bedrooms: 4
Bathrooms: 3 ½

Width: 73' - 8"
Depth: 58' - 6"
Foundation: Crawlspace, Slab, Unfinished Basement

First Floor

Plan: HPK3200451

First Floor: 2,577 sq. ft.
Second Floor: 1,703 sq. ft.
Total: 4,280 sq. ft.
Bedrooms: 4

Bathrooms: 3 ½
Width: 80' - 4"
Depth: 85' - 11"
Foundation: Crawlspace

Second Floor

from the actual blueprints. For more detailed information, please check the floor plans carefully.

Luxury Homes

Plan: HPK3200452

First Floor: 2,961 sq. ft.
Second Floor: 1,338 sq. ft.
Total: 4,299 sq. ft.
Bedrooms: 4
Bathrooms: 3 ½

Width: 100' - 8"
Depth: 73' - 8"
Foundation: Unfinished Walkout Basement

This breathtaking home makes an unforgettable impression, beginning with a two-story sunlit entry. The great room welcomes with an architecturally intriguing coffered ceiling and a two-sided fireplace that shares its glow with the open hearth room.

The kitchen is equipped with plenty of work space and an island that seats five. An adjacent sunroom is a pleasant way to start the day. The master suite is located on this level, complete with a sitting area and lavish bath. Upstairs, three bedrooms have plenty of privacy.

First Floor

Second Floor

Plan: HPK3200453

First Floor: 2,266 sq. ft.
Second Floor: 2,060 sq. ft.
Total: 4,326 sq. ft.
Bedrooms: 5
Bathrooms: 4 ½

Width: 67' - 0"
Depth: 55' - 0"
Foundation: Unfinished
Walkout Basement

Hipped rooflines, muntin windows, and a front porch with stately pillars invite you into this amazing two-story home. Especially appealing inside are the bay-windowed breakfast nook and two-story family room that overlook a rear sundeck. Its hearth fireplace and nearness to the kitchen will surely make the family room the attractive pole of family gatherings. The first level also hosts a guest suite. Four more bedrooms, one a master suite, are upstairs. Homeowners will relax in an oversized shower or oval tub, quietly read in the bay-windowed sitting room, and sleep under a 13-foot tray ceiling. Mammoth His and Hers walk-in closets will adequately provide for their wardrobes. A three-car garage can be entered from a hall that connects to both the kitchen and the laundry.

First Floor

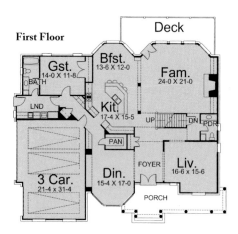

Second Floor

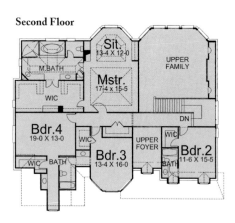

Luxury Homes

Plan: HPK3200454

First Floor: 2,857 sq. ft.
Second Floor: 1,469 sq. ft.
Total: 4,326 sq. ft.
Bonus Space: 473 sq. ft.
Bedrooms: 6

Bathrooms: 4 ½
Width: 89' - 0"
Depth: 62' - 0"
Foundation: Crawlspace

A classic Colonial exterior is the facade for a modern interior layout. A broken pediment and columns grace the entrance to a center-hall foyer that is unconventionally flanked by a dining room and guest room. The family room straight ahead openly leads to a covered porch while double doors separate the space from the more casual kitchen, breakfast area, and morning room. The master suite leaves little to be desired, with such amenities as His and Hers walk-in closets, a master bath, and a separate dressing room. The second floor holds such family-friendly spaces as four bedrooms, a study area, a playroom, and an exercise room, and it is surrounded by thoughtful attic storage.

First Floor

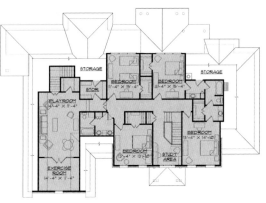

Second Floor

Luxury Homes

From its dramatic front entry to its rear twin turrets, this design is as traditional as it is historic. A two-story foyer opens through a gallery to an expansive gathering room, which shares its natural light with a bumped-out morning nook. A formal living room or study offers a coffered ceiling and a private door to the gallery hall that leads to the master suite. The dining room opens to more casual living space, including the kitchen with its angled island counter. Bonus space may be developed later.

Plan: HPK3200455

Main Level: 2,293 sq. ft.
Upper Level: 949 sq. ft.
Lower Level: 1,088 sq. ft.
Total: 4,330 sq. ft.
Bonus Space: 373 sq. ft.
Bedrooms: 4

Bathrooms: 4 ½
Width: 82' - 6"
Depth: 67' - 2"
Foundation: Finished Walkout Basement

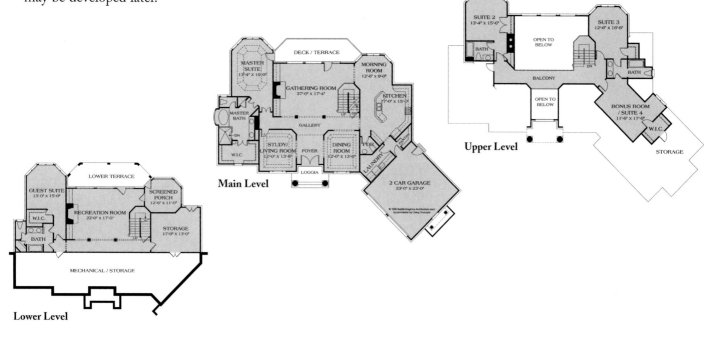

Lower Level

Main Level

Upper Level

Luxury Homes

Plan: HPK3200456

Main Level: 1,737 sq. ft.
Upper Level: 727 sq. ft.
Lower Level: 1,876 sq. ft.
Total: 4,340 sq. ft.
Bonus Space: 376 sq. ft.
Bedrooms: 4

Bathrooms: 2 ½
Width: 65' - 6"
Depth: 53' - 0"
Foundation: Finished Basement

The beauty and warmth of a brick facade adds stately elegance to this traditional design. Its open floor plan is highlighted by a two-story living room and open dining room. The kitchen includes a central cooking island and opens to a bright breakfast area. The master suite offers an ample walk-in closet/dressing area and a bath featuring an exquisite double vanity and a tub with corner windows. A bonus room over the two-car garage offers room for expansion.

Lower Level

Main Level

Upper Level

Plan: HPK3200457

First Floor: 3,056 sq. ft.	Bathrooms: 4 ½
Second Floor: 1,307 sq. ft.	Width: 94' - 4"
Total: 4,363 sq. ft.	Depth: 79' - 2"
Bonus Space: 692 sq. ft.	Foundation: Crawlspace,
Bedrooms: 4	Unfinished Basement

This fantasy begins as soon as you step from the porch into the two-story vaulted foyer. To the right sits the columned elegance of the formal dining room and, to the left, a personal library awaits. Steps away, the entrance to the master suite beckons with promises of a sitting area, morning kitchen, L-shaped walk-in closet, garden tub, separate shower, and dual vanities. The three family bedrooms upstairs each have a full bath and ample closet space. In addition to the bedrooms, the option of a game room/billiards room provides plenty of space for casual entertainment. A three-car garage completes this plan.

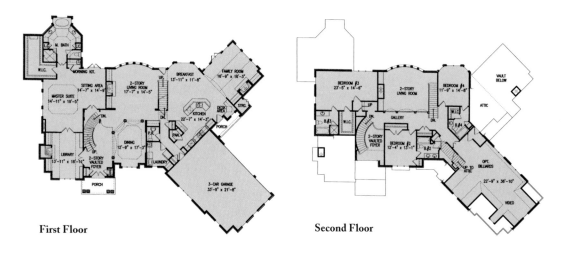

First Floor

Second Floor

Luxury Homes

Photography courtesy of Archival Designs - JoAnne Loftus. This home, as shown in the photography, may differ from the actual blueprints. For more detailed information, please

Plan: HPK3200458

First Floor: 2,914 sq. ft.
Second Floor: 1,450 sq. ft.
Total: 4,364 sq. ft.
Bedrooms: 4
Bathrooms: 4 ½

Width: 67' - 8"
Depth: 70' - 2"
Foundation: Unfinished
Walkout Basement

Keystone arches and a pedimented entry grace the facade of this luxury home. The grand salon, a family room, the dining hall and a library revolve around a central foyer with curved stair. An island gourmet kitchen is open to the family room and a sunny morning room. The master suite is conveniently placed on the first floor and features a bath with spa tub, separate shower and two vanities. The second level holds three bedrooms with walk-in closets and private baths, plus a bonus room that can be developed later.

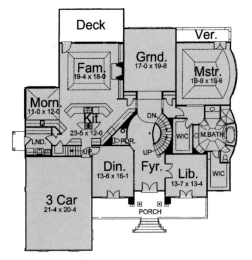

First Floor

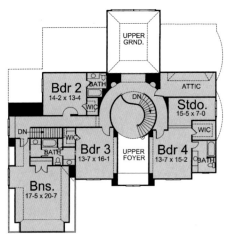

Second Floor

First Floor

Plan: HPK3200459

First Floor: 3,026 sq. ft.   Bathrooms: 3 ½
Second Floor: 1,377 sq. ft.   Width: 87' - 0"
Total: 4,403 sq. ft.   Depth: 80' - 9"
Bedrooms: 4

Rich with character and personality, this luxury home makes a tasteful addition to any fine neighborhood. The recessed entry leads straight ahead to formal living and dining areas defined by columns and graced with arches. Natural light from these rooms illuminates the gallery hall, which leads to a fantastic kitchen and bayed breakfast nook. The family room ushers in sunlight and the warmth of a fireplace. Located at the right rear, the master suite exemplifies splendor; the bedroom is lit by a full bay window, and the opulent bath includes separate His and Hers amenities. A central shower abuts the step-up garden tub. Upstairs, three generous bedrooms delight in dormer windows.

Second Floor

Luxury Homes

Plan: HPK3200460

First Floor: 2,768 sq. ft.
Second Floor: 1,662 sq. ft.
Total: 4,430 sq. ft.
Bedrooms: 4

Bathrooms: 3 ½
Width: 75' - 6"
Depth: 96' - 6"
Foundation: Crawlspace

This country cottage has the style you're looking for and the comforts and amenities you deserve. Across the impressive foyer, the library and dining room face each other, both with cozy fireplaces. A third fireplace is located in the gathering room, where terrace access and a wet bar make it a great place for entertaining. The island kitchen is a chef's delight and easily serves both eating areas. The master suite encompasses the left wing, with the splendor of a tray ceiling, abundant natural light, and a sumptuous bayed-tub bath. Upstairs, two dormer-lit bedrooms share a full bath; the remaining bedroom shares a bath with the recreation room.

First Floor

Second Floor

**Order blueprints anytime at
eplans.com or 1-800-521-6797**

Luxury Homes

This charming ranch home gets its inspiration from classic farmhouses of long ago. Eight columns grace the facade, creating a porch area perfect for enjoying a cool summer evening. As you enter, find a formal dining room to the left and a second bedroom/den to the right—both with cathedral ceilings. Straight ahead, the great room has an impressive view of the backyard through a wall of windows. The kitchen features an eat-in island and flows easily into the nook. An adjacent sunroom has French doors that open to a large wood deck. The master suite features a unique tray ceiling, large walk-in closet, and spa tub. On the lower level, a spacious recreation room with wet bar and three additional bedrooms with walk-in closets serve all your entertainment needs.

Plan: HPK3200461

Main Level: 2,614 sq. ft.
Lower Level: 1,827 sq. ft.
Total: 4,441 sq. ft.
Bedrooms: 5
Bathrooms: 4 ½

Width: 80' - 4"
Depth: 91' - 8"
Foundation: Finished Basement

Main Level

Lower Level

Luxury Homes

Plan: HPK3200462

First Floor: 3,249 sq. ft.	Bedrooms: 4
Second Floor: 1,202 sq. ft.	Bathrooms: 4 ½
Total: 4,451 sq. ft.	Width: 89' - 0"
Bonus Space: 240 sq. ft.	Depth: 65' - 0"

The classic design of this country farmhouse has a comforting appeal. A wide footprint allows for a long front porch that spans across the majority of the facade. Inside, the living room is at the center of activity, with a fireplace flanked by rear-facing windows and the kitchen and nook nearby. A bedroom in upper left corner of the plan gives guests appreciated privacy, while homeowners receive the same luxury from secluded Bedroom 1. This master suite feature such amenities as a compartmented bath and an island walk-in wardrobe. Two more bedrooms—each with a full bath—can be found upstairs, along with a game room that will surely be a popular spot for entertainment.

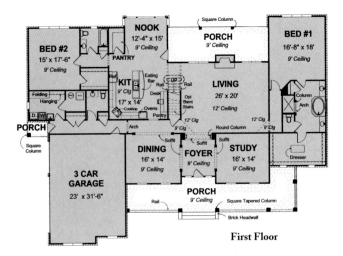

First Floor

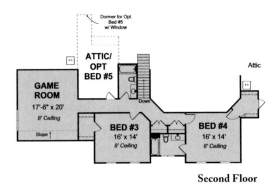

Second Floor

© The Sater Design Collection, Inc.

With European and Southern Colonial influences, this striking five-bedroom stucco home allows plenty of room for family and friends, and every amenity on your wish list. A stylish, open foyer presents access to all living areas. The library/study will delight with a beamed ceiling, built-in shelves, and French doors to a private porch. The formal dining room and two-story living room are elegant and bathed in natural light. The guest suite offers a private bath and double doors to the loggia. A country kitchen, bayed breakfast nook, and leisure room (with a fireplace) are open to each other—a popular feature. Upstairs, three generous family suites access private baths and balconies. The sprawling master suite is lovely and bright, with a private sun porch and a spa bath with a corner whirlpool tub. Not to be missed: a convenient utility room on the upper level.

Plan: HPK3200463

First Floor: 2,164 sq. ft.	Bathrooms: 5 ½
Second Floor: 2,311 sq. ft.	Width: 58' - 0"
Total: 4,475 sq. ft.	Depth: 65' - 0"
Bedrooms: 5	Foundation: Slab

First Floor

Second Floor

Luxury Homes

Plan: HPK3200464

First Floor: 2,267 sq. ft.
Second Floor: 2,209 sq. ft.
Total: 4,476 sq. ft.
Bedrooms: 4

Bathrooms: 3 ½
Width: 67' - 2"
Depth: 64' - 10"
Foundation: Crawlspace

Keystone arches, a wonderful turret, vertical shutters, and decorative stickwork over the entry add to the charm of this fine home. A formal dining room at the front of the plan is complemented by the breakfast bay at the rear. An angled snack bar/counter separates the island kitchen from the gathering room. An adjoining recreation room offers a wet bar and a second flight of stairs to the sleeping quarters. Bay windows brighten the master suite and a second suite, both with private baths. Two more bedrooms share a full bath that includes a dressing area and twin vanities. The laundry room is on this level for convenience.

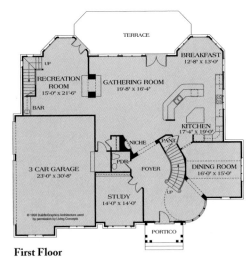

First Floor

Second Floor

Order blueprints anytime at
eplans.com or 1-800-521-6797

Plan: HPK3200465

First Floor: 2,430 sq. ft.	Width: 65' - 0"
Second Floor: 2,050 sq. ft.	Depth: 69' - 0"
Total: 4,480 sq. ft.	Foundation: Unfinished
Bedrooms: 5	Walkout Basement
Bathrooms: 4 ½	

Borrow rooflines from the Norman French, add Palladian windows and a gallantly arched entry, and you'll discover the stunning facade of this estate home. The main level contains spacious living and dining areas that include a grand room with fireplace and deck, a formal dining room, a keeping room, and a casual breakfast nook. The kitchen contains a wonderful walk-in pantry. A home office and self-contained guest suite grace the left side of the main level. Upstairs are a master suite with sitting room and three family bedrooms. Bedroom 2 features a private bath.

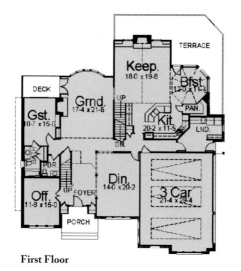

First Floor

Second Floor

Luxury Homes

Photo courtesy of William E. Poole Designs, Inc. Wilmington NC. This home, as shown in the

Plan: HPK3200466

First Floor: 2,968 sq. ft.
Second Floor: 1,521 sq. ft.
Total: 4,489 sq. ft.
Bonus Space: 522 sq. ft.
Bedrooms: 4

Bathrooms: 4 ½ + ½
Width: 82' - 6"
Depth: 81' - 8"
Foundation: Crawlspace

This home—showcasing elegant Georgian architecture—is reminiscent of the grand homes in the battery section of Charleston, South Carolina. The entry opens to the foyer with a grand staircase. To the right is the hearth-warmed library and to the left, the formal dining room. The foyer leads to the family room where a window wall looks out to the covered porch. A central hall passes the study and proceeds to the luxurious master suite, featuring a windowed tub and a huge walk-in closet. The left wing holds the sunny breakfast area, island kitchen, spacious mudroom, and garage. Upstairs, three bedrooms enjoy private baths and ample closet space.

First Floor

Second Floor

First Floor

Second Floor

Plan: HPK3200467

First Floor: 3,143 sq. ft.
Second Floor: 1,348 sq. ft.
Total: 4,491 sq. ft.
Bonus Space: 368 sq. ft.
Bedrooms: 4

Bathrooms: 3 ½
Width: 89' - 4"
Depth: 85' - 9"
Foundation: Crawlspace

A hipped roof, quoins, and both Palladian and sunburst windows present a beautiful exterior on this four-bedroom plan. Flanking the two-story foyer are a formal dining room to the left and a den or study to the right. Straight ahead, under a balcony defined by yet more pillars, is the spacious grand room. A full wall of windows along the back of the grand room will brighten it during the day; the fireplace, set in built-ins, will warm it during the evening. The already large kitchen, complete with an island and a snack-bar counter, is enhanced by a bayed morning nook and a hearth-warmed gathering room that accesses the rear property. The master bedroom suite is lavish with its amenities, which include a bayed sitting area, direct access to the rear terrace, a walk-in closet, and a sumptuous bath.

Luxury Homes

Plan: HPK3200468

First Floor: 2,557 sq. ft.
Second Floor: 1,939 sq. ft.
Total: 4,496 sq. ft.
Bedrooms: 4
Bathrooms: 3 ½ + ½

Width: 97' - 4"
Depth: 53' - 0"
Foundation: Unfinished Basement

The decorative half-timbers and stone-clad exterior on this manor are stately examples of Tudor architecture. A grand double staircase is the highlight of the elegant, two-story foyer that opens to each of the main living areas. The living and gathering rooms are anchored by impressive central fireplaces. Filled with amenities, the island kitchen has a nearby breakfast room for casual meals. The butler's pantry functions with both the kitchen and the formal dining room. The quiet study is accessible from both the gathering and living rooms. The outstanding master suite features a cozy bedroom fireplace, a picturesque whirlpool bath, and a convenient walk-in closet. Three additional second-floor bedrooms include a guest suite with a dressing room and a walk-in closet.

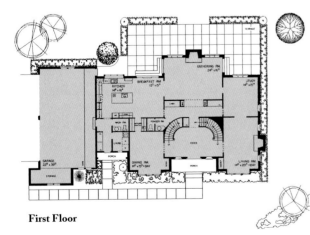

First Floor

Second Floor

Plan: HPK3200469

Main Level: 2,425 sq. ft.
Upper Level: 1,398 sq. ft.
Lower Level: 705 sq. ft.
Total: 4,528 sq. ft.
Bonus Space: 176 sq. ft.
Bedrooms: 4

Bathrooms: 3 ½
Width: 64' - 10"
Depth: 66' - 4"
Foundation: Finished Basement

Stone accents lend European flavor to this enchanting, modern home. A bonus space upstairs and future space in the basement allow endless opportunities for expansion and redesign. The first floor begins with a two-story foyer that opens up to a formal dining room on the left and an expansive gathering room ahead. Adorned by columns, a fireplace, and French doors, the gathering room will be the heart of the home. An open kitchen features "boomerang" counters, one a cooktop island and the other a double-sink serving bar. The sun room opens through French doors to the veranda. On the far right, tucked away for privacy, the master suite is a dream come true. A romantic fireplace, deck access, and a lavish bath with a garden tub are the ultimate in luxury. The upper level can be accessed by two staircases and includes three suites and future space.

Main Level

Lower Level

Upper Level

Luxury Homes

© William E. Poole Designs, Inc.

Plan: HPK3200470

First Floor: 2,998 sq. ft.
Second Floor: 1,556 sq. ft.
Total: 4,554 sq. ft.
Bonus Space: 741 sq. ft.
Bedrooms: 4

Bathrooms: 4 ½
Width: 75' - 6"
Depth: 91' - 2"
Foundation: Crawlspace

The paired double-end chimneys, reminiscent of the Georgian style of architecture, set this design apart from the rest. The covered entry opens to the columned foyer with the dining room on the left and the living room on the right, each enjoying the warmth and charm of a fireplace. Beyond the grand staircase, the family room delights with a third fireplace and a window wall that opens to the terrace. The expansive kitchen and breakfast area sit on the far left; the master suite is secluded on the right with its pampering private bath. The second floor holds three additional bedrooms (including a second master bedroom), three full baths, a computer room, and the future recreation room.

First Floor

Second Floor

Plan: HPK3200471

First Floor: 3,033 sq. ft.
Second Floor: 1,545 sq. ft.
Total: 4,578 sq. ft.
Bedrooms: 4
Bathrooms: 3 ½ + ½

Width: 91' - 6"
Depth: 63' - 8"
Foundation: Crawlspace, Slab, Unfinished Basement

This majestic storybook cottage, from the magical setting of rural Europe, provides the perfect home for any large family. A graceful staircase cascades from the two-story foyer. To the left, a sophisticated study offers a wall of built-ins. To the right, a formal dining room is easily served from the island kitchen. The breakfast room accesses the rear screened porch. Fireplaces warm the great room and keeping room. Two sets of double doors open from the great room to the rear covered porch. The master bedroom features private porch access, a sitting area, lavish bath, and two walk-in closets. Upstairs, three additional family bedrooms offer walk-in closet space galore! The game room is great entertainment for both young and old. A three-car garage with golf-cart storage completes the plan.

First Floor

Second Floor

Luxury Homes

Plan: HPK3200472

First Floor: 2,453 sq. ft.
Second Floor: 2,138 sq. ft.
Total: 4,591 sq. ft.
Bedrooms: 5
Bathrooms: 4

Width: 80' - 0"
Depth: 67' - 0"
Foundation: Unfinished Basement

Accommodate your life's diverse pattern of formal occasions and casual times with this spacious home. The exterior of this estate presents a palatial bearing, while the interior is both comfortable and elegant. Formal areas are graced with amenities to make entertaining easy. Casual areas are kept intimate, but no less large. The solarium serves both with skylights and terrace access. Guests will appreciate a private guest room and a bath with loggia access on the first floor. Family bedrooms and the master suite are upstairs. Note the gracious ceiling treatments in the master bedroom, its sitting room, and Bedroom 2.

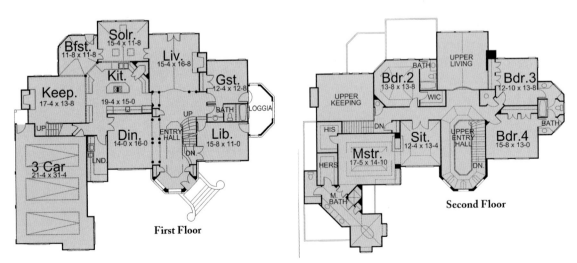

First Floor

Second Floor

The hipped-roof, French Country exterior, and porte-cochere entrance are just the beginning of this unique and impressive design. An unusual Pullman ceiling graces the foyer as it leads to the formal dining room on the right, to the study with a fireplace on the left, and straight ahead to the formal living room with its covered patio access. A gallery directs you to the island kitchen with its abundant counter space and adjacent sun-filled breakfast bay. On the left side of the home, a spectacular master suite will become your favorite haven and the envy of guests. The master bedroom includes a coffered ceiling, a bayed sitting area, and patio access. The master bath features a large, doorless shower, a separate exercise room, and a huge walk-in closet with built-in chests. All of the family bedrooms offer private baths and walk-in closets.

Plan: HPK3200473

Square Footage: 4,615	Width: 109' - 10"
Bedrooms: 4	Depth: 89' - 4"
Bathrooms: 4 ½	Foundation: Slab

Luxury Homes

Plan: HPK3200474

First Floor: 3,337 sq. ft.
Second Floor: 1,292 sq. ft.
Total: 4,629 sq. ft.
Bedrooms: 4

Bathrooms: 4 ½
Width: 84' - 10"
Depth: 102' - 3"

Dreaming of a home with estate-like elegance and cottage allure? Explore this flexible small-scale chateau. Allow your guests the delight of wandering through the garden courtyard just off the dining room before dinner. Retire to the handsome den, with soaring 14-foot ceilings, for a nightcap and conversation. Prepare holiday pastries in the chef's kitchen with friends to keep you company in the comfortable breakfast room. Feel closer without sacrificing space in the open family room fully outfitted with built-ins and a stunning extended-hearth fireplace.

First Floor

Second Floor

Plan: HPK3200475

Main Level: 2,394 sq. ft.	Bathrooms: 4 ½
Upper Level: 792 sq. ft.	Width: 67' - 0"
Lower Level: 1,486 sq. ft.	Depth: 93' - 2"
Total: 4,672 sq. ft.	Foundation: Finished
Bonus Space: 450 sq. ft.	Walkout Basement
Bedrooms: 4	

A trio of gables allow light to filter inside through original and decorative windows on this contemporary design. A side-loading, three-car garage provides more than enough room for the family fleet, and includes storage! Enter from the portico into the foyer and you'll be facing the hearth-warmed great room that connects to the dining room—and each room has sliding-door access to the rear terrace. To the far left is the master bedroom, complete with a reading room and lavish bath. To the far right are the sunroom, breakfast nook, and island kitchen. Two bedrooms, each with a private bath, reside upstairs with the bonus room.

Lower Level

Main Level

Upper Level

Luxury Homes

Plan: HPK3200476

First Floor: 3,248 sq. ft.
Second Floor: 1,426 sq. ft.
Total: 4,674 sq. ft.
Bedrooms: 5
Bathrooms: 5 ½ + ½

Width: 99' - 10"
Depth: 74' - 10"
Foundation: Slab,
Unfinished Basement

Multiple rooflines; a facade of stone, brick, and siding; and an absolutely grand entrance combine to give this home the look of luxury. A striking family room showcases a beautiful fireplace framed with built-ins. The nearby breakfast room streams with light and accesses the rear patio. The kitchen features an island workstation, walk-in pantry, and plenty of counter space. A guest suite is available on the first floor, perfect for when family members visit. The first-floor master suite offers easy access to a large study, bayed sitting room, and luxurious bath. Private baths are also included for each of the upstairs bedrooms.

Luxury Homes

Plan: HPK3200477

First Floor: 2,472 sq. ft.	Width: 80' - 8"
Second Floor: 2,207 sq. ft.	Depth: 52' - 0"
Total: 4,679 sq. ft.	Foundation: Unfinished
Bedrooms: 5	Basement
Bathrooms: 3 ½ + ½	

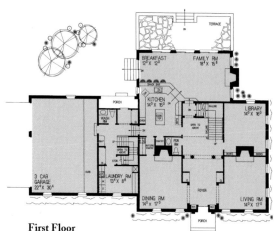

First Floor

Second Floor

Recalling the grandeur of its Maryland ancestors, this manor house is replete with exterior details that make it special: keystoned lintels, fluted pilasters, a dormered attic, and a pedimented doorway. The centerhall floor plan allows formal living and dining areas to the front of the plan. Complementing these are the cozy library and large family room/breakfast room area. A service entrance off the garage holds a laundry room and wash room. Upstairs bedrooms allow more than adequate space. Over the garage is a complete guest apartment with living area, office, bedroom, bath, and kitchen.

Luxury Homes

Plan: HPK3200478

Main Level: 2,563 sq. ft.
Upper Level: 298 sq. ft.
Lower Level: 1,870 sq. ft.
Total: 4,731 sq. ft.
Bonus Space: 532 sq. ft.
Bedrooms: 3

Bathrooms: 3 ½
Width: 84' - 2"
Depth: 89' - 3"
Foundation: Finished
Walkout Basement

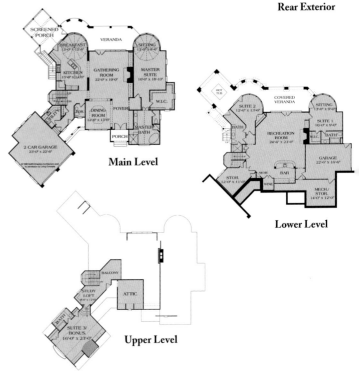

Rear Exterior

Arched gables and windows, a recessed entry, and varied rooflines complement the brick-and-stone facade of this French Country beauty. Inside, beyond the foyer, a generous gathering room with a fireplace awaits. The island kitchen features a breakfast nook, plenty of counter space, and access to a screened porch. The master bedroom is privately tucked away on the right side of the plan, complete with a roomy walk-in closet, an amenity-filled bath, and a sitting area that accesses the veranda. Downstairs houses two additional family bedrooms, each with a full bath and doors leading to the veranda. A wet bar and wine storage area make the recreation room a perfect place to entertain guests. The upper level harbors a fourth bedroom/bonus room, full bath, and study loft.

Main Level

Lower Level

Upper Level

Plan: HPK3200479

First Floor: 2,380 sq. ft.
Second Floor: 2,372 sq. ft.
Total: 4,752 sq. ft.
Bedrooms: 4
Bathrooms: 4 ½ + ½

Width: 82' - 0"
Depth: 59' - 0"
Foundation: Unfinished
Walkout Basement

Designed for a sloping lot, this outstanding stone manor will bring "ooh"s and "aah"s from every passerby. Enter under a beautiful pediment to the grand foyer, expanding to the box-bay family room. Here, arches, columns, and a see-through fireplace make it a special retreat. The kitchen features a large island with seating for four that overlooks the fireplace. A sunny nook opens to the deck and sun porch. The formal dining and living rooms are at the front of the home, taking in plenty of natural light. Four upstairs bedroom suites include a master suite with a romantic fireplace and soothing bath. An upper-level den is a thoughtful touch. A four-car garage completes the plan.

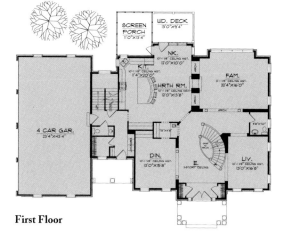

First Floor

Second Floor

Luxury Homes

Plan: HPK3200480

Main Level: 3,040 sq. ft.	Bathrooms: 4 ½ + ½
Lower Level: 1,736 sq. ft.	Width: 106' - 5"
Total: 4,776 sq. ft.	Depth: 104' - 2"
Bedrooms: 5	

Looking a bit like a mountain resort, this fine rustic-style home is sure to be the envy of your neighborhood. Upon entering through the elegant front door, find an open staircase to the right and a spacious great room directly ahead. Here, a fireplace and a wall of windows give a cozy welcome. A lavish master suite begins with a sitting room, complete with a fireplace, and continues to a private porch, large walk-in closet, and sumptuous bedroom. The gourmet kitchen adjoins a sunny dining room that offers access to a screened porch.

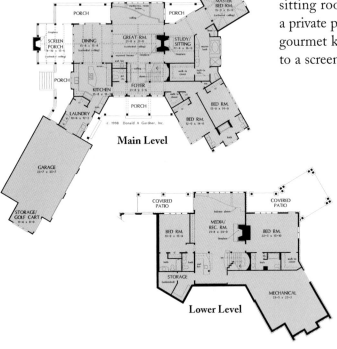

Main Level

Lower Level

Luxury Homes

Plan: HPK3200481

First Floor: 2,810 sq. ft.
Second Floor: 1,990 sq. ft.
Total: 4,800 sq. ft.
Bonus Space: 570 sq. ft.
Bedrooms: 4

Bathrooms: 3 ½ + ½
Width: 72' - 0"
Depth: 87' - 0"
Foundation: Unfinished Basement

Dormers, a brick facade, and a columned entryway splendidly express the inviting decor of this two-story traditional home. Designed to meet the needs of a growing family, the upper level includes three bedrooms, two bathrooms, a playroom, and a library. One of the bedrooms has a sitting area that could also accommodate a desk for a student. Loads of storage space is also available. On the lower level, a living room opens onto a screened veranda. It also has access to the island kitchen, family room, and sunlit breakfast bay. The kitchen opens to a rear patio, adjoins a small office, and is linked to a three-car side-loading garage. A gorgeous master suite features oversized His and Hers walk-in closets.

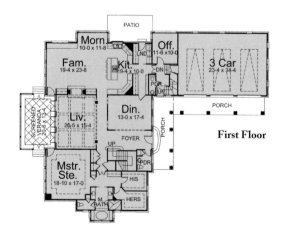

First Floor

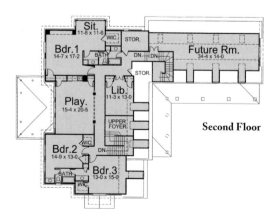

Second Floor

Luxury Homes

Plan: HPK3200482

Main Level: 2,094 sq. ft.
Upper Level: 874 sq. ft.
Lower Level: 1,904 sq. ft.
Total: 4,872 sq. ft.
Bedrooms: 3

Bathrooms: 2 ½
Width: 61' - 6"
Depth: 72' - 8"
Foundation: Finished
Walkout Basement

Indoor-outdoor relationships define this transitional stone-and-stucco home. Positioned to take advantage of natural light, the sunroom provides a great alternative to the lakeside dining room. Both are convenient to the island kitchen. The first-floor master suite provides access to the rear deck. Don't miss the His and Hers walk-in closets and sumptuous bath here. Upstairs, the captain's quarters views not only the hearth-warmed gathering room, but also the rear deck. Two family bedrooms sharing a full bath round out this level.

Lower Level

Main Level

Upper Level

Order blueprints anytime at
eplans.com or 1-800-521-6797

Plan: HPK3200483

First Floor: 3,265 sq. ft.	Width: 73' - 0"
Second Floor: 1,634 sq. ft.	Depth: 84' - 0"
Total: 4,899 sq. ft.	Foundation: Unfinished
Bedrooms: 4	Walkout Basement
Bathrooms: 4 ½ + ½	

An impressive curved stairway greets those who enter this stately Neoclassical manor. Luxury appointments, such as a study, master stateroom, private bath, and oversized walk-in closet, serve to pamper homeowners. The remaining rooms do the same for family and guests. The grand salon, with a robust center fireplace, opens to the dining room, where double doors lead to the more casual atmosphere for the family and morning rooms. All of the public spaces are convenient to an island kitchen with working snack bar. Venture upstairs to find three additional bedroom suites as well as a computer room and a bonus room for future development.

First Floor

Second Floor

Luxury Homes

Photo courtesy of Living Concepts Home Planning. This home, as shown in the photography, may differ from the actual blueprints. For more detailed information, please check the floor plans carefully.

Plan: HPK3200484

First Floor: 2,733 sq. ft.	Bathrooms: 4 ½ + ½
Second Floor: 2,206 sq. ft.	Width: 93' - 7"
Total: 4,939 sq. ft.	Depth: 78' - 8"
Bonus Space: 350 sq. ft.	Foundation: Crawlspace
Bedrooms: 4	

A pedimented entrance leads to a two-story foyer flanked by a formal dining room and a study/living room. The angled kitchen looks into the sunny morning room and the two-story gathering room. Located on the first floor for privacy, the master bedroom suite is sure to please. It includes a huge walk-in closet, a separate shower and tub, and a detailed ceiling. Three suites are upstairs and include private baths. An exercise room, bonus room, and powder room finish this floor.

First Floor

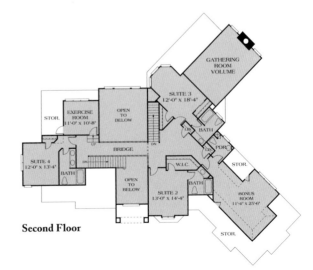

Second Floor

Plan: HPK3200485

First Floor: 2,782 sq. ft.
Second Floor: 2,181 sq. ft.
Total: 4,963 sq. ft.
Bedrooms: 4
Bathrooms: 3 ½

Width: 68' - 0"
Depth: 75' - 4"
Foundation: Unfinished Basement

Large, open rooms and natural light make the interior of this striking brick home a place to remember. The two-story entry and hearth-warmed great room are defined by balcony overlooks from above; a two-story Palladian window graces the great room. On the left, a bayed living room and cozy den provide wonderful spots to relax. The gourmet kitchen features an unusual island with seating for four and effortlessly serves the breakfast nook and elegant dining room. A nearby sunroom offers year-round enjoyment. Upstairs, the master suite reigns supreme with a sitting area, lavish bath, awe-inspiring walk-in closet, and additional storage. Three secondary bedrooms complete the design.

First Floor

Second Floor

Luxury Homes

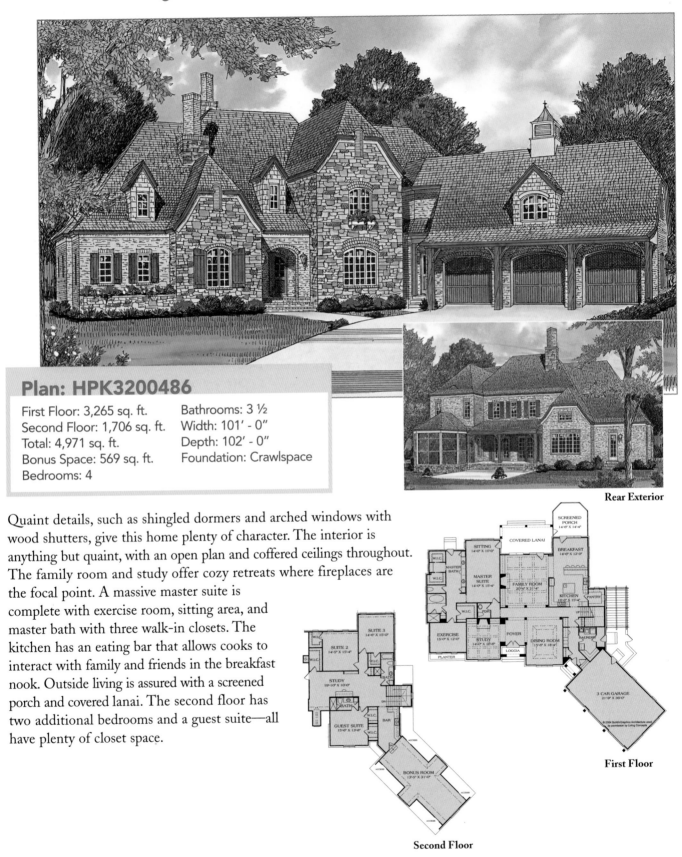

Plan: HPK3200486

First Floor: 3,265 sq. ft.
Second Floor: 1,706 sq. ft.
Total: 4,971 sq. ft.
Bonus Space: 569 sq. ft.
Bedrooms: 4

Bathrooms: 3 ½
Width: 101' - 0"
Depth: 102' - 0"
Foundation: Crawlspace

Rear Exterior

Quaint details, such as shingled dormers and arched windows with wood shutters, give this home plenty of character. The interior is anything but quaint, with an open plan and coffered ceilings throughout. The family room and study offer cozy retreats where fireplaces are the focal point. A massive master suite is complete with exercise room, sitting area, and master bath with three walk-in closets. The kitchen has an eating bar that allows cooks to interact with family and friends in the breakfast nook. Outside living is assured with a screened porch and covered lanai. The second floor has two additional bedrooms and a guest suite—all have plenty of closet space.

First Floor

Second Floor

Plan: HPK3200487

First Floor: 3,378 sq. ft.
Second Floor: 1,631 sq. ft.
Total: 5,009 sq. ft.
Bedrooms: 5
Bathrooms: 3 ½ + ½

Width: 112' - 7"
Depth: 72' - 6"
Foundation: Unfinished Basement

This traditional two-story home features a brick front facade that's sure to grab the attention of family and friends. The spacious floor plan has a large eat-in kitchen with a walk-in pantry. Surrounding the angular two-story entry, is a den, a formal living room with wet bar, a family room, a nook, and a dining room. The master suite is located on the main floor and has His and Hers walk-in closets and a jacuzzi tub. Upstairs, find four additional bedrooms; three of them have walk-in closets and private bathrooms. A computer loft makes the second floor a perfect kid's retreat. The angled three-car garage provides ample storage space for cars and equipment.

First Floor

Second Floor

Luxury Homes

Plan: HPK3200488

First Floor: 3,438 sq. ft.
Second Floor: 1,645 sq. ft.
Total: 5,083 sq. ft.
Bedrooms: 5
Bathrooms: 5 ½ + ½

Width: 92' - 0"
Depth: 68' - 0"
Foundation: Unfinished
Walkout Basement

This manor exudes opulence inside and out. An awe-inspiring portico, formed by full-height brick pilasters, second-floor balcony, pedimented frontispiece, rounded steps, and Palladian windows, shelters the entrance and defines the exterior. Grand double doors open to the foyer, where a sweeping staircase is first to catch one's eye. The great room awaits at the other end, measuring 20 x 17 feet, and featuring a curved window wall for spectacular outdoor views. The decadent master suite constitutes most of the space of the right side of the plan on this level, bearing an opulent sitting room, coffered ceiling, and His and Hers walk-in closets. The left side of the floor hosts an ornate keeping room next to the salon, a kitchen with work island and breakfast nook, and a gorgeous morning room opening onto a veranda. An expansive three-car garage sits at the front.

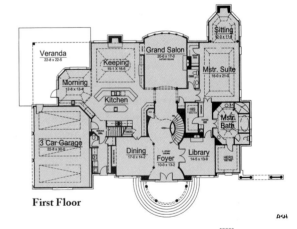

First Floor

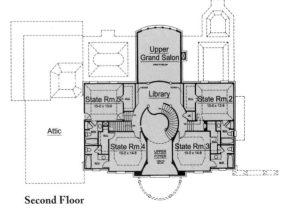

Second Floor

Order blueprints anytime at
eplans.com or 1-800-521-6797

© Larry E. Belk Designs

This elegantly appointed home is a beauty inside and out. A centerpiece stair rises gracefully from the two-story grand foyer. The kitchen, breakfast room, and family room provide open space for the gathering of family and friends. The beam-ceilinged study and the dining room flank the grand foyer, and each includes a fireplace. The master bedroom features a cozy sitting area and a luxury master bath with His and Hers vanities and walk-in closets. Three large bedrooms and a game room complete the second floor. A large expandable area is available at the top of the rear stair.

Plan: HPK3200489

First Floor: 3,170 sq. ft.
Second Floor: 1,914 sq. ft.
Total: 5,084 sq. ft.
Bonus Space: 445 sq. ft.
Bedrooms: 4

Bathrooms: 3 ½
Width: 100' - 10"
Depth: 65' - 5"
Foundation: Crawlspace

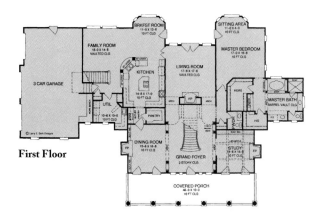

First Floor

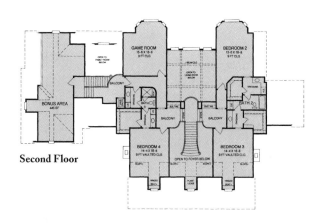

Second Floor

Luxury Homes

Plan: HPK3200490

Main Level: 2,517 sq. ft.	Bathrooms: 3 ½
Upper Level: 722 sq. ft.	Width: 72' - 10"
Lower Level: 1,895 sq. ft.	Depth: 71' - 9"
Total: 5,134 sq. ft.	Foundation: Finished
Bonus Space: 400 sq. ft.	Walkout Basement
Bedrooms: 4	

A stucco facade with detailed embellishments and a full-height, arched loggia with hipped roof strikes a distinctive and stylish tone for this transitional-inspired design. Arched, multipaned windows proliferate, providing charm and an airy feel for the interior. This plan bursts with a cornucopia of amenities: a sunroom, guest-suite/library, enormous master suite, a foyer with lots of openings, functional kitchen with generous breakfast nook, a terrace accessible by the great and dining rooms, and a laundry, powder room, built-in bar, and pantry downstairs. Two family bedrooms with shared bath and a bonus room, plus an interior balcony, are all upstairs.

Lower Level   Main Level   Upper Level

Luxury Homes

First Floor

Second Floor

Plan: HPK3200491

First Floor: 2,864 sq. ft.	Bathrooms: 5 ½ + ½
Second Floor: 2,284 sq. ft.	Width: 71' - 2"
Total: 5,148 sq. ft.	Depth: 67' - 0"
Bedrooms: 5	Foundation: Crawlspace

Traditional elegance characterizes this home both inside and out, while the most up-to-date conveniences make it a joy to inhabit. A wide-open foyer offers the options of heading right into a sophisticated study or left into a formal dining room. Or, pass through the foyer to the arcaded gallery and into the family room, where three sets of French doors offer an invitation to the rear patio. At one end of the gallery lies a spacious guest suite; at the other is the gourmet kitchen, which serves as the hub of the casual living areas. A walk-in pantry and hobby room off the kitchen, along with a toy closet and a mudroom at the rear entrance, provide plenty of hiding places for household clutter. An upstairs laundry room is an additional convenience with its proximity to the master suite and three family bedrooms, each with its own private bath.

Luxury Homes

© 1999 Donald A. Gardner, Inc.

Plan: HPK3200492

First Floor: 3,520 sq. ft.
Second Floor: 1,638 sq. ft.
Total: 5,158 sq. ft.
Bonus Space: 411 sq. ft.

Bedrooms: 5
Bathrooms: 4 ½
Width: 96' - 6"
Depth: 58' - 8"

This custom-designed estate home elegantly combines stone and stucco, arched windows, and stunning exterior details under its formidable hipped roof. Equally remarkable is the generous living room with a fireplace and a coffered two-story ceiling. The kitchen, breakfast bay, and family room with a fireplace are all open to one another for a comfortable, casual atmosphere. The first-floor master suite indulges with numerous closets, a dressing room, and a fabulous bath. Upstairs, four more bedrooms are topped by tray ceilings—three have walk-in closets and two have private baths.

© 1999 Donald A. Gardner, Inc.

Rear Exterior

First Floor

Second Floor

Plan: HPK3200493

First Floor: 2,790 sq. ft.	Bathrooms: 4 ½
Second Floor: 2,382 sq. ft.	Width: 111' - 10"
Total: 5,172 sq. ft.	Depth: 92' - 8"
Bonus Space: 599 sq. ft.	Foundation: Crawlspace
Bedrooms: 5	

Rustic stone accents on the exterior of this home balance the grandeur found inside. A magnificent stairway spirals up through the foyer, which is flanked by a formal living room and a cozier den or study. Elegant ceiling treatments define the open living and dining areas, which are graced by a fireplace, French doors, and a built-in china cabinet. A convenient butler's pantry leads to the spacious island kitchen, where yards of counter space and cabinetry will delight the family chef. The family room is big enough for a reunion, and French doors allow the company to spill out onto the grass. A back stair leads to the second floor, which includes a spacious bonus room, four family bedrooms, two compartmented baths, and a spa-like master suite.

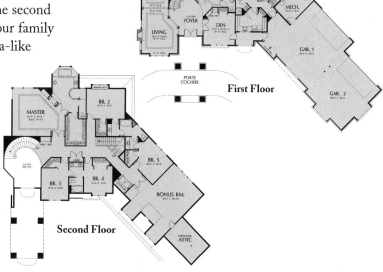

First Floor

Second Floor

Luxury Homes

Plan: HPK3200494

First Floor: 3,030 sq. ft.	Bathrooms: 5
Second Floor: 2,150 sq. ft.	Width: 117' - 6"
Total: 5,180 sq. ft.	Depth: 63' - 6"
Bedrooms: 6	Foundation: Crawlspace

Farmhouse style brings to this home a delightful appeal. A wrapping front porch introduces the plan and offers space to enjoy a cool breeze in the evening. The main floor holds great livability with a great room, a club room, a formal dining room, and a tucked-away office. The work center includes an island kitchen with nook and attached sun room and a craft room is nearby. The second floor holds the master suite and three family bedrooms. The master bedroom has a private deck. An apartment over the three-car garage offers living/dining space, a kitchen, and two bedrooms.

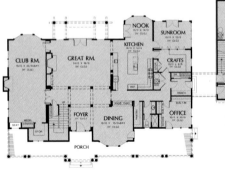
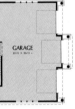

First Floor

Second Floor

COPYRIGHT LARRY E. BELK

Plan: HPK3200495

First Floor: 3,261 sq. ft.
Second Floor: 1,920 sq. ft.
Total: 5,181 sq. ft.
Bedrooms: 4
Bathrooms: 3 ½

Width: 86' - 2"
Depth: 66' - 10"
Foundation: Crawlspace,
Unfinished Basement

This home is elegantly styled in the French Country tradition. A large dining room and a study open off the two-story grand foyer. The large formal living room accesses the covered patio. A more informal family room is conveniently located off the kitchen and breakfast room. The spacious master suite includes a sitting area, a luxurious private bath, and its own entrance to the study. The second floor can be reached from the formal front stair or a well-placed rear staircase. Three large bedrooms and a game room are located on this floor. The walkout basement can be expanded to provide more living space.

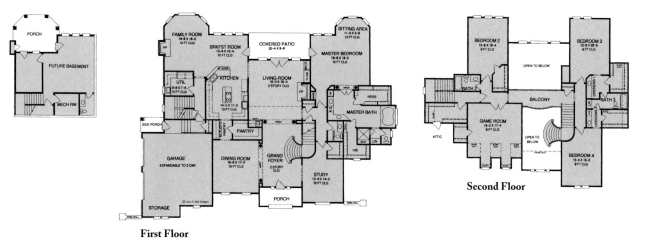

First Floor

Second Floor

Luxury Homes

Plan: HPK3200496

First Floor: 3,322 sq. ft.	Bathrooms: 4 ½
Second Floor: 1,897 sq. ft.	Width: 106' - 6"
Total: 5,219 sq. ft.	Depth: 89' - 10"
Bedrooms: 4	Foundation: Crawlspace

A curved wall of windows leads to the entrance of this fine home. The lavish master suite features two walk-in closets, a deluxe bath with a separate tub and shower and two vanities, a separate lounge, and an exercise room. On the other end of the home, find the highly efficient kitchen, a spacious gathering room, a round morning room and study, and a quiet guest suite. The second level is equally deluxe with two suites, a recreation room, a quiet den, and a large open area called the captain's quarters that opens to an evening deck.

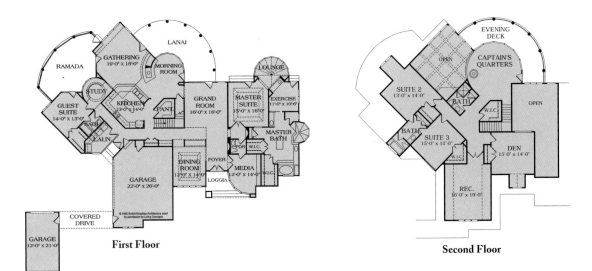

First Floor

Second Floor

Plan: HPK3200497

First Floor: 3,599 sq. ft.	Bathrooms: 5 ½
Second Floor: 1,621 sq. ft.	Width: 108' - 10"
Total: 5,220 sq. ft.	Depth: 53' - 10"
Bonus Space: 537 sq. ft.	Foundation: Slab,
Bedrooms: 4	Unfinished Basement

A grand facade detailed with brick corner quoins, stucco flourishes, arched windows, and an elegant entrance presents this home. A spacious foyer is accented by curving stairs and flanked by a formal living room and dining room. For cozy times, a through-fireplace is located between a large family room and a quiet study. The master bedroom is designed to pamper, with two walk-in closets, a two-sided fireplace, a bayed sitting area, and a lavish private bath. Upstairs, three secondary bedrooms each have a private bath and a walk-in closet. Also on this level is a spacious recreation room, perfect for a game room or children's playroom.

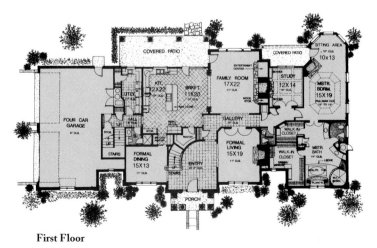

First Floor

Second Floor

Luxury Homes

Plan: HPK3200498

First Floor: 3,594 sq. ft.
Second Floor: 1,656 sq. ft.
Total: 5,250 sq. ft.
Bedrooms: 4
Bathrooms: 4 ½ + ½

Width: 112' - 4"
Depth: 72' - 10"
Foundation: Crawlspace, Slab, Unfinished Basement

Beginning with pleasing curb appeal, this French Country design offers loads of custom home features. A barrel-vaulted ceiling graces the formal living room, which boasts one of three fireplaces found within this home. Across the entry is a formal dining room with a bay window and a wet bar. A gallery leads to the cozy family room, which shares a through-fireplace with the island kitchen and the breakfast nook. The master bedroom will delight with a separate sitting area that includes a fireplace, a private screened porch, and an exercise area and sauna in the master bath. The second floor includes three bedrooms, each with walk-in closets and individual full baths, and a family area with a Pullman ceiling and a half-bath. Notice the utility rooms on both levels.

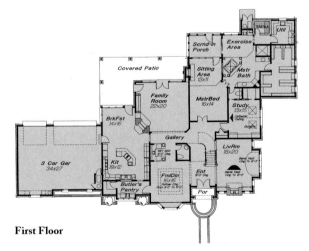

First Floor

Second Floor

A sweeping central staircase is just one of the impressive features of this lovely estate home. Four fireplaces—in the library, family room, grand room, and master-suite sitting room—add a warm glow to the interior; the master suite, grand room, and family room all open to outdoor terrace space. There's plenty of room for family and guests: a guest suite sits to the front of the plan, joining the master suite and two more family bedrooms. Upstairs, a large bonus area—possibly a mother-in-law suite—offers a petite kitchen and walk-in closet; a full bath is nearby.

Plan: HPK3200499

First Floor: 4,107 sq. ft.
Second Floor: 1,175 sq. ft.
Total: 5,282 sq. ft.
Bonus Space: 745 sq. ft.
Bedrooms: 4

Bathrooms: 4 ½
Width: 90' - 0"
Depth: 63' - 0"
Foundation: Unfinished Walkout Basement

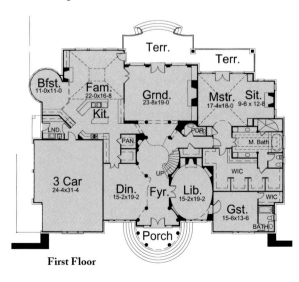

First Floor

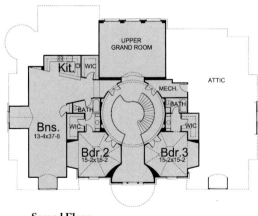

Second Floor

Luxury Homes

Plan: HPK3200500

Main Level: 2,694 sq. ft.
Upper Level: 1,041 sq. ft.
Lower Level: 1,556 sq. ft.
Total: 5,291 sq. ft.
Bonus Space: 389 sq. ft.
Bedrooms: 4

Bathrooms: 3 ½
Width: 74' - 4"
Depth: 82' - 6"
Foundation: Finished Basement

Imagine the fantastic parties that could be hosted in this home, where every space flows into the next. Whether a formal feast in the columned dining room or a casual gathering for drinks and nibbles, the gourmet kitchen can handle it. Guests may congregate for music or games in the large room at the front of the home, spilling out through the French door onto the veranda. Or, move aside the furniture in the gathering room and turn it into a dance floor! A rear deck and an adjacent sunroom beckon guests in need of fresh air or a quieter spot. When the party's over, retreat to the master suite for a soak in the garden tub.

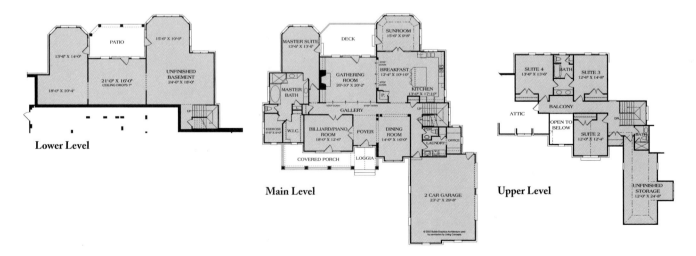

Lower Level

Main Level

Upper Level

First Floor

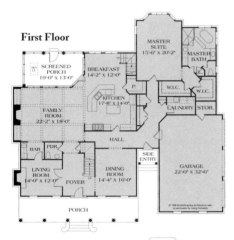

SCREENED PORCH
19'-0" X 13'-0"

BREAKFAST
14'-2" X 12'-0"

MASTER SUITE
15'-6" X 20'-2"

MASTER BATH

KITCHEN
17'-8" X 14'-0"

W.I.C.

W.I.C.

FAMILY ROOM
22'-2" X 18'-0"

LAUNDRY

STOR.

HALL

BAR

PDR

SIDE ENTRY

GARAGE
22'-0" X 32'-6"

LIVING ROOM
14'-0" X 12'-0"

DINING ROOM
14'-4" X 16'-0"

FOYER

PORCH

Second Floor

BATH

W.I.C.

SUITE 5
14'-0" X 19'-8"

W.I.C.

OPEN TO BELOW

SUITE 3
13'-0" X 14'-4"

LOFT
18'-0" X 12'-0"

LIN.

BATH

W.I.C.

BALCONY

BATH

W.I.C.

STOR.

SUITE 2
14'-8" X 16'-0"

OPEN TO BELOW

SUITE 4
14'-4" X 16'-0"

REC. ROOM
14'-8" X 31'-10"

Plan: HPK3200501

First Floor: 2,828 sq. ft.	Bathrooms: 4 ½
Second Floor: 2,483 sq. ft.	Width: 72' - 6"
Total: 5,311 sq. ft.	Depth: 70' - 10"
Bonus Space: 480 sq. ft.	Foundation: Crawlspace
Bedrooms: 5	

This southern plantation home is pure country, graced with multiple arched windows, dormers set into a steeply sloped roof, and a front porch designed for relaxation. The formal entry opens to a bright foyer; French doors on the left leads to a hearth-warmed living room, and an archway on the right reveals the elegant dining room. The family room enjoys a warming fireplace, distinctive coffered ceiling, and a wet bar. The kitchen is ready for any occasion with space for professional-grade appliances and a large center island. The bayed master suite is tucked to the rear, featuring an outstanding resort-style bath that will relax your cares away. On the upper level, four suites (two with private baths) are all lit by charming dormers. A recreation room is a great place for family fun.

Luxury Homes

Plan: HPK3200502

First Floor: 3,307 sq. ft.	Bathrooms: 5 ½ + ½
Second Floor: 2,015 sq. ft.	Width: 143' - 3"
Total: 5,322 sq. ft.	Depth: 71' - 2"
Bonus Space: 373 sq. ft.	Foundation: Crawlspace
Bedrooms: 5	

You'll be amazed at what this estate has to offer. A study/parlor and a formal dining room announce a grand foyer. Ahead, the living room offers a wet bar and French doors to the rear property. The kitchen is dazzling, with an enormous pantry, oversized cooktop island ... even a pizza oven! The gathering room has a corner fireplace and accesses the covered veranda. To the far right, the master suite is a delicious retreat from the world. A bowed window lets in light and a romantic fireplace makes chilly nights cozy. The luxurious bath is awe-inspiring, with a Roman tub and separate compartmented toilet areas—one with a bidet. Upstairs, three family bedrooms share a generous bonus room. A separate pool house is available, which includes a fireplace, full bath, and dressing area.

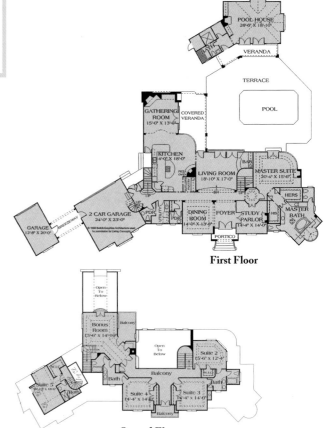

First Floor

Second Floor

Order blueprints anytime at
eplans.com or 1-800-521-6797

Plan: HPK3200503

First Floor: 3,745 sq. ft.
Second Floor: 1,643 sq. ft.
Total: 5,388 sq. ft.
Bonus Space: 510 sq. ft.
Bedrooms: 5
Bathrooms: 4 ½ + ½

Width: 100' - 0"
Depth: 70' - 1"
Foundation: Crawlspace, Slab, Unfinished Basement

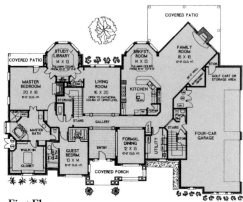

First Floor

Second Floor

Steep rooflines and plenty of windows create a sophisticated aura around this home. Columns support the balconies above as well as the entry below. An angled family room featuring a fireplace is great for rest and relaxation. Snacks and sunlight are just around the corner in the nearby breakfast room and island kitchen. A ribbon of windows in the living room makes for an open feel. A bay-windowed study/library has two sets of French doors: one to the living room and one to the master suite. The master bedroom offers a bath with dual vanities and a spacious walk-in closet. Three family bedrooms are located on the upper level with a recreation/media room and an optional bonus room.

Luxury Homes

Plan: HPK3200504

First Floor: 3,229 sq. ft.	Bathrooms: 5 ½ + ½
Second Floor: 2,219 sq. ft.	Width: 72' - 11"
Total: 5,448 sq. ft.	Depth: 99' - 6"
Bonus Space: 603 sq. ft.	Foundation: Crawlspace
Bedrooms: 5	

Rear Exterior

Stone and stucco topped by varying roof lines and adorning a plan to be envied—this home is magnificent. Through the elegant portico and into the foyer, let your eye wander to the study on the right or the formal dining room on the left. Ahead you'll find a spacious family room joining with an open island kitchen and breakfast nook. The family room provides access to the covered lanai, which leads to a rear patio. The master suite and bath, two powder rooms, an office, and a laundry room complete this level. Find four family bedrooms and private baths, a study, and space for a rec room upstairs.

First Floor   **Second Floor**

Order blueprints anytime at
eplans.com or 1-800-521-6797

Plan: HPK3200505

First Floor: 3,413 sq. ft.
Second Floor: 2,076 sq. ft.
Total: 5,489 sq. ft.
Bedrooms: 4
Bathrooms: 3 ½

Width: 90' - 6"
Depth: 63' - 6"
Foundation: Unfinished
Basement

Classic design combined with dynamite interiors make this executive home a real gem. Inside, a free-floating curved staircase rises majestically to the second floor. The enormous living room, great for formal entertaining, features a dramatic two-story window wall. The family room, breakfast room, and kitchen are conveniently grouped. A large pantry and a companion butler's pantry serve both the dining room and kitchen. Privately located, the master suite includes a sitting area and a sumptuous master bath. The second floor contains Bedroom 2, which has a private bath. Bedrooms 3 and 4 share a bath that includes two private dressing areas. A large game room is accessed from a rear stair.

First Floor

Second Floor

Luxury Homes

Plan: HPK3200506

First Floor: 3,276 sq. ft.
Second Floor: 2,272 sq. ft.
Total: 5,548 sq. ft.
Bedrooms: 5
Bathrooms: 4 ½

Width: 81' - 6"
Depth: 93' - 2"
Foundation: Crawlspace, Slab, Unfinished Basement

This timeless brick exterior showcases slatted shutters and multipaned, oversized windows. The brick portico with contrasting arches and a balcony adds pizazz to this stately facade. The designer thoughtfully utilizes space and includes amenities such as a walk-in pantry, an exercise room, numerous built-ins, a computer room, and skylights over the screened and covered porches. Let guests bring their kids along to play in the upstairs game room/home theater!

First Floor

Second Floor

Plan: HPK3200507

Main Level: 2,137 sq. ft.	Bathrooms: 3 ½
Upper Level: 1,901 sq. ft.	Width: 79' - 4"
Lower Level: 1,528 sq. ft.	Depth: 83' - 3"
Total: 5,566 sq. ft.	Foundation: Unfinished
Bedrooms: 3	Basement

This breathtaking estate offers an impressive floor plan with luxurious amenities and plenty of room to expand. Enter to a two-story foyer; the music room is on the left, warmed by a fireplace. A central staircase defines the family room, graced by natural light, a cozy hearth, and an elegant balcony overlook from above. A cooktop-island kitchen easily serves the bayed breakfast nook and formal dining room. Sleeping quarters are upstairs and begin with two generous secondary bedrooms. The master suite is a refreshing getaway with a bayed sitting area and a resplendent spa bath. A playroom completes this level.

Lower Level

Main Level

Upper Level

Luxury Homes

Plan: HPK3200508

First Floor: 3,722 sq. ft.	Bathrooms: 4 ½
Second Floor: 1,859 sq. ft.	Width: 127' - 10"
Total: 5,581 sq. ft.	Depth: 83' - 9"
Bedrooms: 5	Foundation: Slab

A richly detailed entrance sets the elegant tone of this luxurious design. Rising gracefully from the two-story foyer, the staircase is a fine prelude to the great room beyond, where a fantastic span of windows on the back wall overlooks the rear grounds. The dining room is located off the entry and has a lovely coffered ceiling. The kitchen, breakfast room, and sunroom are conveniently grouped for casual entertaining. The elaborate master suite includes a coffered ceiling, private sitting room, and spa-style bath. The second level consists of four bedrooms with private baths, and a large game room with a rear stair.

First Floor

Second Floor

Plan: HPK3200509

Main Level: 2,732 sq. ft.	Bathrooms: 4 ½ + ½
Upper Level: 1,250 sq. ft.	Width: 97' - 4"
Lower Level: 1,607 sq. ft.	Depth: 69' - 11"
Total: 5,589 sq. ft.	Foundation: Finished
Bedrooms: 5	Walkout Basement

Take advantage of great views on a sloping lot with this multilevel plan. By setting the hearth room and breakfast nook at an angle to the family room, the designer created a panoramic screen across the back of the home. An angled wing provides seclusion for the luxurious master suite and mirrors the opposite wing, embracing an outdoor terrace. A spiraling stair leads to the lower-level terrace, which is an extension of the recreational space downstairs. A full bedroom suite on this level treats guests to ultimate privacy. Three family bedrooms are located on the upper level.

Upper Level

Lower Level

Main Level

Luxury Homes

Plan: HPK3200510

Main Level: 2,734 sq. ft.
Upper Level: 1,258 sq. ft.
Lower Level: 1,839 sq. ft.
Total: 5,831 sq. ft.
Bonus Space: 529 sq. ft.
Bedrooms: 3

Bathrooms: 4 ½
Width: 88' - 0"
Depth: 92' - 8"
Foundation: Finished
Walkout Basement

Rear Exterior

Attractive stone, curved dormers, and varied rooflines give this fine European manor a graceful dose of class. Inside, the foyer introduces a formal dining room defined by columns and a spacious gathering room with a fireplace. The nearby kitchen features a walk-in pantry, beamed ceiling, adjacent breakfast nook, and a screened porch. The first-floor master suite features two walk-in closets, a lavish bath, a corner fireplace, and a sitting room with access to the rear veranda. Upstairs, three suites with walk-in closets surround a study loft. On the lower level, a huge recreation room awaits to entertain with a bar, a fireplace, and outdoor access. A secluded office provides a private entrance—perfect for a home business.

Lower Level

Upper Level

Main Level

Luxury abounds in this graceful manor. The formal living and dining rooms bid greeting as you enter and the impressive great room awaits more casual times with its cathedral ceiling and raised-hearth fireplace. A gallery hall leads to the kitchen and the family sleeping wing on the right and to the study, guest suite, and master suite on the left. The large island kitchen offers a sunny breakfast nook. The master suite includes a bayed sitting area, a dual fireplace shared with the study, and a luxurious bath. Each additional bedroom features its own bath and sitting area. Upstairs is a massive recreation room with a sunlit studio area and a bridge leading to an attic over the garage.

Plan: HPK3200511

First Floor: 5,152 sq. ft.	Bathrooms: 5 ½
Second Floor: 726 sq. ft.	Width: 146' - 7"
Total: 5,878 sq. ft.	Depth: 106' - 7"
Bedrooms: 4	Foundation: Slab

First Floor

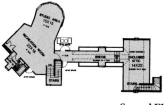

Second Floor

Luxury Homes

Plan: HPK3200512

First Floor: 4,383 sq. ft.	Bathrooms: 4 ½ + ½
Second Floor: 1,544 sq. ft.	Width: 113' - 4"
Total: 5,927 sq. ft.	Depth: 84' - 5"
Bedrooms: 5	Foundation: Slab

Looking for a style superlative? Look no further than this quietly elegant design. A columned entry and Palladian windows add panache and grace. The floor plan was decidedly created for family living. A great room with fireplace and curved staircase, a breakfast area and adjoining family room, the upstairs game room, and the more formal dining and music rooms lend space for all occasions. The master suite is on the first floor but has a private loft overlook above. It has such fine appointments as an exercise room, a fireplace, and a cedar closet. Two of four family bedrooms are also on the first floor. The additional two bedrooms are upstairs. Each has a private bath and walk-in closet.

First Floor

Second Floor

Plan: HPK3200513

First Floor: 3,725 sq. ft.	Bathrooms: 5 ½ + ½
Second Floor: 2,208 sq. ft.	Width: 132' - 0"
Total: 5,933 sq. ft.	Depth: 78' - 0"
Bedrooms: 4	

The neoclassical facade reflects the homes of the Old South. The front of the plan is traditional in its layout, with the dining room on the right of the foyer and the study on the left. A corner fireplace lights and warms the rear living room as the screened porch invites seasonal festivities. The unique design creates bridges off either side of the plan's center. A mudroom with lockers, a laundry room, and a powder room connect the island kitchen to the four-car garage. On the other side of the plan, a library bridges the gap to the master bedroom, for ultimate seclusion. The second floor harbors three bedrooms, three baths, a powder room, and a game room. A front-facing deck off the game room allows outdoor activities.

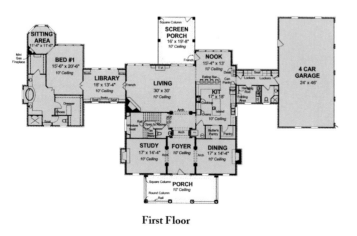

First Floor

Second Floor

Luxury Homes

Plan: HPK3200514

Main Level: 2,534 sq. ft.
Upper Level: 1,578 sq. ft.
Lower Level: 1,857 sq. ft.
Total: 5,969 sq. ft.
Bonus Space: 685 sq. ft.
Bedrooms: 6

Bathrooms: 4 ½ + 2 Half-Baths
Width: 126' - 4"
Depth: 74' - 5"
Foundation: Finished Basement

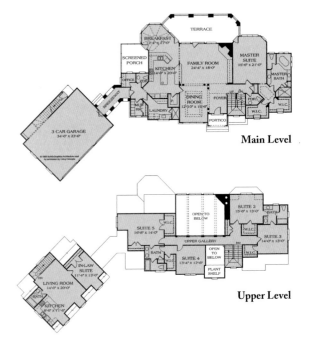

Rear Exterior

Special touches adorn this English country design. A recessed entry leads to a foyer that is open to the formal dining room and the family room, creating a large area for entertaining. A corner fireplace, built-ins, columned arches, and access to the rear terrace highlight the area. An octagonal breakfast nook with an attached screened porch is separated from the kitchen by a snack bar. The master suite is on the first floor, with two walk-in closets, a dressing area, and a compartmented bath designed to pamper. Family sleeping quarters are upstairs and include four bedrooms and two baths.

Main Level

Upper Level

Lower Level

Rear Exterior

Plan: HPK3200515

First Floor: 3,623 sq. ft.	Bathrooms: 4 ½ + ½
Second Floor: 2,507 sq. ft.	Width: 105' - 10"
Total: 6,130 sq. ft.	Depth: 96' - 8"
Bedrooms: 5	Foundation: Slab

First Floor

Second Floor

This thoroughly modern plan meets the needs of busy families. Two studies—one on the first floor, one on the second floor—serve homeowners who require office space for business or a library for leisure. Shared spaces are plentiful, beginning with the large great room, where built-in bookcases and a fireplace structure the layout and allow easy flow from the foyer and breakfast nook. Dual two-car garages form a courtyard "friend's" entry at the left of the home. The oversized utility area will prove to be a must-have room.

Luxury Homes

Plan: HPK3200516

First Floor: 3,889 sq. ft.
Second Floor: 2,288 sq. ft.
Total: 6,177 sq. ft.
Bedrooms: 4

Bathrooms: 5 ½ + ½
Width: 112' - 0"
Depth: 86' - 0"
Foundation: Crawlspace

A palatial facade promises the refinement you're looking for; but a pretty face means nothing without a suitable floor plan. This estate delivers on both aspects. If formal entertaining is part of your lifestyle, the grand room and formal dining hall will serve you well. Casual weekend call for family gatherings? Look to the open family room, island kitchen, and moring room to provide commodious but intimate space. The master suite is gratifying in its own right: His and Hers baths, a huge sitting room with fireplace, and double walk-in closets. The family is also well provided for with three secondary bedrooms with private baths on the upper floor.

First Floor

Second Floor

Rear Exterior

Plan: HPK3200517

Main Level: 3,230 sq. ft.	Bathrooms: 6 ½ + ½
Upper Level: 1,881 sq. ft.	Width: 113' - 8"
Lower Level: 1,847 sq. ft.	Depth: 84' - 6"
Total: 6,958 sq. ft.	Foundation: Finished
Bonus Space: 869 sq. ft.	Walkout Basement
Bedrooms: 5	

The dream of owning a castle can finally be realized. At just under 7,000 square feet, this European beauty exudes the opulence of luxury living. Guests enjoy accommodations on the lower level that includes the option of an early morning workout in the adjacent exercise room. On the main level, common areas flow without the restriction of walls, adding spaciousness. The master suite is a grand retreat for the homeowner. On the upper level, three secondary bedrooms each feature full baths.

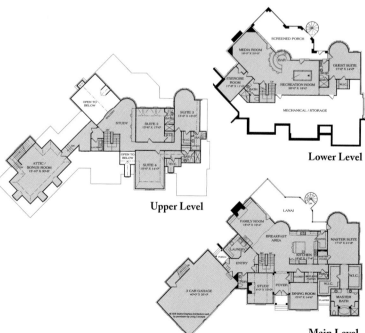

Upper Level

Lower Level

Main Level

Luxury Homes

Plan: HPK3200518

First Floor: 5,394 sq. ft.
Second Floor: 1,305 sq. ft.
Total: 6,699 sq. ft.
Bonus Space: 414 sq. ft.
Bedrooms: 5

Bathrooms: 3 ½ + 2 Half-Baths
Width: 124' - 10"
Depth: 83' - 2"
Foundation: Crawlspace

This elegant French Country estate features a plush world of luxury within. A beautiful curved staircase cascades into the welcoming foyer that is flanked by a formal living room and the dining room with a fireplace. A butler's pantry leads to the island kitchen, which is efficiently enhanced by a walk-in storage pantry. The kitchen easily serves the breakfast room. The covered rear porch is accessed from the media/family room and the great room warmed by a fireplace. The master suite is a sumptuous retreat highlighted by its lavish bath and two huge walk-in closets. Next door, double doors open to a large study. All family bedrooms feature walk-in closets.

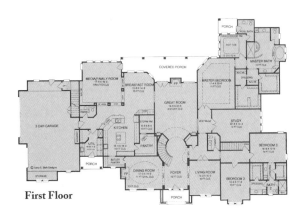

First Floor

Second Floor

Plan: HPK3200519

Main Level: 3,309 sq. ft.	Bathrooms: 5 ½ + 2 Half-Baths
Upper Level: 1,694 sq. ft.	
Lower Level: 2,235 sq. ft.	Width: 112' - 9"
Total: 7,238 sq. ft.	Depth: 97' - 0"
Bedrooms: 6	Foundation: Finished Walkout Basement

Three levels of luxury highlight the livability of this French Country manor. A formal portico welcomes you inside to a foyer that introduces a beautiful curved staircase. To the left, the study features a fireplace with flanking built-ins. To the right, the formal dining room is easily served from the island kitchen. The grand room presents a massive hearth and accesses the rear terrace. The gathering room and nook are also warmed by a fireplace and access a rear screened porch. The first-floor master suite provides a private bath and two walk-in closets. Upstairs, a balcony overlooks the grand room below. Four additional family bedrooms reside on this level. The basement level is reserved for pure entertainment and includes a recreation room, game room complete with a wet bar, a sitting room, future home theater, guest suite, and computer room.

Lower Level

Main Level

Upper Level

Luxury Homes

Plan: HPK3200520

First Floor: 6,198 sq. ft.
Second Floor: 3,547 sq. ft.
Total: 9,745 sq. ft.
Bonus Space: 1,584 sq. ft.
Bedrooms: 5

Bathrooms: 5 + 2 Half-Baths
Width: 112' - 0"
Depth: 139' - 0"
Foundation: Unfinished Walkout Basement

While it would take volumes to explain in detail all of the delights of this home, some of its most notable features include a spectacular grand stair hall, an oval library, a glass-enclosed morning room, an elephantine keeping room, and a two-story grand salon. The master suite is all a homeowner could wish for. It features a separate boudoir, His and Hers closets with built-in dressers, and a uniquely shaped bath. Upstairs family bedrooms include two with private sitting rooms. The skyroom makes use of a glass dome light entertainment space.

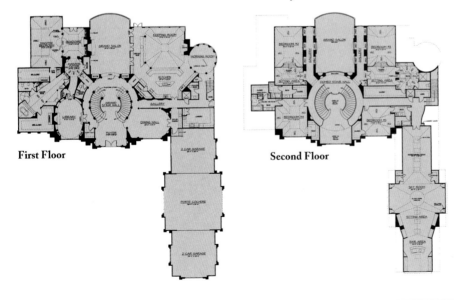

First Floor

Second Floor

Plan: HPK3200521

Main Level: 4,528 sq. ft.	Bathrooms: 5 ½ + 3 Half-Baths
Upper Level: 3,590 sq. ft.	Width: 138' - 2"
Lower Level: 2,992 sq. ft.	Depth: 80' - 10"
Total: 11,110 sq. ft.	Foundation: Finished Basement
Bedrooms: 4	

If you're looking for a home that fits a sloping lot, yet retains a strength and character that matches that of our Colonial forefathers, you need look no further. The front elevation reflects a traditional style that incorporates design elements of an earlier period. However, the floor plan and the rear elevation provide a contemporary twist. Beyond the portico, you'll enter a two-story foyer framed by twin curving staircases. Straight ahead, a spacious great room separates the private master suite to the left from the formal dining room, kitchen, breakfast room, and family/sitting room to the right. The second floor contains three suites—two with bay windows—three full baths, one powder room, a study, and a recreation room. The basement sports a billiards room, two kitchens, an exercise room, a full bath, a game room, and a sitting room.

Lower Level

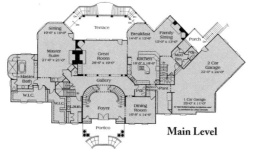

Main Level

Upper Level

Outdoor Living

Designed for families who love outdoor living, this backyard features a deck and patio combination that is perfect for entertaining. It features an area for cooking and dining, as well as space for intimate conversations and relaxing in the sun.

The perfect setting for an outdoor party—or for simply relaxing with family and friends—this backyard features an elegant wooden deck and brick patio that run the length of the house. The deck area on the right (not included in the plans) acts as an outdoor kitchen, featuring a built-in barbecue, serving cabinet, and space enough for a dining table and chairs. For those who opt to mingle with the other guests rather than chat with the cook, a separate area has been provided at the other end.

Built at the same level as the house, and easily accessible from inside, the deck extends the interior living space to the outdoors. Three lovely flowering trees shade the deck and house, while creating a visual ceiling and walls to further reinforce the idea that these areas are outdoor rooms.

Down a few steps from the deck, the brick terrace makes a transition between the house (and deck) and the garden. Open on two sides to the lawn, this sunny terrace feels spacious and open, creating a great place in which people can mingle and talk during a cocktail party or sunbathe on a Saturday afternoon. From here, it's possible to enjoy the garden setting close at hand. The plantings around the perimeter of the yard feature several kinds of tall evergreens to provide privacy. In front of the evergreens, large drifts of flowering perennials are perfectly displayed against the green background. Between the evergreens, masses of shrubbery provide a changing color show from early spring through fall.

Outdoor Living

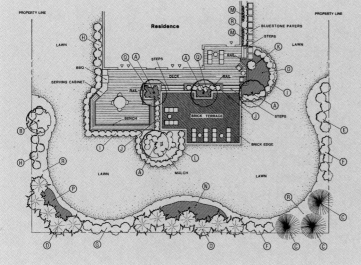

Plan: HPK3200522

Design by Michael J. Opisso
Shown in Spring

Outdoor Living

Shaded yards need not be dark and dull, as this backyard design demonstrates. Here, beneath the shadows of seven mature trees, a colorful collection of shade-loving shrubs, perennials and groundcovers flourishes.

The key to working with large existing trees is to use the shade as an asset, not as a liability, and to choose shade-loving plants to grow beneath them. If the trees have a very dense canopy, branches can be selectively removed to thin the trees and create filtered shade below. In this plan, the designer shapes the lawn and beds to respond to the locations of the trees. Note that all but one of the trees are situated in planting beds, not in open lawn. Placing a single tree in the lawn helps to integrate the lawn and planting beds, creating a cohesive design. At the right, the deep planting area is enhanced by pavers, a bench, and a birdbath, creating an inviting, shady retreat. Near the house, a small patio provides a lounging spot; its shape echoes the curving form of the planting beds. Shaded yards need not be dark and dull, as this backyard design demonstrates. Here, beneath the shadows of seven mature trees, a colorful collection of shade-loving shrubs, perennials, and groundcovers flourishes.

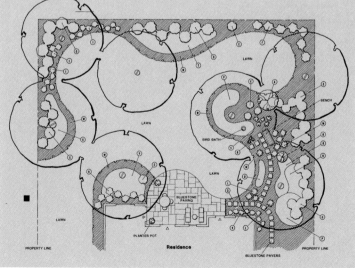

Plan: HPK3200523

Design by Michael J. Opisso
Shown in Summer

Outdoor Living

This formal garden provides a perfect setting for romantic outdoor parties or for simply relaxing in the sun on a Saturday afternoon.

Want to play a role from *The Great Gatsby*? Then close your eyes and imagine being a guest at a large party in this magnificent garden designed for formal entertaining. Imagine standing in the house at the French doors, just at the entrance to the paved area, and looking out at this perfectly symmetrical scene. The left mirrors the right; a major sight line runs straight down the center past the fountain to the statue that serves as a focal point at the rear of the garden. Three perfectly oval flowering trees on each side of the patio frame the sight line, as well as help to delineate the pavement from the planted areas of the garden.

The flagstone patio along the house rises several steps above the brick patio, giving it prominence and presenting a good view of the rest of the property. The change in paving materials provides a separate identity to each area; yet, by edging the brick with bluestone to match the upper patio the two are tied together.

Pink and purple flowering shrubs and perennials provide an elegant color scheme throughout the growing season. A vine-covered lattice panel featuring royal purple flowers that bloom all summer long creates a secluded area that is accessible by paving stones at the rear of the property. What a perfect spot for a romantic rendezvous!

Outdoor Living

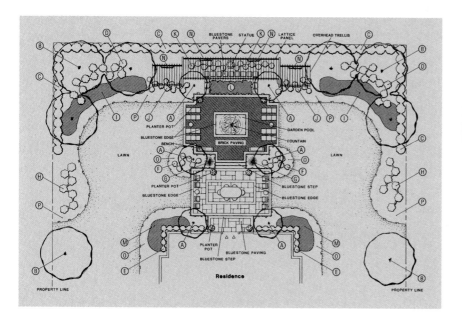

Plan: HPK3200524

Design by Michael J. Opisso
Shown in Summer

Outdoor Living

A second-story deck can be the answer to many difficult landscaping issues. Even a high deck can have two levels and, therefore, two separate use areas, and the designer accomplishes this with this deck. The upper area features a built-in barbecue, service cabinet, and space for dining. The lower area invites family and guests to lounge and relax in the sun. Filled with masses of annuals, the planters bring living color above ground. Without screening, the underside of the deck would be an eyesore when viewed from the yard. The designer solved this problem by enclosing the void beneath the deck with latticework and using a hedge to soften the effect. If the area beneath the deck is to be used as storage, a door can be added to the latticework. Three flowering trees at the corners of the deck anchor this shape and further serve to bring color and greenery up high. Tall evergreens help to screen the deck from the neighbors. High above the rest of the garden, this second-story deck affords a beautiful view of the grounds.

Outdoor Living

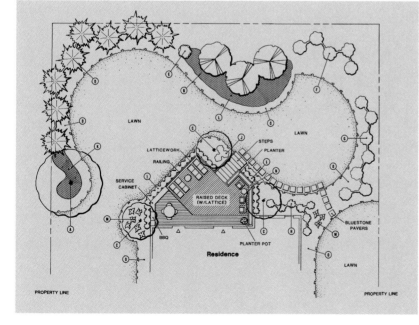

Plan: HPK3200525

Design by Michael J. Opisso
Shown in Summer

Outdoor Living

This design proves that "drought tolerant" and "low maintenance" don't have to mean boring. This attractive backyard looks lush, colorful, and inviting but relies entirely on plants that flourish, even if water is scarce. This means you won't spend any time tending to their watering needs once the plantings are established. Even the lawn is planted with a newly developed turf grass that tolerates long periods of drought.

The designer specifies buffalo grass, a native grass of the American west, for the lawn. The grass has fine-textured, grayish-green leaf blades; tolerates cold; and needs far less water to remain green and healthy than most lawns. It goes completely dormant during periods of extended drought, but greens up with rain or irrigation. To keep the lawn green throughout summer, all you need do is water occasionally if rainfall doesn't cooperate. And mowing is an occasional activity, too! This slow-growing grass needs mowing only a few times in summer to about one inch high. To keep the grass from spreading into the planting borders—and to reduce weeding and edging chores—the designer calls for a decorative brick mowing strip surrounding the lawn.

Deciduous and evergreen trees and shrubs interplanted with long-blooming flowering perennials—all drought-tolerant—adorn the yard, bringing color every season. Against the fence grow espaliered shrubs, which offer flowers in spring and berries in winter. The vine-covered trellis shades the roomy, angular deck, where you can sit in cool seclusion and relax while your beautiful backyard takes care of itself. This environmentally sound landscape plan won't strain the local water supply or burden you with gardening chores because all the plants used here—from grass to flowers to trees—are easy-care, trouble-free kinds that flourish without frequent rain or irrigation.

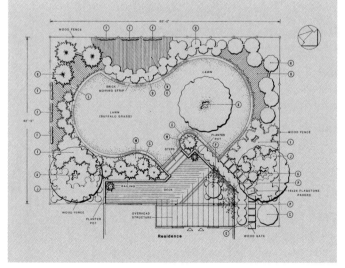

Plan: HPK3200524

Design by Damon Scott
Shown in Summer

Outdoor Living

> **Plan: HPK3200527**
>
> Design by Edward D. Georges
> Shown in Summer

The centerpiece of this landscape, which includes several existing mature trees in the background, is a naturalistic swimming pool. Dark paint helps give the pool the look of a real pond, similar to one you might discover in a wilderness clearing.

To the left of the wooden bridge, a gentle waterfall spills into the 2-foot-deep children's pool. To the right is a 5-foot-deep adults' pool; recessed steps and rocks placed as hand-grips substitute for a ladder. Smooth-edged boulders stud the flagstone coping.

The two irregularly shaped lawn areas flank the children's pool—kids can go from splashing in the pool to frolicking on the grass and back again without missing a beat.

The existing trees give the landscape a head start on privacy. To expand that feeling and to create the effect of a glade, the designer strategically placed additional trees around the yard, but well away from the pool. He also clusters well-behaved shrubs, perennials, and ground-covers—some chosen for their colored foliage and others for their seasonal flowers—around the pool, lawn areas, and deck. For easy maintenance, a thick layer of mulch blankets the soil and smothers weeds in the less visible, less accessible perimeter of the yard.

Many of the deciduous and ever-green shrubs in this landscape feature colorful foliage or bark, providing easy-care color and texture through the seasons. Chosen for their small leaves and restrained growth habits, the trees and shrubs won't add to pool maintenance or overrun the lawn areas.

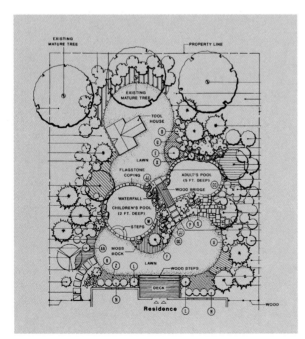

Outdoor Living

A spacious deck with an outdoor kitchen is effectively incorporated into this design for a medium-sized backyard.

Here's a wonderful plan for the serious backyard gardener and outdoor chef: a yard featuring a raised-bed vegetable garden and a spacious deck with an outdoor kitchen for serving and enjoying the homegrown bounty. And the plan doesn't neglect floral beauty for the sake of produce; large patches of easy-care, long-blooming perennials catch the eye, while flowering shrubs and evergreens provide privacy and beauty.

This plan is designed with raised beds to provide visual structure and, at the same time, improve growing conditions by creating warmer, better-drained and more fertile soil. The size of the beds in this garden permits easy tending, because all the plants are within an arm's reach and grow closely together to discourage weeds. Wood chips cover the permanent pathways to reduce mud and improve the garden's appearance. The storage shed and compost area for recycling garden and kitchen waste are located conveniently close to the vegetable beds, but they're attractively screened by evergreens.

Outdoor Living

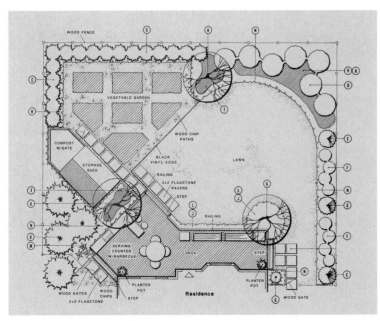

Plan: HPK3200528

Design by Michael J. Opisso
Shown in Summer

Outdoor Living

The flagstone patio, nestled among the flowers near the center of the yard, brings you away from the house. This is a perfect place for a table and chairs to dine during a summer evening. The swing and arbor (not included in the plan) provide a cool spot to relax.

Instead of a pure grass lawn, the designer specified a lawn composed of mixed clover and grass. The abundant flowers in this backyard turn it into a paradise for butterflies as well as for garden lovers. Dozens of different kinds of nectar-rich plants, blooming from spring through fall, provide the necessary blossoms to lure the ephemeral beauties not only to stop and pay a visit, but perhaps to stay and set up a home.

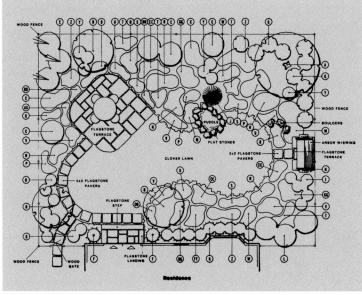

Plan: HPK3200529

Design by Edward D. Georges
Shown in Summer

Outdoor Living

Birds flock to this border, which provides them with ample supplies of food and water and locations for nesting and bathing.

This border includes everything birds need— food, water, and nesting sites—and encourages them to become permanent residents of your yard. The design curves inward, creating a sense of enclosure and a sanctuary that appeals to even the shiest of birds. The border's attractive design includes a pond, birdhouse, and birdbath, which act as focal points and make the garden irresistible to people as well.

The large variety of pretty fruiting shrubs offers birds natural nourishment throughout much of the year, but you can supplement the food supply with store-bought bird food if you wish. Deciduous and evergreen trees provide shelter and nesting places, while the mulched areas give birds a place to take dust baths and to poke around for insects and worms.

Because water is so important to birds, the garden includes two water features: a small naturalistic pond and a birdbath set in a circular bed. Both offer spots for perching, bathing, and drinking. In cold-weather climates, consider adding a special heater to the birdbath to keep the water from freezing; water attracts birds in winter even more than birdseed. Note: The pond is not included in the landscape plans.

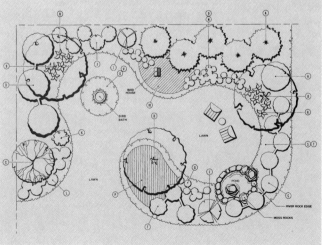

Plan: HPK3200530

Designed by Michael J. Opisso
Shown in Summer

With more than 50 years of experience in the industry and millions of blueprints sold, Hanley Wood is a trusted source of high-quality, high-value pre-drawn home plans.

Using pre-drawn home plans is a **reliable, cost-effective way** to build your dream home, and our vast selection of plans is second-to-none. The nation's finest designers craft these plans that builders know they can trust. Meanwhile, our friendly, knowledgeable customer service representatives can help you every step of the way.

WHAT YOU'LL GET WITH YOUR ORDER

The contents of each designer's blueprint package is unique, but all contain detailed, high-quality working drawings. You can expect to find the following standard elements in most sets of plans:

1. FRONT PERSPECTIVE

This artist's sketch of the exterior of the house gives you an idea of how the house will look when built and landscaped.

2. FOUNDATION AND BASEMENT PLANS

This sheet shows the foundation layout including concrete walls, footings, pads, posts, beams, bearing walls, and foundation notes. If the home features a basement, the first-floor framing details may also be included on this plan. If your plan features slab construction rather than a basement, the plan shows footings and details for a monolithic slab. This page, or another in the set, may include a sample plot plan for locating your house on a building site. Additional sheets focus on foundation cross-sections and other details.

3. DETAILED FLOOR PLANS

These plans show the layout of each floor of the house. Rooms and interior spaces are carefully dimensioned, doors and windows located, and keys are given for cross-section details provided elsewhere in the plans.

4. HOUSE AND DETAIL CROSS-SECTIONS

Large-scale views show sections or cutaways of the foundation, interior walls, exterior walls, floors, stairways, and roof details. Additional cross-sections may show important changes in floor, ceiling, or roof heights, or the relationship of one level to another. These sections show exactly how the various parts of the house fit together and are extremely valuable during construction. Additional sheets may include enlarged wall, floor, and roof construction details.

5. FLOOR STRUCTURAL SUPPORTS

The floor framing plans provide detail for these crucial elements of your home. Each includes floor joist, ceiling joist, spacing, direction, span, and specifications. Beam and window headers, along with necessary details for framing connections, stairways, or dormers are also included.

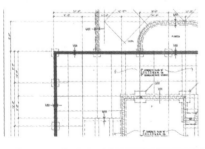

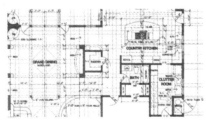

6. ELECTRICAL PLAN

The electrical plan offers suggested locations with notes for all lighting, outlets, switches, and circuits. A layout is provided for each level, as well as basements, garages, or other structures. This plan does not contain diagrams detailing how all wiring should be run, or how circuits should be engineered. These details should be designed by your electrician.

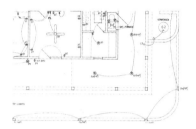

7. EXTERIOR ELEVATIONS

In addition to the front exterior, your blueprint set will include drawings of the rear and sides of your house as well. These drawings give notes on exterior materials and finishes. Particular attention is given to cornice detail, brick and stone accents, or other finish items that make your home unique.

ROOF FRAMING PLANS — PLEASE READ

Some plans contain roof framing plans; however because of the wide variation in local requirements, many plans do not. If you buy a plan without a roof framing plan, you will need an engineer familiar with local building codes to create a plan to build your roof. Even if your plan does contain a roof framing plan, we recommend that a local engineer review the plan to verify that it will meet local codes.

BEFORE YOU CALL

You are making a terrific decision to use a pre-drawn house plan—it is one you can make with confidence, knowing that your blueprints are crafted by national-award-winning certified residential designers and architects, and trusted by builders.

Once you've selected the plan you want—or even if you have questions along the way—our experienced customer service representatives are available 24 hours a day, seven days a week to help you navigate the home-building process. To help them provide you with even better service, please consider the following questions before you call:

■ Have you chosen or purchased your lot?
If so, please review the building setback requirements of your local building authority before you call. You don't need to have a lot before ordering plans, but if you own land already, please have the width and depth dimensions handy when you call.

■ Have you chosen a builder?
Involving your builder in the plan selection and evaluation process may be beneficial. Luckily, builders know they can have confidence with pre-drawn plans because they've been designed for livability, functionality, and typically are builder-proven at successful home sites across the country.

■ Do you need a construction loan?
Construction loans are unique because they involve determining the value of something that is not yet constructed. Several lenders offer convenient contstruction-to-permanent loans. It is important to choose a good lending partner—one who will help guide you through the application and appraisal process. Most will even help you evaluate your contractor to ensure reliability and credit worthiness. Our partnership with IndyMac Bank, a nationwide leader in construction loans, can help you save on your loan, if needed.

■ How many sets of plans do you need?
Building a home can typically require a number of sets of blueprints—one for yourself, two or three for the builder and subcontractors, two for the local building department, and one or

more for your lender. For this reason, we offer 5- and 8-set plan packages, but your best value is the Reproducible Plan Package. Reproducible plans are accompanied by a license to make modifications and typically up to 12 duplicates of the plan so you have enough copies of the plan for everyone involved in the financing and construction of your home.

■ Do you want to make any changes to the plan?
We understand that it is difficult to find blueprints for a home that will meet all of your needs. That is why Hanley Wood is glad to offer plan Customization Services. We will work with you to design the modifications you'd like to see and to adjust your blueprint plans accordingly—anything from changing the foundation; adding square footage, redesigning baths, kitchens, or bedrooms; or most other modifications. This simple, cost-effective service saves you from hiring an outside architect to make alterations. Modifications may only be made to Reproducible Plan Packages that include the license to modify.

■ Do you have to make any changes to meet local building codes?
While all of our plans are drawn to meet national building codes at the time they were created, many areas required that plans be stamped by a local engineer to certify that they meet local building codes. Building codes are updated frequently and can vary by state, county, city, or municipality. Contact your local building inspection department, office of planning and zoning, or department of permits to determine how your local codes will affect your construction project. The best way to assure that you can make changes to your plan, if necessary, is to purchase a Reproducible Plan Package.

■ Has everyone—from family members to contractors—been involved in selecting the plan?
Building a new home is an exciting process, and using pre-drawn plans is a great way to realize your dreams. Make sure that everyone involved has had an opportunity to review the plan you've selected. While Hanley Wood is the only plans provider with an exchange policy, it's best to be sure all parties agree on your selection before you buy.

CALL TOLL-FREE 1-800-521-6797

Source Key
HPK32

CUSTOMIZE YOUR PLAN –
HANLEY WOOD CUSTOMIZATION SERVICES

Creating custom home plans has never been easier and more directly accessible. Using state-of-the-art technology and top-performing architectural expertise, Hanley Wood delivers on a long-standing customer commitment to provide world-class home-plans and customization services. Our valued customers—professional home builders and individual home owners—appreciate the convenience and accessibility of this interactive, consultative service.

With the Hanley Wood Customization Service you can:

■ Save valuable time by avoiding drawn-out and frequently repetitive face-to-face design meetings

■ Communicate design and home-plan changes faster and more efficiently
■ Speed-up project turn-around time
■ Build on a budget without sacrificing quality
■ Transform master home plans to suit your design needs and unique personal style

All of our design options and prices are impressively affordable. A detailed quote is available for a $50 consultation fee. Plan modification is an interactive service. Our skilled team of designers will guide you through the customization process from start to finish making recommendations, offering ideas, and determining the feasibility of your changes. This level of service is offered to ensure the final modified plan meets your expectations. If you use our service the $50 fee will be applied to the cost of the modifications.

You may purchase the customization consultation before or after purchasing a plan. In either case, it is necessary to purchase the Reproducible Plan Package and complete the accompanying license to modify the plan before we can begin customization.

Customization Consultation $50

TOOLS TO WORK WITH YOUR BUILDER

Two Reverse Options For Your Convenience –
Mirror and Right-Reading Reverse (as available)

Mirror reverse plans simply flip the design 180 degrees—keep in mind, the text will also be flipped. For a minimal fee you can have one or all of your plans shipped mirror reverse, although we recommend having at least one regular set handy. Right-reading reverse plans show the design flipped 180 degrees but the text reads normally. When you choose this option, we ship each set of purchased blueprints in this format.

Mirror Reverse Fee (indicate the number of sets when ordering) $55
Right Reading Reverse Fee (all sets are reversed) $175

A Shopping List Exclusively for Your Home – Materials List

A customized Materials List helps you plan and estimate the cost of your new home, outlining the quantity, type, and size of materials needed to build your house (with the exception of mechanical system items). Included are framing lumber, windows and doors, kitchen and bath cabinetry, rough and finished hardware, and much more.

Materials List . . . .$85 each
Additional Materials Lists (at original time of purchase only) . .$20 each

Plan Your Home-
Building Process – Specification Outline

Work with your builder on this step-by-step chronicle of 166 stages or items crucial to the building process. It provides a comprehensive review of the construction process and helps you choose materials.

Specification Outline . . . .$10 each

Learn the Basics of Building – Electrical, Plumbing, Mechanical, Construction Detail Sheets

If you want to know more about building techniques—and deal more confidently with your subcontractors—we offer four useful detail sheets. These sheets provide non-plan-specific general information, but are excellent tools that will add to your understanding of Plumbing Details, Electrical Details, Construction Details, and Mechanical Details.

Electrical Detail Sheet $14.95
Plumbing Detail Sheet $14.95
Mechanical Detail Sheet $14.95
Construction Detail Sheet $14.95

SUPER VALUE SETS:
Buy any 2: $26.95; Buy any 3: $34.95; Buy All 4: $39.95

Best
Value

MAKE YOUR HOME TECH-READY — HOME AUTOMATION UPGRADE

Building a new home provides a unique opportunity to wire it with a plan for future needs. A Home Automation-Ready (HA-Ready) home contains the wiring substructure of tomorrow's connected home. It means that every room—from the front porch to the backyard, and from the attic to the basement—is wired for security, lighting, telecommunications, climate control, home computer networking, whole-house audio, home theater, shade control, video surveillance, entry access control, and yes, video gaming electronic solutions.

Along with the conveniences HA-Ready homes provide, they also have a higher resale value. The Consumer Electronics Association (CEA), in conjunction with the Custom Electronic Design and Installation Association (CEDIA), have developed a TechHome™ Rating system that quantifies the value of HA-Ready homes. The rating system is gaining widespread recognition in the real estate industry.

Developed by CEDIA-certified installers, our Home Automation Upgrade package includes everything you need to work with an installer during the construction of your home. It provides a short explanation of the various subsystems, a wiring floor plan for each level of your home, a detailed materials list with estimated costs, and a list of CEDIA-certified installers in your local area.

Home Automation Upgrade $250

GET YOUR HOME PLANS PAID FOR!

IndyMac Bank, in partnership with Hanley Wood, will reimburse you up to $750 toward the cost of your home plans simply by financing the construction of your new home with IndyMac Bank Home Construction Lending.

IndyMac's construction and permanent loan is a one-time close loan, meaning that one application—and one set of closing fees—provides all the financing you need.

Apply today at www.indymacbank.com, call toll free at 1-800-847-6138, or ask a Hanley Wood customer service representative for details.

DESIGN YOUR HOME — INTERIOR AND EXTERIOR FINISHING TOUCHES

Be Your Own Interior Designer! — Home Furniture Planner

Effectively plan the space in your home using our Hands-On Home Furniture Planner. It's fun and easy—no more moving heavy pieces of furniture to see how the room will go together. The kit includes reusable peel-and-stick furniture templates that fit on a 12"x18" laminated layout board—enough space to lay out every room in your house.

Home Furniture Planning Kit $15.95

Enjoy the Outdoors! — Deck Plans

Many of our homes have a corresponding deck plan, sold separately, which includes a Deck Plan Frontal Sheet, Deck Framing and Floor Plans, Deck Elevations, and a Deck Materials List. A Standard Deck Details Package, also available, provides all the how-to information necessary for building any deck. Get both the Deck Plan and the Standard Deck Details Package for one low price in our Complete Deck Building Package. See the price tier chart below and call for deck plan availability.

Create a Professionally Designed Landscape — Landscape Plans

Many of our homes have a front-yard Landscape Plan that is complementary in design to the house plan. These comprehensive Landscape Blueprint Packages include a Frontal Sheet, Plan View, Regionalized Plant & Materials List, a sheet on Planting and Maintaining Your Landscape, Zone Maps, and a Plant Size and Description Guide. Each set of blueprints is a full 18" x 24" with clear, complete instructions in easy-to-read type. Our Landscape Plans are available with a Plant & Materials List adapted by horticultural experts to eight regions of the country. Please specify your region when ordering your plan—see region map below. Call for more information about landscape plan availability and applicable regions.

LANDSCAPE & DECK PRICE SCHEDULE

PRICE TIERS	1-SET STUDY PACKAGE	5-SET BUILDING PACKAGE	1-SET REPRODUCIBLE*	1-SET CAD*
P1	$25	$55	$145	$245
P2	$45	$75	$165	$280
P3	$75	$105	$195	$330
P4	$105	$135	$225	$385
P5	$175	$205	$405	$690
P6	$215	$245	$445	$750
D1	$45	$75**	$90	$90
D2	$75	$105**	$150	$150

PRICES SUBJECT TO CHANGE * REQUIRES AN E-MAIL ADDRESS OR FAX NUMBER
** 3-SET BUILDING PACKAGE

TERMS & CONDITIONS

OUR 90-DAY EXCHANGE POLICY

Hanley Wood is committed to ensuring your satisfaction with your blueprint order, which is why a we offer a 90-day exchange policy. With the exception of Reproducible Plan Package orders, we will exchange your entire first order for an equal or greater number of blueprints from our plan collection within 90 days of the original order. The entire content of your original order must be returned before an exchange will be processed. Please call our customer service department at 1-888-690-1116 for your return authorization number and shipping instructions. If the returned blueprints look used, redlined, or copied, we will not honor your exchange. Fees for exchanging your blueprints are as follows: 20% of the amount of the original order, plus the difference in cost if exchanging for a design in a higher price bracket or less the difference in cost if exchanging for a design in a lower price bracket. (Because they can be copied, Reproducible blueprints are not exchangeable or refundable.) Please call for current postage and handling prices. Shipping and handling charges are not refundable.

ARCHITECTURAL AND ENGINEERING SEALS

Some cities and states now require that a licensed architect or engineer review and "seal" a blueprint, or officially approve it, prior to construction. Prior to application for a building permit or the start of actual construction, we strongly advise that you consult your local building official who can tell you if such a review is required.

LOCAL BUILDING CODES AND ZONING REQUIREMENTS

Each plan was designed to meet or exceed the requirements of a nationally recognized model building code in effect at the time and place the plan was drawn. Typically plans designed after the year 2000 conform to the International Residential Building Code (IRC 2000 or 2003). The IRC is comprised of portions of the three major codes below. Plans drawn before 2000 conform to one of the three recognized building codes in effect at the time: Building Officials and Code Administrators (BOCA) International, Inc.; the Southern Building Code Congress International, (SBCCI) Inc.; the International Conference of Building Officials (ICBO); or the Council of American Building Officials (CABO).

Because of the great differences in geography and climate throughout the United States and Canada, each state, county, and municipality has its own building codes, zone requirements, ordinances, and building regulations. Your plan may need to be modified to comply with local requirements. In addition, you may need to obtain permits or inspections from local governments before and in the course of construction. We authorize the use of the blueprints on the express condition that you consult a local licensed architect or engineer of your choice prior to beginning construction and strictly comply with all local building codes, zoning requirements, and other applicable laws, regulations, ordinances, and requirements. Notice: Plans for homes to be built in Nevada must be redrawn by a Nevada-registered professional. Consult your local building official for more information on this subject.

TERMS AND CONDITIONS

These designs are protected under the terms of United States Copyright Law and may not be copied or reproduced in any way, by any means, unless you have purchased a Reproducible Plan Package and signed the accompanying license to modify and copy the plan, which clearly indicates your right to modify, copy, or reproduce. We authorize the use of your chosen design as an aid in the construction of ONE (1) single- or multifamily home only. You may not use this design to build a second dwelling or multiple dwellings without purchasing another blueprint or blueprints or paying additional design fees. Multi-use fees vary by designer—please call one of experienced sales representatives for a quote.

DISCLAIMER

The designers we work with have put substantial care and effort into the creation of their blueprints. However, because we cannot provide on-site consultation, supervision, and control over actual construction, and because of the great variance in local building requirements, building practices, and soil, seismic, weather, and other conditions, WE MAKE NO WARRANTY OF ANY KIND, EXPRESS OR IMPLIED, WITH RESPECT TO THE CONTENT OR USE OF THE BLUE-PRINTS, INCLUDING BUT NOT LIMITED TO ANY WARRANTY OF MERCHANTABILITY OR OF FITNESS FOR A PARTICULAR PURPOSE. ITEMS, PRICES, TERMS, AND CONDITIONS ARE SUBJECT TO CHANGE WITHOUT NOTICE.

CALL TOLL-FREE
1-800-521-6797
OR VISIT
EPLANS.COM

IMPORTANT COPYRIGHT NOTICE

From the Council of Publishing Home Designers

Blueprints for residential construction (or working drawings, as they are often called in the industry) are copyrighted intellectual property, protected under the terms of the United States Copyright Law and, therefore, cannot be copied legally for use in building. The following are some guidelines to help you get what you need to build your home, without violating copyright law:

1. HOME PLANS ARE COPYRIGHTED

Just like books, movies, and songs, home plans receive protection under the federal copyright laws. The copyright laws prevent anyone, other than the copyright owner, from reproducing, modifying, or reusing the plans or design without permission of the copyright owner.

2. DO NOT COPY DESIGNS OR FLOOR PLANS FROM ANY PUBLICATION, ELECTRONIC MEDIA, OR EXISTING HOME

It is illegal to copy, change, or redraw home designs found in a plan book, CDROM or on the Internet. The right to modify plans is one of the exclusive rights of copyright. It is also illegal to copy or redraw a constructed home that is protected by copyright, even if you have never seen the plans for the home. If you find a plan or home that you like, you must purchase a set of plans from an authorized source. The plans may not be lent, given away, or sold by the purchaser.

3. DO NOT USE PLANS TO BUILD MORE THAN ONE HOUSE

The original purchaser of house plans is typically licensed to build a single home from the plans. Building more than one home from the plans without permission is an infringement of the home designer's copyright. The purchase of a multiple-set package of plans is for the construction of a single home only. The purchase of additional sets of plans does not grant the right to construct more than one home.

4. HOUSE PLANS IN THE FORM OF BLUEPRINTS OR BLACKLINES CANNOT BE COPIED OR REPRODUCED

Plans, blueprints, or blacklines, unless they are reproducibles, cannot be copied or reproduced without prior written consent of the copyright owner. Copy shops and blueprinters are prohibited from making copies of these plans without the copyright release letter you receive with reproducible plans.

5. HOUSE PLANS IN THE FORM OF BLUEPRINTS OR BLACKLINES CANNOT BE REDRAWN

Plans cannot be modified or redrawn without first obtaining the copyright owner's permission. With your purchase of plans, you are licensed to make non-structural changes by "red-lining" the purchased plans. If you need to make structural changes or need to redraw the plans for any reason, you must purchase a reproducible set of plans (see topic 6) which includes a license to modify the plans. Blueprints do not come with a license to make structural changes or to redraw the plans. You may not reuse or sell the modified design.

6. REPRODUCIBILE HOME PLANS

Reproducible plans (for example sepias, mylars, CAD files, electronic files, and vellums) come with a license to make modifications to the plans. Once modified, the plans can be taken to a local copy shop or blueprinter to make up to 10 or 12 copies of the plans to use in the construction of a single home. Only one home can be constructed from any single purchased set of reproducible plans either in original form or as modified. The license to modify and copy must be completed and returned before the plan will be shipped.

7. MODIFIED DESIGNS CANNOT BE REUSED

Even if you are licensed to make modifications to a copyrighted design, the modified design is not free from the original designer's copyright. The sale or reuse of the modified design is prohibited. Also, be aware that any modification to plans relieves the original designer from liability for design defects and voids all warranties expressed or implied.

8. WHO IS RESPONSIBLE FOR COPYRIGHT INFRINGEMENT?

Any party who participates in a copyright violation may be responsible including the purchaser, designers, architects, engineers, drafters, homeowners, builders, contractors, sub-contractors, copy shops, blueprinters, developers, and real estate agencies. It does not matter whether or not the individual knows that a violation is being committed. Ignorance of the law is not a valid defense.

9. PLEASE RESPECT HOME DESIGN COPYRIGHTS

In the event of any suspected violation of a copyright, or if there is any uncertainty about the plans purchased, the publisher, architect, designer, or the Council of Publishing Home Designers (www.cphd.org) should be contacted before proceeding. Awards are sometimes offered for information about home design copyright infringement.

10. PENALTIES FOR INFRINGEMENT

Penalties for violating a copyright may be severe. The responsible parties are required to pay actual damages caused by the infringement (which may be substantial), plus any profits made by the infringer commissions to include all profits from the sale of any home built from an infringing design. The copyright law also allows for the recovery of statutory damages, which may be as high as $150,000 for each infringement. Finally, the infringer may be required to pay legal fees which often exceed the damages.

BLUEPRINT PRICE SCHEDULE

PRICE TIERS	1-SET STUDY PACKAGE	5-SET BUILDING PACKAGE	8-SET BUILDING PACKAGE	1-SET REPRODUCIBLE*	1-SET CAD*
A1	$470	$520	$575	$700	$1,055
A2	$510	$565	$620	$765	$1,230
A3	$575	$630	$690	$870	$1,400
A4	$620	$685	$750	$935	$1,570
C1	$665	$740	$810	$1,000	$1,735
C2	$715	$795	$855	$1,065	$1,815
C3	$785	$845	$910	$1,145	$1,915
C4	$840	$915	$970	$1,225	$2,085
L1	$930	$1,030	$1,115	$1,390	$2,500
L2	$1,010	$1,105	$1,195	$1,515	$2,575
L3	$1,115	$1,220	$1,325	$1,665	$2,835
L4	$1,230	$1,350	$1,440	$1,850	$3,140
SQ1				$0.40/SQ. FT.	$0.68/SQ. FT.
SQ3				$0.55/SQ. FT.	$0.94/SQ. FT.
SQ5				$0.80/SQ. FT	$1.36/SQ. FT.
SQ7				$1.00/SQ. FT.	$1.70/SQ. FT.
SQ9				$1.25/SQ. FT.	$2.13/SQ. FT.
SQ11				$1.50/SQ. FT.	$2.55/SQ. FT.

PRICES SUBJECT TO CHANGE

* REQUIRES AN E-MAIL ADDRESS OR FAX NUMBER

PLAN #	PRICE TIER	PAGE	MATERIALS LIST	DECK	DECK PRICE	LANDSCAPE	LANDSCAPE PRICE	REGIONS
HPK3200001	A3	6	Y					
HPK3200002	A2	11						
HPK3200003	A2	12						
HPK3200004	A3	12						
HPK3200005	A3	13	Y					
HPK3200006	A4	13						
HPK3200007	A2	14						
HPK3200008	A4	14						
HPK3200009	A4	15						
HPK3200010	A2	15						
HPK3200011	A4	16						
HPK3200012	A3	16	Y					
HPK3200013	A2	17	Y					
HPK3200014	C2	17						
HPK3200015	A3	18						
HPK3200016	A4	18	Y					
HPK3200017	A4	19	Y					
HPK3200018	A3	19						
HPK3200019	A4	20	Y					
HPK3200020	A4	20	Y					
HPK3200021	A4	21	Y					
HPK3200022	A2	21	Y					
HPK3200023	A4	22	Y					
HPK3200024	A4	22	Y					
HPK3200025	A3	23						
HPK3200026	A4	23	Y					
HPK3200027	A3	24						
HPK3200028	A4	24	Y					
HPK3200029	A3	25						
HPK3200030	A4	25						
HPK3200031	A4	26	Y					
HPK3200032	A3	26						
HPK3200033	A3	27	Y					
HPK3200034	C2	27						
HPK3200035	A4	28						
HPK3200036	A3	28	Y					
HPK3200037	C3	29	Y					
HPK3200038	A3	29	Y					
HPK3200039	A3	30						
HPK3200040	C3	30	Y					
HPK3200041	A3	31	Y					
HPK3200042	A3	31						
HPK3200043	A4	32	Y					
HPK3200044	A3	32						
HPK3200045	A3	33	Y					
HPK3200046	C3	33	Y					
HPK3200047	A4	34						
HPK3200048	A3	34						
HPK3200049	A3	35						
HPK3200050	A4	35						
HPK3200051	A4	36						
HPK3200052	A3	36	Y					
HPK3200053	C3	37	Y					
HPK3200054	A4	38						
HPK3200055	A3	38						
HPK3200056	A4	39						
HPK3200057	A3	39	Y					
HPK3200058	C1	40						
HPK3200059	A3	40	Y					
HPK3200060	A4	41	Y					
HPK3200061	A4	41	Y					
HPK3200062	A3	42	Y					
HPK3200063	A4	42	Y					
HPK3200064	A4	43	Y					
HPK3200065	A4	44						
HPK3200066	C1	45	Y					
HPK3200067	A3	46	Y					
HPK3200068	A3	47	Y					
HPK3200069	A4	48	Y					
HPK3200070	A4	49						
HPK3200071	A3	50						
HPK3200072	A3	51						
HPK3200073	A4	52	Y					
HPK3200074	A3	53	Y		OLA004	P3	123568	
HPK3200075	C1	54	Y					
HPK3200076	A3	55	Y					
HPK3200077	A4	56	Y					
HPK3200078	A4	57						
HPK3200079	A4	58	Y					
HPK3200080	C2	59	Y					
HPK3200081	A4	60						
HPK3200082	A4	61	Y					
HPK3200083	A3	62						
HPK3200084	A4	63	Y					
HPK3200085	A4	64	Y					
HPK3200086	C3	65						

PLAN #	PRICE TIER	PAGE	MATERIALS LIST	DECK	DECK PRICE	LANDSCAPE	LANDSCAPE PRICE	REGIONS
HPK3200087	C1	66						
HPK3200088	C1	67						
HPK3200089	A3	68						
HPK3200090	A3	69						
HPK3200091	A3	70	Y					
HPK3200092	C2	71						
HPK3200093	A4	72	Y					
HPK3200094	A4	73						
HPK3200095	A4	74						
HPK3200096	A3	75						
HPK3200097	A4	76	Y					
HPK3200098	A3	77						
HPK3200099	C1	78	Y					
HPK3200100	A3	79						
HPK3200101	A3	80						
HPK3200102	A4	81	Y					
HPK3200103	C1	82						
HPK3200104	A3	83						
HPK3200105	A4	84						
HPK3200532	A4	84						
HPK3200106	A3	85						
HPK3200107	A3	86						
HPK3200108	A4	87	Y					
HPK3200109	A4	88	Y					
HPK3200110	C1	89	Y					
HPK3200111	C1	90	Y					
HPK3200112	A4	91	Y					
HPK3200113	A4	92	Y					
HPK3200114	A3	93	Y					
HPK3200115	A3	94	Y					
HPK3200116	A3	95	Y					
HPK3200117	A3	96						
HPK3200118	A3	97	Y					
HPK3200119	A4	98	Y					
HPK3200120	A4	99	Y					
HPK3200121	C1	100	Y			OLA017	P3	123568
HPK3200122	C3	101						
HPK3200123	A4	106	Y					
HPK3200124	C1	107	Y					
HPK3200125	C1	107						
HPK3200126	A4	108	Y					
HPK3200127	A4	108	Y					
HPK3200128	A3	109						
HPK3200129	A4	109	Y					
HPK3200130	C1	110						
HPK3200131	C2	110	Y					
HPK3200132	A4	111	Y					
HPK3200133	A4	111	Y	ODA006	D1	OLA001	P3	123568
HPK3200134	C2	112						
HPK3200533	C1	112						
HPK3200534	C1	113						
HPK3200535	C1	113						
HPK3200135	C1	114	Y					
HPK3200536	C1	114						
HPK3200136	C1	115						
HPK3200137	C1	115	Y					
HPK3200138	C4	116	Y					
HPK3200139	A4	116						
HPK3200140	C2	117						
HPK3200141	A4	117	Y					
HPK3200142	C2	118						
HPK3200537	C1	118						
HPK3200143	C2	119						
HPK3200144	C1	119	Y					
HPK3200145	C4	120						
HPK3200146	A4	120						
HPK3200147	C4	121						
HPK3200148	C3	121						
HPK3200149	C1	122	Y					
HPK3200150	C1	122	Y					
HPK3200151	C1	123						
HPK3200152	A4	123	Y					
HPK3200153	C1	124						
HPK3200154	C1	124	Y					
HPK3200155	C2	125						
HPK3200156	C1	125						

PLAN #	PRICE TIER	PAGE	MATERIALS LIST	DECK	DECK PRICE	LANDSCAPE	LANDSCAPE PRICE	REGIONS
HPK3200157	C2	126						
HPK3200158	C1	126						
HPK3200159	C2	127						
HPK3200160	C3	127						
HPK3200161	C1	128	Y					
HPK3200162	C1	128						
HPK3200163	C1	129	Y					
HPK3200164	A4	129						
HPK3200165	A4	130	Y					
HPK3200166	C1	130						
HPK3200167	C4	131	Y					
HPK3200168	C4	131	Y					
HPK3200169	C2	132						
HPK3200170	C1	132						
HPK3200171	C3	133						
HPK3200172	A4	133	Y					
HPK3200173	C1	134	Y					
HPK3200174	C1	134						
HPK3200175	C1	135	Y			OLA025	P3	123568
HPK3200538	C1	135						
HPK3200176	A4	136	Y					
HPK3200177	C1	136	Y					
HPK3200178	C1	137						
HPK3200179	C2	137						
HPK3200180	A4	138						
HPK3200539	C1	138						
HPK3200181	SQ1	139	Y					
HPK3200182	C1	139	Y					
HPK3200183	A4	140	Y					
HPK3200184	C1	140						
HPK3200185	C3	141						
HPK3200186	A4	141	Y					
HPK3200187	C2	142	Y					
HPK3200540	C2	142						
HPK3200188	C1	143	Y					
HPK3200189	C2	144						
HPK3200190	C1	145						
HPK3200191	C1	146	Y					
HPK3200192	C1	147	Y					
HPK3200193	A4	148						
HPK3200194	A4	149						
HPK3200195	A4	150						
HPK3200196	A4	151						
HPK3200197	C1	152	Y					
HPK3200198	C2	153	Y					
HPK3200199	C2	154	Y					
HPK3200200	C1	155						
HPK3200201	C2	156						
HPK3200202	C2	157	Y					
HPK3200203	C3	158						
HPK3200204	C2	159	Y					
HPK3200205	C3	160						
HPK3200541	C2	161						
HPK3200206	C1	162	Y					
HPK3200207	C2	163	Y					
HPK3200208	C3	164						
HPK3200209	C2	165	Y					
HPK3200210	C1	166						
HPK3200211	C3	167						
HPK3200212	C2	168	Y					
HPK3200213	C2	169	Y					
HPK3200214	C1	170	Y					
HPK3200215	C1	171						
HPK3200216	C1	172	Y					
HPK3200217	C1	173	Y					
HPK3200218	C2	174	Y					
HPK3200219	C1	175	Y					
HPK3200220	C1	176						
HPK3200221	C4	177						
HPK3200222	C1	178	Y					
HPK3200223	C1	179	Y					
HPK3200224	C1	180	Y					
HPK3200225	C4	181						
HPK3200226	C2	182						
HPK3200227	C1	183						
HPK3200228	C2	184						

PLAN #	PRICE TIER	PAGE	MATERIALS LIST	DECK	DECK PRICE	LANDSCAPE	LANDSCAPE PRICE	REGIONS
HPK3200229	C2	185	Y					
HPK3200230	C3	186						
HPK3200231	C1	187						
HPK3200232	C2	188						
HPK3200233	C3	189						
HPK3200234	C2	190	Y					
HPK3200235	C1	191	Y					
HPK3200236	C3	192						
HPK3200237	C1	193	Y					
HPK3200238	C3	194						
HPK3200239	C1	195	Y			OLA010	P3	1234568
HPK3200240	C3	196						
HPK3200241	C4	197						
HPK3200242	SQ1	198	Y					
HPK3200243	C4	199	Y					
HPK3200244	C2	200	Y					
HPK3200245	C4	201						
HPK3200246	C1	202						
HPK3200247	C1	203						
HPK3200248	C2	204	Y			OLA007	P4	1234568
HPK3200249	C3	205						
HPK3200250	C2	206	Y					
HPK3200251	C2	207	Y					
HPK3200252	C3	208	Y					
HPK3200253	C3	209						
HPK3200254	C2	210	Y					
HPK3200255	C4	211						
HPK3200256	SQ1	212						
HPK3200257	C4	217						
HPK3200258	C2	218						
HPK3200259	C4	218						
HPK3200260	C4	219						
HPK3200261	C3	219						
HPK3200262	C2	220						
HPK3200263	C4	220	Y					
HPK3200264	C3	221						
HPK3200265	C3	221	Y					
HPK3200266	C3	222	Y					
HPK3200267	C2	222						
HPK3200268	C4	223						
HPK3200269	C2	223						
HPK3200270	C2	224						
HPK3200271	C4	224	Y					
HPK3200272	C2	225						
HPK3200273	C3	225	Y					
HPK3200274	C3	226	Y	ODA007	D2	OLA018	P3	12345678
HPK3200275	C2	226						
HPK3200276	C2	227						
HPK3200277	C4	227						
HPK3200278	C3	228	Y					
HPK3200279	C4	228						
HPK3200280	C4	229	Y					
HPK3200281	SQ1	229	Y					
HPK3200282	C3	230	Y					
HPK3200283	C4	230						
HPK3200284	C3	231	Y					
HPK3200285	C4	231						
HPK3200286	L1	232						
HPK3200287	C3	232	Y					
HPK3200288	C4	233						
HPK3200289	C4	233						
HPK3200290	C2	234	Y					
HPK3200291	C4	234						
HPK3200292	C3	235	Y					
HPK3200293	C3	235						
HPK3200294	C2	236						
HPK3200295	C2	236						
HPK3200296	C3	237						
HPK3200297	C3	237	Y					
HPK3200298	C3	238	Y					
HPK3200299	C3	238	Y					
HPK3200300	C4	239						
HPK3200301	C3	239						
HPK3200302	C3	240						
HPK3200303	C4	240	Y					
HPK3200304	C4	241	Y					
HPK3200305	C4	241	Y					
HPK3200306	C3	242						
HPK3200307	C3	242						
HPK3200308	C3	243						
HPK3200309	C3	243						
HPK3200310	C3	244	Y					
HPK3200311	C2	244						
HPK3200312	C4	245						
HPK3200313	C2	245	Y					
HPK3200314	C2	246						
HPK3200315	C2	246	Y					
HPK3200316	C2	247						
HPK3200317	C2	247						
HPK3200318	C4	248						
HPK3200319	C4	248						
HPK3200320	C4	249						
HPK3200321	C4	249						
HPK3200322	C4	250	Y					
HPK3200323	C4	250						
HPK3200324	C4	251						
HPK3200325	C3	252						
HPK3200326	C4	253						
HPK3200327	C4	254						
HPK3200328	C4	255						
HPK3200329	C4	256						
HPK3200330	C4	257						
HPK3200331	C2	258						
HPK3200332	C3	259	Y					
HPK3200333	C4	260						
HPK3200334	C2	261						
HPK3200335	C4	262						
HPK3200336	C4	263						
HPK3200337	C4	264						
HPK3200338	C4	265						
HPK3200339	C2	266	Y					
HPK3200340	C4	267						
HPK3200341	C2	268						
HPK3200342	C2	269						
HPK3200343	C4	270	Y					
HPK3200344	C3	271	Y			OLA010	P3	1234568
HPK3200345	C4	272						
HPK3200346	C4	273	Y					
HPK3200347	C3	274						
HPK3200348	C3	275	Y					
HPK3200349	C4	276						
HPK3200350	C4	277						
HPK3200351	C2	278						
HPK3200352	C4	279						
HPK3200353	C3	280	Y			OLA008	P4	1234568
HPK3200354	C4	281						
HPK3200355	C4	282						
HPK3200356	C4	283						
HPK3200357	C4	284						
HPK3200358	C3	285						
HPK3200359	C4	286						
HPK3200360	C4	287	Y					
HPK3200361	C4	288						
HPK3200362	C4	289						
HPK3200363	C4	290						
HPK3200364	C4	291						
HPK3200365	C4	292						
HPK3200366	C4	293						
HPK3200367	C4	294						
HPK3200368	C4	295						
HPK3200369	L1	296	Y	ODA011	D1	OLA028	P4	12345678
HPK3200370	C3	297						
HPK3200371	C4	298						
HPK3200372	C4	299						
HPK3200373	C3	300	Y	ODA016	D1	OLA006	P3	123568
HPK3200374	C4	301	Y					
HPK3200375	C4	302	Y					
HPK3200376	C3	303						
HPK3200377	L1	304						
HPK3200378	C3	305						
HPK3200379	C4	306	Y					
HPK3200380	C4	307						

PLAN #	PRICE TIER	PAGE	MATERIALS LIST	DECK	DECK PRICE	LANDSCAPE	LANDSCAPE PRICE	REGIONS
HPK3200381	C3	308						
HPK3200382	C3	309						
HPK3200383	C4	310						
HPK3200384	C4	311						
HPK3200385	C4	312						
HPK3200386	C4	313						
HPK3200387	C4	314						
HPK3200388	SQ1	315	Y					
HPK3200389	C4	316						
HPK3200390	C3	317	Y					
HPK3200391	C4	318						
HPK3200392	C3	319	Y					
HPK3200393	L1	320	Y					
HPK3200394	C3	321	Y					
HPK3200395	L1	322						
HPK3200396	L1	323	Y	ODA012	D2	OLA017	P3	123568
HPK3200397	C3	324	Y					
HPK3200398	C3	325						
HPK3200399	C4	326						
HPK3200400	C3	327						
HPK3200401	C4	328						
HPK3200402	SQ1	329	Y					
HPK3200403	SQ1	330						
HPK3200404	L1	331						
HPK3200405	C3	332	Y					
HPK3200406	SQ1	333						
HPK3200407	C4	334						
HPK3200408	C4	335	Y					
HPK3200409	L1	336						
HPK3200410	C4	337						
HPK3200411	L1	338						
HPK3200412	C4	339						
HPK3200413	L2	340	Y	ODA004	D1	OLA004	P3	123568
HPK3200414	L1	341	Y					
HPK3200415	SQ5	342						
HPK3200416	L2	343						
HPK3200417	L1	348	Y	ODA002	D1	OLA015	P4	123568
HPK3200418	L2	349						
HPK3200419	C4	349						
HPK3200420	C4	350	Y					
HPK3200421	L1	350						
HPK3200422	SQ1	351						
HPK3200423	L1	351						
HPK3200424	C4	352						
HPK3200425	L1	352						
HPK3200426	C4	353	Y					
HPK3200427	SQ1	353						
HPK3200428	L1	354						
HPK3200429	C4	354	Y					
HPK3200430	L2	355	Y	ODA012	D2	OLA025	P3	123568
HPK3200431	L1	355						
HPK3200432	C4	356						
HPK3200433	SQ1	356	Y					
HPK3200434	SQ1	357	Y					
HPK3200435	C4	357						
HPK3200436	C4	358	Y					
HPK3200437	L2	358						
HPK3200438	C4	359	Y	ODA008	D2	OLA017	P3	123568
HPK3200439	L1	359	Y					
HPK3200440	C4	360	Y					
HPK3200441	L1	360						
HPK3200442	C4	361	Y					
HPK3200443	L1	361	Y					
HPK3200444	C4	362						
HPK3200445	SQ3	362						
HPK3200446	L1	363						
HPK3200447	SQ1	363						
HPK3200448	L2	364						
HPK3200449	L1	364						
HPK3200450	L1	365	Y			OLA008	P4	1234568
HPK3200451	L1	365						
HPK3200452	C4	366						
HPK3200453	L1	367						
HPK3200454	C4	368						
HPK3200455	L1	369	Y					
HPK3200456	L1	370	Y					
HPK3200457	SQ3	371	Y					
HPK3200458	L1	372						
HPK3200459	C4	373						
HPK3200460	L1	374						
HPK3200461	C4	375						
HPK3200462	C4	376	Y					
HPK3200463	L2	377	Y					
HPK3200464	L1	378						
HPK3200465	L2	379						
HPK3200466	L1	380						
HPK3200467	L1	381						
HPK3200468	C4	382	Y	ODA008	D2	OLA019	P4	1234568
HPK3200469	L2	383						
HPK3200470	L1	384						
HPK3200471	C4	385	Y					
HPK3200472	L2	386						
HPK3200473	L1	387	Y					
HPK3200474	C4	388						
HPK3200475	L2	389						
HPK3200476	SQ1	390	Y					
HPK3200477	L1	391	Y	ODA006	D1	OLA019	P4	1234568
HPK3200478	L2	392						
HPK3200479	C4	393						
HPK3200480	L2	394	Y					
HPK3200481	L2	395						
HPK3200482	L2	396						
HPK3200483	L2	397						
HPK3200484	L2	398						
HPK3200485	C4	399						
HPK3200486	L2	400						
HPK3200487	L3	401						
HPK3200488	SQ1	402						
HPK3200489	L1	403	Y					
HPK3200490	L3	404						
HPK3200491	L3	405						
HPK3200492	L3	406	Y					
HPK3200493	L1	407	Y					
HPK3200494	L1	408	Y					
HPK3200495	L1	409						
HPK3200496	L3	410	Y					
HPK3200497	SQ1	411	Y					
HPK3200498	L2	412						
HPK3200499	SQ1	413						
HPK3200500	L3	414						
HPK3200501	L3	415						
HPK3200502	L3	416	Y					
HPK3200503	SQ1	417						
HPK3200504	L3	418						
HPK3200505	L1	419						
HPK3200506	L1	420	Y					
HPK3200507	L3	421						
HPK3200508	SQ1	422	Y			OLA017	P3	123568
HPK3200509	L3	423						
HPK3200510	L3	424	Y					
HPK3200511	SQ1	425	Y					
HPK3200512	L1	426						
HPK3200513	L1	427	Y					
HPK3200514	L3	428	Y					
HPK3200515	SQ7	429						
HPK3200516	SQ1	430						
HPK3200517	L4	431						
HPK3200518	SQ1	432	Y					
HPK3200519	L4	433						
HPK3200520	SQ1	434						
HPK3200521	L4	435						
HPK3200522	P3	436						
HPK3200523	P3	438						
HPK3200524	P4	440						
HPK3200525	P3	442						
HPK3200526	P3	444						
HPK3200527	P4	446						
HPK3200528	P3	448						
HPK3200529	P4	450						
HPK3200530	P3	452						

Beauty in Simplicity

Break away from conventional ideas of starter homes. Hanley Wood titles prove that "budget" homes don't have to be boring homes. Elegant, yet affordable plans show how beautiful home design is available at every price range.

NEW!

325 New Home Plans 06/07

The 5th volume in the popular "New Home Plans" series offers all new plans for 2006 and 2007. Every plan is guaranteed to be new and exciting, and updated with the most popular trends in residential architecture.

$10.95 U.S. (*256 pages*)
ISBN-10: 1-931131-65-1
ISBN-13: 978-1-931131-65-0

NEW!

DREAM HOME SOURCE:
350 Two-Story Home Plans

Perfect for families of all sizes and ages, two-story homes offer the universal appeal that has made them among the most popular home plan styles in the country.

$12.95 U.S. (*384 pages*)
ISBN-10: 1-931131-66-X
ISBN-13: 978-1-931131-66-7

NEW!

Big Book of Designer Home Plans

This fabulous compilation profiles ten top designers and reveals dozens of their most popular home plans.

$12.95 U.S. (*464 pages*)
ISBN-10: 1-931131-68-6
ISBN-13: 978-1-931131-68-1

200 Budget-Smart Home Plans

Finally, a collection of homes in all sizes, styles, and types that today's home-owner can really afford to build. This complete selection of houses meets smaller and modest building budgets.

$8.95 U.S. (*224 pages*)
ISBN-10: 0-918894-97-2

The Big Book of Home Plans

Finding paradise at home is even easier with this collection of 500+ home and landscaping plans, in every style.

$12.95 U.S. (*464 pages*)
ISBN-10: 1-931131-36-8

DREAM HOME SOURCE:
350 One-Story Home Plans

A compendium of exclusively one-story homes, for the homeowners that know what they are looking for. Plans run the gamut in both style and size, offering something for everyone.

$12.95 U.S. (*384 pages*)
ISBN-10: 1-931131-47-3

DREAM HOME SOURCE:
300 Affordable Home Plans

There's no need to sacrifice quality to meet any budget— no matter how small. Find stylish, time-proven designs, all in homes that fit small and modest budgets.

$12.95 U.S. (*384 pages*)
ISBN-10: 1-931131-59-7
ISBN-13: 978-1-931131-59-9

DREAM HOME SOURCE:
350 Small Home Plans

A reader-friendly resource is perfect for first-time buyers and small families looking for a starter home, this title will inspire and prepare readers to take the initial steps toward homeownership.

$12.95 U.S. (*384 pages*)
ISBN-10: 1-931131-42-2

Hanley Wood Books

One Thomas Circle, NW | Suite 600 | Washington, DC 20005
877.447.5450 | www.hanleywoodbooks.com

HPK32